ZELDA

For Yuna and Isia B.

Zelda. The history of a legendary saga.
by Nicolas Courcier and Mehdi El Kanafi
Published by Third Éditions
32 rue d'Alsace-Lorraine, 31000 Toulouse, France
contact@thirdeditions.com
www.thirdeditions.com

Follow us: 🐦 @Third_Editions – ⓕ Facebook.com/ThirdEditions

Edited by: Nicolas Courcier et Mehdi El Kanafi
Texts by: Nicolas Courcier and Mehdi El Kanafi
Chapter on "Link: A Character and His Evolution": Selami Boudjerda
Chapter on "Music in *Zelda*": Damien Mecheri
Proofreading and page layout: Thomas Savary
Covers: Nicolas Courcier and Mehdi El Kanafi
Cover assembly: Frédéric Tomé
Translated from French by: Keith Sanders (ITC Traductions)

This educational work is Third Éditions' tribute to the classic *Zelda* video game series. The authors present an overview of the history of the *Zelda* games in this one-of-a-kind volume that lays out the inspirations, the context and the content of these titles through original analysis and discussion.

Nicolas Courcier

Mehdi El Kanafi

ZELDA

THE HISTORY OF A LEGENDARY SAGA

03rd. THIRD éditions

This book is dedicated to Justin Carroz, to his family, to his friends and everyone who loves the legend. Remember, the world can always use another hero. May the Triforce guide you on all your adventures. Never stop working for a better future.

CONTENTS

ZELDA

THE HISTORY OF A LEGENDARY SAGA

PREFACE

n February 2016, the Zelda saga celebrated its thirtieth anniversary. More than a quarter-century later, Nintendo's hit series is still very much a standard-bearer for the brand, alongside its iconic *Mario* series. Created by Shigeru Miyamoto in 1986, the saga is still viewed by players with a certain reverence. Each individual title has a strong reputation, and the series as a whole enjoys a level of prestige that is rarely called into question. With installments available on all of Nintendo's different platforms, this flagship franchise has also served as a showcase for the Kyoto-based developer's technical and design prowess.

The first episode of *Zelda* made a powerful impression upon its release, introducing a new approach to the action-adventure genre. One *Zelda* installment followed another in sure-footed succession, displaying an impressively consistent level of quality that few other series have been able to match. Although the franchise has appeared in many incarnations in a variety of media (manga, animated series, merchandise), it has above all been a source of inspiration to other games that have taken it as a model. Those titles, ranging from *Ōkami* and *Darksiders* to *Alundra* and *3D Dot Game Heroes*, all of them heirs to the original ideas first set forth by Miyamoto, have helped to popularize and build upon the Japanese designer's vision for video games.

What is it that defines the *Zelda* series more than anything else? We might start by mentioning the world in which it takes place, Hyrule, along with its three main characters: Link, Princess Zelda and the evil Ganon. We might also mention the Triforce, the magical artifact that everyone covets. However, as part of the more rigorous and analytical approach that we intend to take here, we will instead focus on its gameplay system, quite innovative for 1986, which ties the hero's development of new skills to exploration and the acquisition of precious new objects. To complete his quest, Link has to visit villages, explore dungeons, and battle tough bosses, all within a well-defined framework that is re-used in one episode after another.

We can also quite reasonably argue that the essence of *Zelda* lies first and foremost in Nintendo's skill in game design. In these games, the developer has chosen to express its own vision of what an adventure game should be: a seamless blend of action, adventure and role-playing (stripped of the genre's unwieldier aspects), yielding a gameplay experience that is not only simple, but deeply intuitive. This original structure reflects a certain philosophy towards video games, manifested on screen in the character of Link—so very appealing, and yet so very silent.

Just as in the *Mario* and *Donkey Kong* games, players find themselves on familiar ground from the very first moments of a *Zelda* game. In fact, this sense of familiarity goes well beyond visual impressions. It's something you experience with the controller in your hands, through a control scheme that instantly feels natural and immediate. Anyone returning to the world of *Zelda* has the chance to re-experience the unique science of its gameplay, in which the individual elements (story, level design, difficulty) are masterfully combined in service of a single goal: player enjoyment.

Nicolas Courcier and Mehdi El Kanafi

Fascinated by print media since childhood, Nicolas Courcier and Mehdi El Kanafi wasted no time in launching their first magazine, *Console Syndrome*, in 2004. After five issues with distribution limited to the Toulouse region of France, they decided to found a publishing house under the same name. One year later, their small business was acquired by another leading publisher of works about video games. In their four years in the world of publishing, Nicolas and Mehdi published more than twenty works on major video game series, and wrote several of those works themselves: *Metal Gear Solid. Hideo Kojima's Magnum Opus*, *Resident Evil. Of Zombies and Men*, and *The Legend of Final Fantasy VII* and *IX*. Since 2015, they have continued their editorial focus on analyzing major video game series at a new publishing house that they founded together: Third.

CHAPTER I

THE LEGEND OF ZELDA

n the kingdom of Hyrule, a legend has been passed down since the beginning of time: A mysterious artifact known as the Triforce, symbolized by three golden triangles arranged to form a fourth triangle, is said to possess mystical powers.

It is hardly surprising that this object has been coveted by many power-hungry men over the centuries. One day, the evil Ganon, the Prince of Darkness whose ambition is to subjugate the entire world to his will, sends his armies to attack the peaceful kingdom. He manages to capture one of the fragments of the Triforce, the triangle of power.

Daughter of the king of Hyrule, Princess Zelda is terrified at the prospect of seeing Ganon's armies swarming over the world. She, too, seizes a fragment of the Triforce, the triangle of wisdom, and chooses to break it into eight pieces, which she then scatters across the world, hiding them to prevent Ganon from ever acquiring them. She then orders her faithful nursemaid Impa to go forth and seek a warrior brave enough to challenge Ganon.

As Impa roams the kingdom of Hyrule in the hope of finding a savior, Ganon learns of Zelda's plans and has her locked up before sending his men to track down the nursemaid. Surrounded by these ruthless creatures, Impa is saved by a young boy named Link at the very moment when it appears that all is lost. As unbelievable as it may seem, Link has been chosen by the golden triangle of courage, and thus holds a part of the Triforce himself. Convinced that she has finally found the one who will save the kingdom, Impa hurries to tell him her story. Link accepts his mission to rescue Zelda without hesitation. Before confronting Ganon, however, he will have to gather the eight fragments of the triangle of wisdom, which are his only hope of gaining entry to the dungeon deep beneath Death Mountain where the Prince of Darkness hides. His quest has only just begun.

A SUCCESSFUL PREMIERE

The Legend of Zelda was released in Japan on February 21, 1986, on the Famicom Disk System, an extension that sat on top of the Famicom console and allowed it to read games from floppy disks. But this first installment of the *Zelda* series appeared in the familiar cartridge format when it came out for the NES the following year in the United States and Europe. The rest, of course, is history: The game made an exceptionally strong impression and became an unbelievable critical and commercial success, selling more than 6.5 million copies. It was the start of one of Nintendo's most prestigious series, one which continues to fascinate and inspire players to this day.

THE BIRTH OF ZELDA...

Much like another little game known as *Super Mario Bros.*, which was also a huge success on the NES, *Zelda* was created by Shigeru Miyamoto. It was thanks to his father, a friend of Nintendo president Hiroshi Yamauchi, that Miyamoto—trained as an industrial engineer—was able to find a job at the company. Initially tasked with designing arcade cabinets, Shigeru Miyamoto was assigned in 1981 to direct the *Donkey Kong* project, which was destined to become a major hit. It was soon followed by *Mario Bros.* (1983) and *Super Mario Bros.* (1985), after which Miyamoto set to work on *Zelda*. He decided to give his new game a very different structure from that of *Super Mario*; the idea was to provide an open environment that players could explore however they saw fit. But first, let's back up a bit in order to more fully understand the origin of this first episode of *Zelda*.

In 1984, two new role-playing games were all the rage. Created by Namco, the first was entitled *The Tower of Druaga* and took video arcades by storm. The second, *Hydlide*, was a highly popular RPG from T&E Soft. Like many of his peers, Miyamoto was a fan of *The Tower of Druaga*—so much so that he even had a coin-op machine of the game delivered directly to his office! This action RPG would turn out to be an inspiration to the entire Japanese video game industry—and Miyamoto and his future *Zelda* series were no exception. In December 1984, just after the release of *Devil World* and *Excitebike*, Miyamoto chose to move forward immediately with two new projects. The first one starred a plumber with an impressive mustache and a spring in his step. The second, known at the time as *Adventure Title*, was intended for release as a coin-op arcade game. As you may have guessed, it was *Adventure Title* that would go on to become the first chapter in the *Zelda* saga. As in *The Tower of Druaga*, the initial concept went no further than exploring the different levels of a citadel. At this stage of the project, there

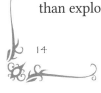

was not yet any thought of allowing the player to explore the great outdoors. However, the game already had a distinct focus on puzzles. It had even started to look like one big two-dimensional puzzle: "The game was becoming more and more puzzle-oriented," Miyamoto explains in the official guide to *A Link to the Past*. "So much so that I sometimes wondered whether it was really still an adventure game." There was even a plan to include "random" and "edit" modes, in which dungeons would be randomly generated by the console or created by the player, respectively.

The character of Link started to take shape in the first few weeks of the project: the hero of *Adventure Title* was soon equipped with a sword, bombs and a bow. To complete what would soon become a familiar arsenal, a variety of objects were planned, including keys, candles, flasks, a genie's lamp, and logs. Aside from these last two accessories, we can see that the basic equipment was already in place.

As the weeks went by, however, the project and its designers' ambitions continued to evolve. Before long, *Adventure Title* was no longer destined for release as a coin-op arcade game, but rather for the Famicom Disk System. For Miyamoto, the fact that Nintendo's new peripheral allowed for rewriting data was the perfect way to allow any player to create their own dungeons and challenge others to solve them.

An amusing anecdote has it that in his efforts to use as many of the options available to him as he could, Miyamoto even briefly explored the idea of using the Zapper and the microphone of the Famicom controller. But weak sales of the infrared pistol accessory, and the lack of a microphone in Western versions of Nintendo hardware, proved fatal to some of Miyamoto's and Takashi Tezuka's more unusual ideas. A little-known but incredibly important figure at Nintendo, Tezuka was Miyamoto's right-hand man, and co-director of the first episodes of the *Mario* and *Zelda* series.

As mentioned earlier, the other game that had the greatest influence on Miyamoto was *Hydlide*. To ensure that his nascent *Zelda* game would fit in with other games of the time, Miyamoto integrated new ideas inspired directly by the popular title from T&E Soft. This was how *Adventure Title* began to take on certain features that were quite different from those of the original project. The game was initially designed as a series of underground dungeons around what would eventually become one of the series' best-known locations: Death Mountain. However, as we will see, this early iteration of *Zelda* would soon break free of this template and its influences.

The area that would come to be known as Hyrule Field was born of Miyamoto's wish to offer players more than just a series of dungeons. His desire to break with tradition was becoming increasingly clear. The 128 KB of disk space

available with the Disk System gave the men behind *The Legend of Zelda* an opportunity to bring their hero out from underground and offer players a kind of "open world." So Miyamoto and Tezuka got started on designing these vast landscapes.

They began by drawing their immense map on large sheets of graph paper, and filling in even the tiniest details: "We wanted to present an above-ground world outside of the dungeons, so we added forests and lakes, and Hyrule Field started to take shape little by little," recalls Miyamoto in the book *Hyrule Historia.* Exploration was on its way to becoming the heart of the *Zelda* experience. For Miyamoto, "it's a game where we can explore mysterious places on our own." "A child's state of mind as he enters a cave all alone— the game has to capture that. As he makes his way in, he has to feel the cold air around him. He discovers a fork in the path and has to decide whether to explore it or not. Sometimes he will get lost," he adds in an interview with *Rolling Stone* in January 1992. We mentioned the idea of an "open world" a moment ago, albeit somewhat hesitantly; in any event, it is clear that Miyamoto wished to offer players a more open-ended experience than in other games of the era. His main ambition was to imbue the game with a feeling of discovery—even to the point of obscuring how players should go about achieving their goals in his game. For Hiroshi Yamauchi, the president of Nintendo, this last point was something of a shock: "We can't sell a game where the player doesn't know where their goal is!"

Miyamoto decided to convince his boss of his approach by presenting the start of the adventure, when the hero is completely alone and unarmed. In this situation, both player and avatar feel a bit lost, and are forced to search for and discover a solution on their own. To provide players with a bit of much-needed guidance, he placed "a cave they couldn't possibly miss" on the very first screen of the game. Miyamoto also notes that "*The Neverending Story* got really popular around that time. It was a world that started off with a message like: 'Here kid, take this sword.' In a word, it was plain," he acknowledged in an "Iwata Asks" interview. Presumably, that's precisely the template he had in mind when he began to design the opening moments of his game.

... OF ITS WORLD...

In creating the world of the future *Zelda* games, Miyamoto took inspiration from his own personal experience. As a child, and later as a teenager, he loved to explore the forest, getting lost in unfamiliar environments and discovering a lake here, a cave or an abandoned house there. It was his own sense of wonder

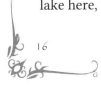

that he hoped to capture in *Zelda*, even going so far as to say that he hoped to make a game that players could use as a sort of "miniature garden" to visit at their leisure. It seems that when Miyamoto visits an unfamiliar place, he prefers to discover it for himself, without seeking out any information at all about it beforehand. That's probably the reason why, when entering a dungeon in *Zelda*, Link has to go through a number of different rooms before finding the map and the compass that will help him find his way to the exit. Miyamoto has said that Ridley Scott's *Legend* (1985), starring a young Tom Cruise, was a source of inspiration for the game's world. The story of this feature film was based in a classic world of fantasy: Jack, a sort of wood elf with a strong connection to the natural world, is in love with the beautiful princess Lily. But the Lord of Darkness desires her as well. The living incarnation of Evil itself, he seeks to bring darkness upon the world by killing the two unicorns who are the guardians of peace in the kingdom.

The team's press agent came to Miyamoto with the idea of publishing a book of illustrations that would introduce the world of the game in more detail, providing an opportunity not only to present images of the game's different characters, but more importantly, to reveal the beauty of the princess that players would be asked to save. During the discussion, the press agent brought up the example of Zelda Fitzgerald, the wife of the famous American novelist F. Scott Fitzgerald. "The book project didn't interest me at all, but I loved the name Zelda, so I asked him if we could just use the name. He said yes, and that's how *The Legend of Zelda* was born," Miyamoto explains. Although it's surely a coincidence, it is amusing to note that Zelda is a short form of the Italian name Griselda (itself most likely of Germanic origin), which originally meant "gray warrior."

Zelda was Miyamoto's first game to include end credits. Before the advent of floppy disks, the Famicom didn't have any way to display text on-screen, so movie-style credits had never been possible before. Players may be surprised to note that Miyamoto's name does not appear in the credits! But a certain "Miyahon" does appear in the appropriate place. The other half of the dynamic duo behind this installment of *Zelda*, Takashi Tezuka, appears under the name of "TenTen." Obscuring the creators' names in this way was a common practice at the time, intended to prevent other companies from poaching top talent.

... AND OF LINK

As for the process of creating the character of Link, Miyamoto would not share any details until much later. In November 2012, the French journalist William Audureau asked the Japanese designer directly as part of an interview for the Gamekult website. His response: "Actually, it was Tezuka-san who designed the sprite for Link. As you know, the NES was very limited at the time, and we could only use three different colors. But we still wanted a recognizable character. What I wanted above all was for him to use his sword or his shield, and for that to be visible. So we gave him these big weapons so that you could recognize them on the screen. Then we needed to create a hero that people would be able to distinguish from his weapons, despite his small size. So we thought of giving him a long hat and big ears. That made us think of a fairy-tale character, so we went with the idea of making him look like an elf. At the time, a character with pointy ears immediately made you think of Peter Pan, and since I like Disney a lot, we started to take inspiration from that. Not only from that, of course—that wouldn't have turned out so great... At that point, I figured that Peter Pan green was perfect for our character. Now, since we were limited to three colors and there were lots of forest environments in the game, that worked out pretty well, so we just kept going with that idea."

With the similarities to *Peter Pan* now an official part of the design and a carefully considered decision on the part of the creators, the team then went even further with other analogies to J. M. Barrie's classic work. For instance, consider the Kokiri in *Ocarina of Time*, a society of children (also dressed in green) who never grow up. Much like Peter Pan and his tribe of Lost Boys, they remain forever young.

When the same journalist went on to ask where their character's name came from, Miyamoto responded: "It's not a very well-known story, but back when we first started designing *The Legend of Zelda*, we imagined that the fragments of the Triforce were actually electronic chips! It was supposed to be a video game that took place in both the past and the future. Since our hero was the link between those two times, we decided to use the English word 'link' for his name. But ultimately, Link never went to the future, and the game remained as a work of heroic fantasy. As a matter of fact, there turned out to be nothing futuristic about it at all! [*laughs*]" The idea was abandoned in the end, not because of any requirements imposed by the story, but for much more prosaic reasons: this futuristic world would have required the creation of an entirely new science-fiction universe.

Finally, note that the second quest owes its existence entirely to a mistake made by Tezuka. When creating all of the game's dungeons, he only used half

of the available memory. To fill up the remaining fifty percent, Miyamoto had the idea of adding a second quest.

SOLID GAMEPLAY MECHANICS

Right from the beginning, *The Legend of Zelda* immerses you completely in the kingdom of Hyrule, which takes the form of an open world. You play as Link, a young hero dressed in green whose mission is to save Princess Zelda. At the time, one especially noteworthy aspect of the game was its choice of a top-down perspective, allowing players to move around in two dimensions. The player moves freely from one screen to the next, able to retrace their steps at any time. In all, the world of Hyrule as seen in this first installment consists of one hundred and twenty-eight screens. To move the story forward, Link must reconstruct the triangle of wisdom after finding its eight fragments, hidden in various dungeons where he must triumph over adversity. He will find a number of objects along the way to assist him in his journey: for example, the raft will allow him to travel to lands surrounded by water, while other found objects serve to increase his strength. Both within the dungeons and in the outside world, the core gameplay is focused on combat—no surprise when we remember that Miyamoto's initial idea was that the dungeons would be Zelda's only playable zones. The idea of a world map connecting the dungeons to one another was not added until later. However, this action-oriented aspect of the game is balanced by the adventure and exploration aspect: the player must continually observe the environment and keep an eye out for any secret passages or mechanisms to open hidden doors.

TWO APPROACHES TO ROLE-PLAYING GAMES

1986 saw the creation of two of gaming's greatest classics. Without knowing it, the two Japanese publishers Nintendo and Enix had each been working to design a game based around an open world. These parallel developments culminated in the release of *Zelda* and *Dragon Quest*, the founding works of two distinct branches within the genre that would later become known as JRPGs (for "Japanese role-playing games"). Miyamoto (at Nintendo) and the duo of Yuji Horii and Koichi Nakamura (at Enix) did not have the same ambitions, to be sure: whereas *Zelda* was built around the idea of exploration, *Dragon Quest* was obviously intended as a response to American role-playing games, and especially to *Wizardry* on the Apple II, which Horii and Nakamura had discovered with great excitement in 1983 while attending Applefest in San Francisco. While Enix was seeking inspiration from role-playing games on microcomputers, Nintendo's approach would turn out to be both more personal and more visceral. Although Shigeru Miyamoto, as we have seen, was not completely free of outside influences, his primary concern was to give life to an internal vision, closely tied to his own personal experience. No sooner had the JRPG genre been established than it began to diverge into two clearly distinct orientations. On the one hand, *Dragon Quest* offered an epic quest in which the player was responsible for controlling an entire team. To acquire the experience needed to progress in the game, the heroes were required to do battle with monsters. These clashes made use of a different on-screen representation than the one used for the map exploration phase; in addition, they cropped up at random moments during play. In the Enix title, then, the team's increasing strength was quantified in numbers: accumulated experience allowed heroes to level up, which led to an increase in the number of points to be distributed over a long list of attributes (hit points, magic, defense, etc.). In *Zelda*, on the other hand, Link's increasing strength was tied to the acquisition of specific objects, and was not expressed in numerical terms.

Another point of distinction between the two productions is accessibility. Since 1986, Miyamoto has displayed a truly unique sensibility which is nevertheless on its way to becoming a universal one, recognized by players all around the world. *Zelda* was extremely ambitious for its time, as we have already noted. And yet its mechanics are extremely simple ones, allowing even the youngest players to pick them up almost immediately. Unlike its "competitor," *Zelda* does not provide the player with any information about the effects of player or enemy attacks; the action is presented in a transparent style. *Dragon Quest*, meanwhile, has a substantially richer interface in this regard, offering various menus and a multitude of options during battles—elements that Miyamoto chose not to include in *Zelda*. Therefore, there is no need for a system of menus to manage the heroes' statistics, their progression, their equipment, and so on; the same is true of the sections that take place in villages or shops, in which every interaction is pared down to its simplest form. This accessibility clearly made it easier for the game to find an audience outside of Japan, thereby contributing to its worldwide success. The first *Dragon Quest* was not so lucky on that front: although sales were impressive within Japan (1.3 million copies), the game fell short of that success in foreign markets. In the United States, the series was known as *Dragon Warrior*, and the franchise didn't make it to European stores until the eighth installment.

But lest we leave the reader with the impression that *Zelda* and *Dragon Quest* were the very first role-playing games to appear on consoles, let's not

forget examples like *Advanced Dungeons & Dragons: Cloudy Mountain* and its sequel, *Advanced Dungeons & Dragons: Treasure of Tarmin*, which came out for Intellivision in 1982 and 1983. Still, the creations of Horii and Miyamoto were the first representatives of the JRPG genre, which has since gone on to widespread fame and launched a long line of descendants. While *Dragon Quest* has rightly earned its reputation as the genre's gold standard, *Zelda* was the game that established the style now known as action RPGs, a genre that persisted by influencing many other publishers to produce games like *Secret of Mana*, *Secret of Evermore*, and *Illusion of Time*—or, more recently, *Kingdom Hearts*.

THE HERO

As the hero of the *Zelda* saga, Link's defining look and personality traits are definitively established from the very first episode: he is a young boy dressed in green, with an elf-like appearance, whose much-vaunted courage has earned him the right to bear the corresponding triangle from the Triforce. We never see the character speak, although subsequent episodes make it clear that he can communicate perfectly well with the various inhabitants of Hyrule. His words simply never directly appear in the game (whether in written or spoken form), except for a few brief interjections. In this first *Zelda* game, Link is a perfect example of the classic video game hero: altruistic and brave, but without much real substance. He does have one unique feature, though: he's left-handed! As in most games at the time, his personality is little more than a sketch, his character is rather simple, or even stereotypical—and his one, crystal-clear objective is as straightforward as can be: to save the princess. In that sense, *Zelda* is much like other leading games of that era such as *Super Mario Bros.*, *Ghosts 'n Goblins*, and others. In order to encourage players to form an attachment to their avatar, the game also allowed them to choose their own name—as did *Dragon Quest*, for that matter.

THE MYTHOLOGY OF HYRULE

While the character of Link turns out to be a mere outline at this point, the mythology in which he takes part is a fairly rich one from the outset. At the heart of a perpetual conflict lies the Triforce, a mythical artifact symbolizing three values (power, wisdom and courage) that each correspond to one of the main characters: Ganon, Zelda, and Link, respectively. The backdrop to this struggle is the world of Hyrule, with a wide variety of environments (lakes, forests, mountains, etc.) inspired by fantasy stories and home to fairies and monsters. As we saw earlier, Link's appearance also evokes the typical image of an elf, even if the word "elf" is never mentioned explicitly.

The origins, appearance and role of elves in mythology remain largely unclear. In Germanic myths, for example, they are never really described, even though they are always a "part of the scenery." In Nordic mythology, elves even live in their own territory, known as Álfheim. Although the etymology of the word *elf* has been the subject of various interpretations and hypotheses, the term is generally traced back to the Indo-European root *albh*, meaning *white*. The elf is considered to be a benevolent being with supernatural powers. Note in this connection that the mandrake, a plant traditionally associated with magical rituals, is called *Alraune* in German; the Proto-Germanic roots of this word are said to signify *secret of the elves*. Elves' virtuous character and pointed ears were clearly the basis for the character of Link. However, the hat worn by the hero is more typically associated with gnomes or leprechauns. Fairies, meanwhile, are part of medieval Western folklore. Traditional Romanesque and Celtic imagery represents them as playing the role of protectors, lovers, or even wives; believed to be agents of fate, fairies are closely associated with notions of dreams and destiny, which are referred to in Latin with the term *phantasia*, originally of Greek origin. Frequently combining animal and humanoid traits, fairies are often associated with the color white (symbol of the supernatural), and are considered as protective figures. It was said that they would choose a person as their lover and take charge of their fate.

Hyrule is presented as a small kingdom. Insofar as neither the king nor his army appear in this first episode, however, Zelda alone, whom we suppose to be the king's daughter, is the embodiment of authority. With a few rare exceptions (a couple of old wise men and merchants), Link never has the chance to meet any friendly inhabitants of the kingdom in the first episode, and he never enters a single village. His primary interactions are thus limited to battles against a variety of enemies, including a confrontation at the end of each dungeon with an iconic adversary who guards one of the fragments of the Triforce: a dragon, a giant spider, a dinosaur, and so on.

The theme of a knight battling a tyrant in a world where elves and fairies coexist with humans clearly goes back to heroic fantasy and to the literary genre of fairy tales. Originally part of the oral tradition, fairy tales take place "outside of time" and reject the notion of realism. Fairy tales rarely provide even the slightest information about the time or place in which their story is set, but they do generally display a significant concern for aesthetics. Aiming at universality, fairy tales are often based around a conflict between good and evil, with an emphasis on archetypes like the beautiful princess or the courageous

prince, thus inviting the audience to focus their attention on the action. And while they often communicate a message along with certain values, fairy tales' main purpose is to entertain. All of this applies perfectly to *Zelda*, even if the title of the first installment would seem to align the game more closely with legends than with fairy tales. Unlike traditional fairy tales, which come from the oral tradition, a legend is first and foremost a *written* story (*legenda* is Latin for "things to be read"); the content of a legend is still just as fictitious, but it often mingles with real elements as well. With more focus on detail than in a fairy tale, a legend is often centered on a specific person, place or event—all elements that we find in *The Legend of Zelda*.

A FEELING OF GREAT FREEDOM

Pixel soup! That would be one way to summarize the graphics in games for the Famicom and competing platforms of its era. And yet, children of the 1980s can't help but feel a bittersweet twinge of nostalgia when they remember their video gaming experiences of that time. The stories were simple, the quality of the graphics was poor, and any broader sense of setting was nonexistent. Nevertheless, players used their imaginations to transcend these limits, transforming these adventures into true interactive fairy tales. In this sense, the most important aspects of games from this era came to life inside our minds. The structure of the stories was similar from one game to the next, so much so that the ins and outs of the narrative felt completely obvious after just a few hours of play. But once again, that wasn't what players were really concerned with. In fact, the absence of narrative and graphical detail actually served to stimulate the imagination, allowing each player to shape their own world. Video games from the era of the Famicom/NES, Master System, and their contemporaries relied much more on suggestion and implication than modern titles do. Taking advantage of how the medium has evolved, today's games put the emphasis on showing the action in a spectacular or even bombastic way.

We can consider these 8-bit games as lying along a narrow fringe at the border between literature and cinema. Whereas literature invites the reader to construct a mental world drawn from the author's prose, movies give viewers the chance to ride along on an intoxicating visual journey. Halfway between these two modes of expression, video games of the 1980s present simple imagery, consisting of colors and situations, which nevertheless give free rein to personal interpretation. We can go further with our cinematic analogy by comparing video games of this era to silent movies. These early films also guided the audience with music and images, while leaving their imaginations free to fill in the gaps inherent to the medium. Indeed, the films of Keaton and Chaplin relied on a similar grammar to those of video games in the NES era. With live interpretation by an orchestra or pianist to accompany the action, the music of the first movies finds an echo in the music of these video games, designed to guide the player's path. The dialog in the first *Zelda* game is also similar to the title cards in silent films, thus justifying the comparison to works from the first few decades of the cinema. Finally, what better way to describe Link, the game's hero who has no voice and expresses himself solely through gestures, than as a bridge between written stories and silent film?

Allowing players to let their imaginations roam freely reinforces the sense of freedom already built into the very design of the game. At the start of his adventure, the hero, and by extension the player, is desperately alone— alone, but therefore free to go wherever he chooses. Right from its very first installment, *Zelda* breaks through the boundaries that had kept players trapped inside of self-contained levels, with invisible walls like those that forced Mario to keep moving forward without ever stopping, and a dynamic screen-scrolling mechanism that created a constant sense of urgency. Although the goal is the same in both games (to free the princess), we do not feel this same sense of urgency in *Zelda*—because in fact, saving the captured princess is not really what motivates the player.

What truly electrifies the player and incites their passion for the game is adventure in its truest form, the kind that puts us face-to-face with ourselves and leaves us to our own fate. The game does very little to force the player's path; from the very first second, the world of Hyrule is largely open to us. The idea of a game like *Grand Theft Auto* had not yet even crossed the minds of the creative forces at DMA Design, but even in this early era, *Zelda* was already offering the vision of an open world. Of course, that vision was still light years away from what an "open world" means to the young players of today. Nevertheless, Nintendo deserves credit for having brought to life a real feeling of freedom with this game.

A FASCINATING STORY… TOLD MOSTLY IN THE MANUAL

Nowadays, video games can draw on a toolbox of their own genre-specific codes to tell a story, or on the tools of the cinema. But in the mid-1980s, all of those tools had yet to be invented. The games of the era reflect the emergence of this new mode of storytelling, often awkward and stumbling at this early stage. As explained earlier, it was *Zelda* and *Dragon Quest* that first cleared the path for a discussion in Japan about the best way to bring engaging adventures to life through video games. In fact, however, the fable told in *Zelda* is not much more ambitious than the story of Mario's mission to rescue Princess Peach. Despite this, Nintendo's new title had a distinctly more epic character, and even if the story as presented was every bit as simplistic as that of its platformer cousin, the player taking on the role of Link was meant to be filled with a sense of courage and valor. This was a daunting challenge for the designers, who obviously had to deal with the very limited resources available on the consoles of that era. Clearly, the available capacities of the Famicom and its Disk System would not allow them to construct their story through a series of close-ups and wide-angle shots. The most obvious solution for the team was to present a brief summary of the story on the game's title screen after a short pause. Only the broadest outlines were explained there. In addition, nothing forced players to read the synopsis; this showed that the narrative aspect was never intended to get in the way of pure gameplay, the true heart of the experience. The first few seconds of *Zelda* made clear the vocabulary that Nintendo would be using: with no further explanation, Link is dropped into a vast and hostile open world. The hero is completely free to take all the time he wants to accomplish his mission. Such freedom of action would be almost unthinkable today: even as players strive to break free of any and all restrictions, they still prefer that their games be structured by a consistent story to guide them and provide them with goals.

To compensate for the lack of raw computing power that prevented the creators from expressing themselves however they wished, the team had no choice but to make use of another source that was available to everyone who bought the game: the user's manual! Utterly outdated today, this little booklet was an essential reference at the time, allowing game designers to share tips and instructions that were absent from the game itself. The gameplay mechanics in *Zelda* are not comparable in any way to those of today's games. The playable tutorial sequence, designed to teach players the basic rules of the game, had not been invented yet. Reading the manual was therefore an essential step in learning to play the game. The developers took advantage of this to make the manual a full-fledged narrative tool in its own right. In reading through the booklet that came with the cartridge, the player could learn the details of the plot, alongside illustrations of the different protagonists in the adventure. These few pages were an indispensable supplement to the game, and provided information that would have been impossible to present on the consoles of the time. In addition to the manual, Nintendo decided to include a map of all the lands of Hyrule in the game box. This map was another concrete object that allowed the designers to provide the player with essential information that did not appear in the game; but more importantly, in this specific context, it served as a connection between the player and the game. The *Zelda* cartridge came equipped with a save chip—a first. However, each time the game was started, and after every "game over" screen, players found themselves back at the starting point of the game: any objects or rupees that they had collected would be saved, but not the place where they died. Players therefore had to make their own way back to where they had left off, and without a map, this would have been an arduous task. This is where the map provided by Nintendo turned out to be truly useful. It would be an exaggeration to call this an early instance of transmedia storytelling, a systematic approach first discussed in theoretical terms in the early 2000s by which multiple different media are used together in synergy to develop a multifaceted fictional world. Still, it is interesting to note the recent trend back towards *objects*, with a game like Level-5's *Ni no Kuni* including a real spell book with its DS version—an apparent echo of Nintendo's choice with *The Legend of Zelda*.

At the end of the text that scrolls across the screen after starting the game, the developers at Nintendo advise the player to read the manual to learn more about the world of *Zelda*. Nevertheless, this part of the manual was still an entirely optional narrative tool. Players who chose not to read it were not prevented from making progress in the adventure. Recall that at the time, the story underlying a video game was far from the top priority: the market primarily targeted children, and as a new medium, games focused almost exclusively on the gameplay aspect of the experience. With imagination of their own to spare, young minds could take inspiration from the clunky patterns of pixels on their cathode ray tube TVs to make up their own adventures, and turn them into magical tales.

LAYING THE FOUNDATIONS

As with many Nintendo licenses that would drive the company's success for years to come, this first installment of Link's adventures has everything it takes to found a franchise; and indeed, it determined the course of all the *Zelda* games that would follow it. Right away, all of the foundations are laid. The world of Hyrule, the Triforce, and the connections between Link, Zelda and Ganon would serve as the basis for the story of most later episodes, each one tirelessly relating the struggles among the different protagonists within the kingdom, with some seeking to conquer and others to protect. The gameplay would continue to maintain a tight connection between action and exploration, along with the iconic top-down view in the 2D episodes—except for the second episode. Players loved the music as well, especially Koji Kondo's famous theme, which fans looked forward to hearing again in each new episode. Finally, we can conclude by evoking a number of small details scattered throughout *Legend of Zelda* that were to become permanently associated with the series: the hidden heart containers that extend the player's life meter; the ability to map items to controller buttons and see them on the screen; the rupees used as a local currency (although they were referred to as "rubies" in the original game manual); the compass and the map that showed the layout of a dungeon and the location of the boss; and of course the indispensable bow, bombs, boomerang, shield, and other essential accessories.

A LEGENDARY GAME

The first episode of *Zelda* made a huge impression when it was released. It offered players a colossal adventure in comparison to other games of its era, requiring players to explore a gigantic world—not to mention that by completing the adventure once, or by choosing "ZELDA" as the name of their hero, players could take part in a new quest, with a slightly modified world map and different dungeons. The presence of battery-powered RAM for saved games (a first for the era) was a clear indication of the size of the task that awaited young adventurers. Link's increasing power as he collected new objects throughout the game provided a real sense of experiencing an epic quest, punctuated by battles in increasingly complex dungeons. Although the gameplay obviously feels dated today, and the narration a bit abrupt, this first installment still holds an undeniable attraction for many players. But let's not forget how difficult this adventure was. Producer Eiji Aonuma even admits that he has never finished this episode. "I actually never got to the end of it. I think there's practically no other game that's more difficult than that one. Every time I've tried to play it, I wind up with too many 'game over' screens and I end up quitting. After playing the original *Zelda* for the first time, I couldn't even imagine wanting to make a game like that." It was the pleasure of exploration that he felt while playing the third *Zelda* that finally got him hooked on the series. Miyamoto, on the other hand, has stated that the first episode is still his favorite. Although it is not always easy for modern players—perhaps too used to being led by the hand—to figure out where to go in this installment, it is still quite possible with a bit of perseverance to enjoy a replay of this timeless 8-bit Nintendo console classic.

CHAPTER II

ZELDA II: THE ADVENTURE OF LINK

ust a few months after Link's victory over Ganon, the kingdom of Hyrule again finds itself under threat. Although the Prince of Darkness has disappeared, the hate in his heart has continued to spread chaos: many of Ganon's allies still hope for his return. A new rumor has begun to make its way around Hyrule: the evil prince could be brought back to life if Link were sacrificed so that his blood could be sprinkled over Ganon's ashes.

A little while later, on the day of his sixteenth birthday, Link sees the symbol of the Triforce appear on the back of his left hand. Hoping to learn the reason for what he interprets as a dark omen, our young hero goes to seek Impa's advice. Zelda's nursemaid takes him to a palace and brings him to a mysterious door. Impa places Link's left hand on the door, and it opens immediately. Within the secret room, Link is surprised to discover Zelda lying on a slab, apparently asleep. Impa then begins to tell Link the legend of Zelda, passed down from generation to generation in the kingdom.

A long time ago, a noble ruler brought peace to the kingdom of Hyrule, thanks to the power of the Triforce. When the old monarch died, his son had only inherited one fragment of the sacred object when he ascended to the throne. He therefore embarked on a quest to find the other two parts, but in vain. A mysterious magician who had once been close to the king then informed his successor that the only other person who knew of the Triforce's existence was the prince's younger sister, Princess Zelda. The two men thus went to find her, in the hope of learning where the two missing pieces were located. When the young girl refused to cooperate, the magician cast an evil spell on her, sending her into a deep slumber. This act, however, drained the magician of his power, and cost him his life. Overwhelmed with grief, the young king placed Zelda in a secret chamber to wait for her awakening. He then issued a royal decree that in memory of his sister, all girls born to the royal family must be given the name Zelda.

Having finished her story, Impa shows Link an old parchment, as well as six crystals. According to her, these objects will be needed on the day when a new great king shall rise. Although the manuscript appears to be written in an unknown language, Link is able to read it without difficulty. For Impa, this text contains the key to finding the Triforce: Link is in fact the chosen one, the only one able to take possession of the Triforce of Courage, hidden in the great palace in the Valley of Death. To succeed, the hero must first defeat six guardians, then set a crystal into each of the six statues he will find, in order to break the seal that prevents him from entering the final temple. Impa finishes with these words: "Link, you must find the Triforce to save Hyrule and Princess Zelda."

THE HITS KEEP COMING

Less than a year after the first episode, *Zelda II: The Adventure of Link* came out for the Famicom Disk System in January 1987, then at the end of 1988 in the United States and Europe on the NES. The quick turnaround between the two releases can be explained by the fact that, at the time, game development required less time and fewer financial and staff resources than it does today. Nowadays, if a publisher puts out a new game once a year in a given franchise (as with *Call of Duty, Assassin's Creed,* and *Pro Evolution Soccer*), it is likely to draw the ire of many players who assume, sight unseen, that the game will be lacking in ambition. In the NES era, however, it was very common for studios to pump out sequels at a steady rate, as with *Castlevania, Mega Man,* and others. Although *Zelda II* may have surprised players with some unexpected design decisions, it was nevertheless a big commercial success, selling more than 4.4 million copies worldwide.

A NEW FOUNDATION

This second episode of *Zelda* reflects a clear desire for innovation, partly due to a new team of designers—even though Shigeru Miyamoto remained in charge of the project. Among other changes, composer Koji Kondo was replaced by Akito Nakatsuka. Right out of the gate, the number *II* in the game's title removed all doubt as to the creators' intentions: the new game would be a direct follow-up to the first episode. This time, Link gets a turn in the spotlight thanks to the subtitle *The Adventure of Link*. However, the continuity at the story level was accompanied by a sharp break in terms of gameplay, and even

in the world of the game. Despite the immense success of the first *Zelda*, and of the action RPG genre that it helped to create, the Nintendo team chose to take much of their inspiration from the role-playing games that had had such an impact on the Japanese video game industry, especially *Dragon Quest*—just as Square would later do with *Final Fantasy*. The decision caused as much shock as one might expect: the previous installments of *Zelda* and *Dragon Quest* had come out in the same year, and the former had, after all, sold more copies than the latter.

TWO INSPIRATIONS

Influenced by the hit game from Enix, Nintendo based its new *Zelda* game on a classic RPG template. But *Dragon Quest* was not Miyamoto's only source of inspiration; he also drew ideas from the platformer genre that had first made him famous with *Donkey Kong* and *Mario*.

Like the first *Zelda* game, this second installment finds young Link all alone in an open world in which wandering and exploration are the order of the day. The perspective is a more distant one, however: the camera is placed higher up to reveal a wider view of the mountains and plains of Hyrule. Enemies appear on this map, but this is not where the battles take place. When meeting an enemy, the image freezes and the perspective changes to show Link from the side; only then can the battle begin. This alternation between battles and map-based exploration sequences inevitably recalls the *Ultima* series and *Dragon Quest*. The influence is even more obvious in the level progression system, which is now based on increasing quantitative statistics rather than on collecting items. By killing monsters, Link collects experience points that allow him to become stronger. Each time Link levels up, the player can spend these points to increase the hero's strength, magic or life meter, up to a maximum of eight points in each category. Here and there throughout this episode of *Zelda*, we find various details that either evoke *Dragon Quest* directly, or at least reflect a strong affinity for the classic role-playing game. Besides the use of experience points and a clear distinction between combat and exploration sequences, Link also acquires magical skills like healing, fire, and thunder—and the creatures he encounters in this episode even include little blue and red monsters that strongly resemble the "slimes" from the Enix RPG. Hyrule's civilization seems to have spread to the plains, where a number of little villages have now sprung up. And although interactions with NPCs (non-player characters) are not a central aspect of the gameplay, meeting certain villagers allows Link to recover life and magic points—a function usually reserved to inns and churches in classic RPGs. In these villages, rushing off to rescue a widow or an orphan also allows players to acquire certain magical skills, but only after completing an optional side mission like giving a drink to a dying girl, bringing a child back to its frantic mother, and other helpful actions to make Link a hero of the people.

Even with this link to RPGs, the second chapter of the *Zelda* saga doesn't hesitate to show off its love for the platformer genre. At the time, studios were releasing a growing number of games in this category, many of which brought new critical acclaim to the genre: *Wonder Boy* (1986), *Ghosts'n Goblins* (1985), *Castlevania* (1986), and of course *Super Mario Bros.* (1985) were each drawing their share of attention in the video game industry. In changing the top-down perspective of the first *Zelda* game to adopt the side view used in leading platformers like these, Miyamoto emphasized the relationship between his latest work and the platform games of the era. Previously somewhat flattened by the overhead view, Link was suddenly taller than ever. The dungeons, meanwhile, lost none of their labyrinthine character, despite the new perspective. Exploring them truly put players' skills to the test: besides avoiding different traps and snares, Link also has to deal with swarms of enemies. The rhythm is quicker and the action more precise than in *The Legend of Zelda*: the player must approach the deadly pits cautiously and cross them deftly, and the battles are difficult and varied. No longer is a single stroke of the sword enough to drive back enemies; high attacks, low attacks, and well-timed jumps are useful and even essential techniques for players to emerge victorious in battle. The game's overall atmosphere also evokes the other big hits of the era at certain points. The color palette, as well as certain dungeons and enemies, often recall games like *Mario* or *Castlevania*. Like his high-jumping counterparts in those games, Link even has multiple lives now. When he runs out of them, the hero dies—another reflection of the heritage shared by *Zelda* and the platformer genre.

In terms of its design, then, *The Adventure of Link* breaks with the legacy of the first episode, recent as it was, and changes many of its key elements. Rupees are no longer used in the land of Hyrule; the iconic items from the first game have changed (the boomerang and the bow have been replaced by the hammer and the cross, both used exclusively in exploration sections); and Link can use magic, even though only his sword allows him to actually defeat his attackers. More mature than its predecessor, this design fit with Nintendo's desire to reach a wider audience—but exchanged the first game's atmosphere of heroic fantasy for an aesthetic that evoked Greco-Roman mythology, albeit somewhat loosely. The identity of *Zelda II* thus emerged as a combination of the two genres of

RPG and platform games. As blatant as they were, the aspects borrowed from other leading games of the era were put to skillful use. Precision, patience and skill were the new virtues that players had to cultivate if they ever hoped to complete this exceptionally challenging adventure.

A RADICAL EVOLUTION

Much like its hero, the *Zelda* saga had already grown and evolved in the space of just two episodes. At sixteen years old, Link was not far from adulthood. At the start of the adventure, he is seen as a hero by the people of Hyrule, as evidenced by the title on the game cartridge. But had the child grown up too quickly?

Nowadays, a change as drastic as the transition from the first game to *Zelda II* would be simply unthinkable. Changing the formula of a game that had sold more than 6.5 million copies to produce a radically different sequel would seem like financial suicide. The industry was different back then, due in part to the lower production costs—but that doesn't change the fact that Nintendo's sharp left turn with a valued franchise was a remarkable and courageous act. This shift to a more mature and serious game, in which the hero took on more realistic proportions and the atmosphere borrowed more extensively from mythology than from heroic fantasy, reflected an overall turn that Nintendo was beginning to take towards a somewhat more grown-up sensibility—as *Metroid* had already shown in the previous year. The company would continue this process with its launch of the NES in the United States: rather than continuing to present its console as a toy, the manufacturer chose to present it for the first time as an electronic device, along the same lines as a VCR. We can therefore assume that it was with an eye towards this new orientation that the gameplay in *Zelda II* was so fundamentally changed. Whereas the first *Zelda* was known for being highly accessible, its successor aimed to be more demanding—and woe be to any player who came to the game with a casual attitude! This episode turns out to be an unusually difficult one: enemies are tough, dungeons are bigger than before, and mistakes carry a high cost. When the player loses all their lives, they are sent straight back to Zelda's bedside... at the very start of the adventure. At times, the player is also obliged to grind their way through "level up" sessions, drawing out the exploration sections longer than strictly necessary in order to battle more monsters outside the dungeons and thereby collect much-needed experience points—a favorite method of character progression in *Dragon Quest* as well. Finally, *The Adventure of Link* adopts a more serious tone, and the atmosphere is less playful; the game is completely devoid of humor. The conclusion, in which Link confronts his evil alter ego, also leaves the player with something to think about.

In sum, *Zelda II* is defined by the many ways in which it differs from its predecessor and establishes its own unique identity. And it was to remain a unique case, set apart from the other games in the series. In the end, this game is more like a medieval epic, indulging our urge to go forth into knightly battle on a tougher and less forgiving quest than the colorful introductory tale of the first episode.

Nintendo's change in direction with *The Adventure of Link* stands in stark contrast to the choices it made for another iconic series, the *Super Mario* games. After the huge initial success of the first game in each series, both Miyamoto productions were followed up with a second installment less than a year later. As we have just seen, *Zelda II* chose to throw its fans a curveball by changing the original formula. Conversely, *Super Mario Bros.: The Lost Levels* and its predecessor are like two peas in a pod. Nintendo chose to apply two diametrically opposed strategies for its two flagship series. Even though *The Adventure of Link* is considered to this day to be the most difficult game in the series, it is nevertheless a full-fledged *Zelda* game like any other, contributing to the series' legacy and influencing later games. And above all, it was a commercial success in its own right, with more than 4.38 million copies sold—hardly a disappointing result.

THE "BAD" GAME

In a June 2013 interview as part of the promotion of *Pikmin 3*, Miyamoto answered in the affirmative when asked by a journalist from *Kotaku* whether he had ever worked on a bad game. Taken aback, the journalist pressed him for more details. Immediately softening his remarks, Miyamoto explained himself as follows: "I wouldn't say that I've ever made a 'bad' game per se, but a game I think we could have done more with was *Zelda II*. When we're designing games, we have our plan for what we're going to design, but in our process it evolves and grows from there. In *Zelda II*, unfortunately all we ended up creating was what we had originally planned on paper." When the journalist asked him what he would have liked to change, Miyamoto replied: "Speed up the switch between the side-scrolling and overhead scenes... and it would have been nice to have had bigger enemies." Both limitations were imposed by the the NES console's modest abilities.

CHAPTER III
A LINK TO THE PAST

good creation myth has to go back to time immemorial, when a still-pristine world was only waiting for the first spark to set its story in motion. The tale of the how the land of Hyrule was created is no exception. In the beginning, three goddesses descended from the heavens to create life. The goddess of power formed the landscape of Hyrule by shaping the curves of its mountains and plains. The goddess of wisdom created science and magic, and gave life to the plants. Finally, the goddess of courage gave birth to all the animals, from creeping insects to birds soaring high across the sky. Having finished their creation, the three goddesses departed from this new world, but left behind a golden triangle that was itself made up of three smaller equilateral triangles. This mystical object contained the essence of each of the goddesses, and was intended to help guide the course of life in Hyrule with wisdom and discernment. Although it had no mind of its own, this golden triangle was able to assign three titles by conferring a corresponding power on each of the designated title bearers: the Forger of Strength, the Keeper of Knowledge, and the Juror of Courage. It was in reference to this extraordinary property that the object came to be known as the Triforce. Ever since it was hidden in the Golden Land where the goddesses had left it, the Triforce had been calling on the Hylians to seek it; but only an exceptional being who deserved to receive its divine abilities would ever be able to find it.

Born of the three goddesses, the Hylians had extraordinary powers and a deep knowledge of the magic arts. It is said that their long pointed ears allowed them to hear the messages spoken to them by their ancestors. Most of the inhabitants of Hyrule therefore continued to honor the goddesses. As the generations passed, the Hylians' descendants spread out across the world, bringing their knowledge to places beyond the mountains. However, it was not long before this great scholarly tradition began to change, and eventually disappeared completely. The legends make frequent mention of a number of religious buildings. Now a mere shadow of their former glory, these ruins are closely related to the Triforce; some of them are even said to be home to the Triforce itself. The symbolism of the Triforce alone was enough to spark the desires of many. But it was a verse from the Book of Mudora, which contained all the legends and knowledge of the Hylians, that fanned that spark into a flame: "In a realm beyond sight, / The Sky shines gold, not blue. / There, the Triforce's might / Makes mortal dreams come true."

Many people spent their lives searching for this much-coveted object. And yet, no one knew where it was located, not even the Seven Sages. Some believed that the Triforce lay deep beneath the desert sands; others were convinced that it could be found in a graveyard in the shadow of Death Mountain. But no one ever found it. The quest for the great golden triangle gradually became an all-consuming obsession for many, fed by greed and a thirst for power that inevitably led to much bloodshed.

One day, a band of thieves using black magic opened the gateway to the Golden Land—almost by accident. It was these thieves who had the incredible honor to discover the resting place of the Triforce, a land like none other that had ever been seen. Even as the darkness of night began to spread, the Triforce shone brightly from its resting place far above their heads. The group's power-hungry leader fought a long battle against his own companions, and defeated them one by one. When, in his triumph, he finally held the Triforce between his blood-stained hands, he heard a voice whispering in his mind: "If you have an insatiable desire or an impossible dream, make a wish..." The bandit leader burst out in diabolical laughter, so monstrous that its echoes were heard in even the most distant corners of Hyrule. The name of this despicable creature was Ganondorf Dragmire, but he was better known as Mandrag Ganon in reference to his clan of "enchanted thieves."

No one knew what wish he had made that day. From that day forward, however, an evil force began to spread forth from the Golden Land, exerting its pull on wicked men who sought to join Ganon's army. Black clouds began to fill the sky, and innocent lands were rocked by disaster after disaster. Without hesitation, the king of Hyrule ordered the Seven Sages and his most valiant knights to seal the gateway to the Golden Land. To preserve peace in their world, the inhabitants of Hyrule forged an exceptional sword, able to resist magic and repel all evil. This extraordinary weapon was known as the Master Sword. To master it, the one who held the sword had to possess both physical strength and purity of heart. Even as the Seven Sages searched for a person who was fit to wield the Master Sword, Ganon's diabolical army left the Golden Land to attack the king's castle. The sages and knights of Hyrule joined forces

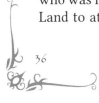

to fight back against this infernal horde. The knights managed to push back the assault, and the Seven Sages sealed the entrance to the Golden Land, imprisoning Ganon inside.

Centuries went by after this fearsome battle. The land of Hyrule bandaged its wounds, and the memory of this terrible conflict faded as the generations passed. The people of Hyrule lived happily for many years...

No one was prepared to confront the next disaster: plagues and droughts began to ravage the kingdom, and magic proved powerless against them. After seeking the counsel of the Sages, the king of Hyrule decided to find out whether Ganon had managed to escape the Dark World, as the Golden Land had been known since the defeat of Ganon's troops. But the seal forged by the Sages in those long-ago days turned out to still be intact. The king then promised a reward to whomever could discover the source of the kingdom's troubles. A stranger by the name of Agahnim appeared, and managed to put a stop to the disasters by using a previously unknown form of magic. To thank him, the king appointed Agahnim as his chief counselor, and he became a hero to the people of Hyrule.

However, it was not long before Agahnim's reputation was tarnished by rumors that the king's chief counselor was conducting strange magical rituals in the tower of the castle. Fear began to take hold of the people of Hyrule— and their concern soon proved to be justified when Agahnim pushed the king aside to seize the throne for himself. But his Machiavellian plan did not end there: one by one, he expelled the descendants of the Seven Sages from his court in order to tighten his grip and break the seal that kept the forces of evil trapped inside the Dark World. Zelda, the daughter of the rightful king, did all that she could to prevent the gateway to the former Golden Land from being opened. From deep within the dark, dank dungeons of the castle, she sent out a telepathic call. The call was heard by the young hero Link, awakening him from his sleep. The boy immediately turned to his uncle, who set out to rescue the girl. Disobeying his uncle's instructions, the daring young lad could not stop himself from hurrying along after him.

A SPECTACULAR RETURN TO THE PAST

Fans had been waiting for four long years for Link's latest adventure to come out—and with the arrival of a new console, the wait was richly rewarded. The Super NES had only been out for a year when the third game in the series, *The Legend of Zelda: A Link to the Past*, was released. As Nintendo's leading title for its new console, this episode marked the transition to the 16-bit architecture

with a sumptuous new look and sound. It will remain forever etched into the memories of those who played it at the time—for its indisputable inherent quality as a game, of course, but also for the skillful way in which it passed the baton to a new generation of consoles. At first, *A Link to the Past* was a visual shock for players: the power of the Super Nintendo allowed Shigeru Miyamoto to express his excitement at creating a new *Zelda* game through the use of brilliant new colors and detailed animations, along with a whole range of improvements that added greater depth to the kingdom of Hyrule. The game's world came to life like never before. In addition, the sound quality available on the new machine could finally do justice to the charming melodies of Koji Kondo, who returned to the series in this episode. And "Mode 7," a graphics mode that provided a breathtaking impression of perspective, also did its part to astound players. In their quest to push the boundaries of the era as far as they could, the designers had worked to enrich the gameplay in every possible way. For a while, they even planned to allow Link to eat and dance in the game! Although these ideas were eliminated from the final version, they reflect the immense freedom with which the designers could express themselves on the Super Nintendo.

Zelda I and *II* had each presented their own distinct take on the series, but A Link to the Past didn't necessarily seek to forge a third path of its own. An admission of failure? A new acceptance of lessons learned? An expression of authentic intent? Whatever the reason, the new title went back to the template of the first episode, and marks the return of the top-down view. The first *Zelda* had been seen as a game that was free of other video game influences and offered a natural approach to character progression. After a very different second episode that clearly had one eye on the competition, Nintendo now chose to return to its origins, and thus to reaffirm and strengthen its original inspiration.

The third *Zelda* also represents the end of the brief timeline that ties the different installments to one another. Although the plot of *The Adventure of Link* appeared to follow up on that of the first title in the series, the observant player will notice certain inconsistencies: the Princess Zelda who was presented in *Zelda II* as having been asleep for centuries—although she was clearly awake in the first episode—was only one of many. The storyline in those two games was apparently not the designers' highest priority, so much so that even at that point, the internal consistency of the series was somewhat fragile. *A Link to the Past* starts by muddying the waters: Ganon is no longer presented as the main enemy, a role which falls this time to the wizard Agahnim. The rest of the game reveals an entirely different reality, but it seems that the new installment preserves only three concrete elements from the previous games to set up its own foundation and tie it to the rest of the series: the world known as Hyrule;

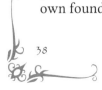

a courageous hero, Link, who risks his life to save a princess named Zelda; and, finally, the big bad guy, Ganon. During the development of *A Link to the Past*, Miyamoto even bemoaned the game's atmosphere of heroic fantasy: although the genre was not yet well-known when the first episode was developed, it had become fairly commonplace since then. Trapped in this straitjacket, the *Zelda* series could hardly change its setting to a completely different kind of world. As someone who was always eager to experiment with new ideas, Miyamoto was saddened by this situation. That may have been the reason for the existence of a parallel world alongside Hyrule in the story of *A Link to the Past*, within which the Japanese designer was able to explore a few new directions— a good way to let his imagination run free.

BACK TO "NORMAL"

The third *Zelda* game thus saw Miyamoto's teams going back to the foundations of the first episode, and opting once again for a top-down perspective on the world. With that framework in place, the evolution on display in the new game is nevertheless so extensive as to make the original *Zelda* look like a simple sketch that was now appearing in a grander, more developed and more beautiful form. For example, gameplay in this episode is more flexible and less punishing than that of the first two games—thanks especially to the new moves now available to Link, including a spinning sword attack and the ability to dash when wearing the Pegasus Boots. In addition, players no longer have to position their attacks down to the millimeter in order to slay an enemy. The increased tolerance and flexibility make the adventure even more enjoyable to play. The world of Hyrule seems more alive than ever, and Link can now interact with his environment in a wider variety of ways.

As part of his progression, our hero will of course have to emerge victorious from all the battles that await him in the twisting passages of the many dungeons he will encounter. The level design in those dungeons is far more ingenious and complex than in previous games—a pattern that was to become a hallmark of the series—and each dungeon also has its own distinct character. Each time Link explores one of these places, he acquires a precious object (hookshot, mirror shield, hammer, etc.) which often turns out to be an essential tool in the boss fight for that dungeon. This, too, would become a signature aspect of the series in later installments.

Also notable in *A Link to the Past* is the care that goes into the connection between story and gameplay. Breaking with the sparse and rough-edged approach of the earlier episodes, the third *Zelda* game marks the start of a

new era in video games, in which story and narrative design start to come into their own; this approach would be revisited a few years later by *Final Fantasy IV* (initially released in North America under the title *Final Fantasy II*), which would become a lasting milestone in the history of the Super Nintendo. As the game begins, the adventure is presented in a lightly "scripted" form, though in a sense quite distinct from what is meant by this term in more modern productions: the first thing the player sees is Link's dream. When he wakes up (surely one of the RPG genre's most well-worn clichés), our young hero immediately sets out on his adventure. The sky is dark and the rain pours down in sheets, and within just a few minutes, the hero has acquired a sword from his uncle, whom he finds injured in an underground tunnel leading to the princess's castle. The RPG aspect is also reflected in how the hero's equipment evolves throughout the game: an increasingly powerful sword (Master Sword, Tempered Sword, Golden Sword), shields and coats of chain mail with improved damage resistance, and so on. Acquiring better equipment makes the player's character stronger, which in turn makes exploration easier. We also encounter gameplay elements that have since become standard features of any good roleplaying game, such as the ocarina—still referred to as a "flute" in this episode, and destined to become one of the saga's most iconic items—which summons a bird that can take the player instantly to any place in the kingdom. This function was also found in many other RPGs of the era. Link also uses a much wider range of equipment in this game, and can acquire even more items by spending time on different side quests that are offered along the way. These include collecting various bottles that can be used to hold health potions or fairies, increasing the number of arrows or bombs Link can carry, and making improvements to his shield or his boomerang—not to mention the search for Pieces of Heart, which allow the hero to extend his health bar.

The adventure ultimately turns out to be one of considerable scope, and one which keeps the player interested at every turn. Exploring the world is easier now with the help of an in-game map, which appears in spectacular form thanks to the console's famous "Mode 7"; the idea of including a printed version with the manual is thereby rendered obsolete. In this episode, then, *Zelda* ignites the player's curiosity and taste for discovery more than ever before.

HYRULE COMES INTO ITS OWN

In expanding on the ideas of the first *Zelda* game, the third installment goes beyond merely adding new gameplay mechanics. For example, the world of Hyrule as a whole has been developed in significantly more detail, and now

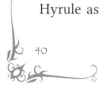

appears in its "definitive" form—or at least, in the form that has found the most lasting place in fans' hearts. The technical capabilities of the Super Nintendo have allowed the designers to build on their achievements from the NES era. Forests, lakes, underground tunnels and villages are now even more majestic, and each different region has its own native population (an aspect which would be developed still further on the Nintendo 64). It all contributes to an in-game universe that feels more fleshed-out and more believable. The people of Hyrule even have their own myths and legends, as we discover through the quest for the Master Sword. Let us note in passing that the Japanese developers obviously took their inspiration from the Arthurian myth of Excalibur to forge the legend of Link's sword, a blade with fantastic powers that was embedded in a stone from which only the chosen one could remove it.

The triad of Link, Zelda and Ganon is further strengthened; the diabolical Lord of Evil, in particular, is fleshed out through the gradual revelation of a deeply cunning and duplicitous plan, setting him up as our hero's eternal antagonist. Putting the finishing touches on Hyrule's new face, a number of new sound effects that have since become legendary make their first appearance, along with new melodies like Zelda's and Ganon's themes. The world in this third *Zelda* game is revealed to be even more enormous when Link discovers the existence of a parallel world. It is interesting to note that the designers' initial vision even included a third world, but the idea was ultimately abandoned for fear of confusing the unfortunate player.

As we have seen, the power of the new Super Nintendo gave Miyamoto and his team the opportunity to fully realize their vision for the world of Hyrule. The graphics were more detailed, allowing for a few unique touches. Link is cuter than ever and meticulously animated—still left-handed (for any players who still hadn't noticed after two episodes) and with pink hair hidden under his pointed green hat (a curiosity that is difficult to explain without directly asking the man who created the character). The hero's facial expressions are irresistible: the little drops of sweat that stand out on his forehead when he lifts a heavy object, the bizarre scowl on his face when he gets electrocuted, and so on. They lead to a noticeable change in the game's atmosphere, compared to the two previous episodes; the tone is lighter and more relaxed, allowing humor to make its way into the series for the first time. The overall look is not unlike a cartoon, reinforcing the sensation of discovering a living and coherent world—and making that world all the more fascinating to players. In this episode, Link really looks like a child—for which he is ruthlessly mocked by certain guards. In the role of a cute little hero like this one, players don't mind a few silly moments: discovering their passion for mowing the lawn, teasing chickens, picking up jars and throwing them in other characters' faces, and so on. Players can spend hours like this, just having fun with their environment.

THE TRUE HEART OF THE SAGA

Two components of the title *The Legend of Zelda: A Link to the Past* seem to support the ideas developed above. The first part of the title, "*The Legend of Zelda,*" is simply a repetition of the first game's title; this might be seen as a way of distancing the game from *Zelda II*, whose full title focused on the character of Link. The young hero is not left out, however. His name appears here again, albeit in the form of a pun rather than a direct reference, in the second part of the title: *A Link to the Past.* In both a literal and figurative sense, Link represents the *link* between the different games in the *Zelda* series. He is truly a link in a chain, exploring the world of Hyrule and connecting it to its inhabitants. And yet, the hero of this third installment has little in common with the Link of the previous chapters. To be sure, his name and general appearance have been preserved, but he has gone back to being a child, and his story is completely different. The same can be said of the other pillars of the series—Hyrule, Zelda and Ganon—whose story has been developed in much more detail, even if it leads to inconsistencies with the first two installments.

A LEGEND IS BORN

Although the first two episodes were resounding commercial successes, the legend of *Zelda* doesn't truly begin until *A Link to the Past.* The 1990s were a kind of golden age in which players experienced a constant rush of discovery, emotion and wonder. On the Super Nintendo, standing out among competitors like *Final Fantasy IV, Dragon Quest V*, and *Super Castlevania IV* was no mean feat.

Miyamoto not only managed it, but by offering a game of exceptionally vast scope in which the actual adventure didn't start until after several hours of play, with its two worlds, a meticulously developed setting and breathtakingly beautiful graphics, he succeeded in setting a new standard. Each with its own unique structure and atmosphere, the dungeons turned the already convoluted challenges of the previous episodes into bona fide architectural puzzles—soon to become one of the cornerstones of the series. The choice to return to the template established by the first *Zelda*, which was already associated with impeccable gameplay, ensured *A Link to the Past*'s place as the ultimate, unassailable standard against which all later installments would inevitably be judged.

CHAPTER IV

LINK'S AWAKENING

he evil Ganon is no more. After a hard-fought battle, peace has finally been restored to the kingdom of Hyrule. Strangely enough, however, our hero Link has not found peace of mind. He is uncertain of his ability to confront future threats and protect Princess Zelda's life. Seeking to regain his self-confidence and improve his skill in combat, he decides to embark on a voyage that will help him to reach a new level of perfection. After a long trek, punctuated by bitter struggles and long wanderings in uncharted lands, the young hero finally feels ready to return to those he is bound to defend. He thus takes to the sea to return to his native land, but the ocean has a different idea: as smooth as glass just a moment before, the surface of the water begins to roll and churn, tossing Link's boat around more and more violently. As a series of crashing waves sets to smashing his ship to pieces, lightning strikes the mast at full force, as if to seal our hero's tragic fate. With a final burst of effort, Link manages to grab hold of a board, but quickly sinks beneath the waves as if pulled under by the inky depths.

Released from the icy embrace of the sea, Link washes up on the island of Koholint. The young hero is awakened from his stupor by a familiar sound, convinced that he has heard Zelda's voice. He is mistaken: standing before him is not the princess of Hyrule, but a girl named Marin. After discovering Link lying on the beach, she decides to take him back to Mabe Village. At home, Marin explains to Link that the island of Koholint lies at the foot of an immense mountain, with a giant egg nestled at its peak. According to legend, the Wind Fish sleeps inside the egg. She tells him that she has waited a long time for the chosen one who can awaken the fish by playing a melody on the eight Instruments of the Sirens. Marin is sure beyond a doubt that Link is the chosen one, and our hero finds himself taking on a new quest: he will not be able to leave the island of Koholint until his mission is complete. Guided by young Marin and a mysterious owl, the young Hylian thus sets off on a new adventure.

A SEQUEL?

Although the timeline relating the different games to one another is not clearly established, a number of clues seem to suggest that *Link's Awakening* is indeed the direct continuation of one of Link's previous adventures. For instance, Link already knows Princess Zelda when his new quest begins, and mistakes Marin for Zelda when he awakens on the beach. He also has a sword and a shield with him, implying that his status as a hero, or at least as a knight, is already established; and he has already mastered his famous spinning attack. In fact, we already know the reason for his voyage: Link was returning from a training journey, specifically intended to make him strong enough to fend off the dangers that might still threaten Zelda. A final intriguing detail: a pair of related *Zelda* games that appeared later, *Oracle of Ages* and *Oracle of Seasons*—although not released until eight years after *Link's Awakening*! —reveals the real end of the adventure in a new cutscene, which players can only see if they complete both games by using the save file from one game to continue the story in the second. These images show Link stepping onto a ship, in a scene that clearly evokes the opening of *Link's Awakening*. Are we to conclude that these two games, which we will discuss in a later chapter, chronologically precede the present installment?

A SEARCH FOR NEW HORIZONS

In just under three years, Nintendo's Game Boy had completely conquered players' hearts. And yet, no adventure truly deserving of the name had yet graced the screen of this portable console. In the hopes of filling that gap, the Japanese publisher decided in 1993 to bring the *Zelda* franchise to the Game Boy. The astounding success of *A Link to the Past* and good console sales helped to spur this project on. Development began after the creation of another roleplaying game, *Kaeru no Tame ni Kane wa Naru* (never released outside of Japan), with which *Link's Awakening* shared its graphics engine and its rounded, cartoonish aesthetic. By the standards of that era, the graphics were magnificent.

The opening and closing cutscenes are incredible for a portable console. A prestigious license, top-notch visuals, and an epic tale that took full advantage

of the Game Boy's capabilities: all the factors were in place for a truly great *Zelda* game.

The Game Boy is known for its immense autonomy, the perfect feature for offering gamers a chance to escape with their console in hand on a grand nomadic adventure. And what better theme to inspire that feeling than the subject of dreams? Nintendo's choice of subject for the game would allow it to set aside certain cornerstones of the series. Princess Zelda and Ganon are nowhere to be seen here—at least, not before the final battle, but we'll come back to that—and the adventure does not take place within the kingdom of Hyrule. More importantly still, the primary goal is completely different. Link's mission this time is to awaken the Wind Fish, a mission that does not at any time involve yet another effort to rescue Princess Zelda. Besides allowing Nintendo to step outside the limits of its established format, the subject of dreams also helped to create a very specific atmosphere with no precedent in other games in the series. Surprisingly, the tone of this *Zelda* for Game Boy is revealed early on to be darker and more grown-up than that of the other installments, with a number of references to death and a more melancholy feeling overall—though it is not without certain touches of humor (as any player who tried stealing an object from the shop, only to find themselves labeled a "Thief" for the rest of the game, will recall to this day). All in all, *Link's Awakening* is a dreamlike adventure in which the imagery of sleep, dreams and nightmares yields an atmosphere so unique that few other games can even be compared to it. However, let us be sure to mention the lovely epic saga of *Alundra*, another action RPG which came out five years later, in which the hero travels through people's dreams in order to free them of their nightmares. With its mix of fantasy and dreamlike imagery, and of scenes both sad and strange, *Alundra* seems quite clearly to have drawn from the teachings of *Link's Awakening* for its psychological and philosophical dimension.

In 1998, Nintendo re-released the game for the Game Boy Color as part of a so-called "Deluxe" collection. Trading black-and-white graphics for color, this version enhances the basic structure of the game with a few well-placed additions. The photographer character makes his appearance, allowing the player to see certain specific moments of the adventure immortalized on film (twelve in all). These snapshots could then be printed on the Game Boy Printer, an accessory that had come out not long before. However, the DX version's biggest addition was an entirely new dungeon: the Color Dungeon. Accessible once the player has acquired the Pegasus Boots, this optional challenge is built entirely around the use of colors, and the puzzles call on the player's sense of observation. If Link succeeds in completing this quest, he is allowed to choose between two special tunics, one blue and one red.

The former gives him increased attack strength, while the latter improves his resistance to weapons and electric shocks—but it is impossible to obtain more than one of them. Starting in June 2011, this DX version of *Link's Awakening* was made available again on the Nintendo eShop, the download platform for the Nintendo 3DS.

SMALL, BUT TOUGH

It would be a grave mistake to assume that its appearance on the Game Boy meant that *Link's Awakening* was a cut-rate *Zelda* title. The small handheld console has plenty of power under the hood, and was determined to prove it by flawlessly reproducing the extremely rich gameplay of its predecessor, *A Link to the Past*. The reuse of mechanics from the third *Zelda* game is a sign of the designers' great skill. Players were thrilled to rediscover the distinctive features that had already become the hallmark of the saga. It only takes a few seconds to get used to the overhead view, and the first dungeon makes it clear to players that the routines they used in the previous *Zelda* will work just as well here. The game's approach to the dungeons thus remains the same: each one has its own unique theme, and the player has to acquire a specific object in order to beat the boss at the end of the level, then use that object to discover new regions of Koholint. For the first time, the world map is revealed only a bit at a time. We also find the same ingenious level design that was the signature element of *A Link to the Past*—with a special nod to the seventh dungeon (the Eagle's Tower), in which the player has to make the fourth floor collapse into the third, and which remains one of the most memorable challenges in the game.

Every bit as intense at its predecessor on the Super Nintendo, *Link's Awakening* turns out to be even more effectively paced: the dungeons are better designed, and the adventure as a whole is enriched by a variety of side quests. This is also the episode that introduces fishing, which was to become an iconic minigame in later *Zelda* games as well. For example, to earn the level two sword, which allows Link to shoot beams of light, he has to collect various shells that are hidden around Koholint. Finally, as a backdrop to the main quest, Link has to engage in a vast trading game which, in exchange for services rendered to different inhabitants of the island, allows him to acquire first the magnifying lens, and then the boomerang. Alongside the classic search for Pieces of Heart, this continuing theme turns out to provide some fun and exciting moments— and offers a clever way to break out of the routine imposed by the game's main path, which would otherwise lead the player unceasingly from one dungeon to the next.

We have seen how the second episode of *Zelda* managed to break with its predecessor. *Link's Awakening* does not completely reject that game's legacy, making use as it does of a similar side view for underground exploration sequences. As Link enters a staircase, a cellar or cave, or even a boss fight, the perspective changes to show him from the side; these alternating viewpoints bring a new dimension to the game, and help to make certain action-packed sequences even more dynamic. The game also finds other ways to add a quick jolt of energy, as when Link slays an enemy and finds a triangular Piece of Power or a Guardian Acorn beneath the monster's remains. The former doubles the hero's attack strength, and the latter makes him invincible for a short period of time. While the use of such temporary power-ups clearly evokes games in the shooter genre, it also recalls the *Mario* saga (with its star of invincibility), as does another nod to that series: the feather, which allows Link to jump, was also featured in *Super Mario World* and in *Mario Kart*, where it provided the same type of ability.

Although the gradual way in which the map is revealed over the course of the adventure preserves a sense of mystery about lands yet to be discovered, *Link's Awakening* also provides players with enough guidance to keep them from feeling abandoned. A number of helpful additions now make Link's task a bit easier: The map is still his most important tool when finding his way through dungeons, but in addition to showing the location of treasure chests and the main boss, the compass now also sounds a tone to help him find keys. The owl also gives frequent advice to our hero, both inside and outside the dungeons. These quick bits of guidance help to avoid the kind of frustration that a player might feel when getting stuck or lost, which could be detrimental to their sense of freedom within the game. In this episode, that freedom even applies to the choice of equipment: for the first time in a *Zelda* game, players are no longer required to use the sword and shield as their weapons. The A and B buttons can be easily assigned to any object in their inventory. It may not always be pleasant to have to switch back and forth between gameplay and menus, but the highly original combinations that players can set up with this new system are a definite plus.

DREAM THEATER

Link's Awakening has a certain charm that is difficult to describe, much like its main theme: the world of dreams. The adventure is marked by a melancholy,

almost morose atmosphere, but with a deeply optimistic message at its core. Before turning to the subject of dreams and its relevance to the game, let us consider the end of this episode, an essential aspect that will be useful for the rest of our analysis. Those who have not yet reached the end of the game may wish to skip the next paragraph if they prefer, quite understandably, to discover the final moments of the story for themselves—one of the finest endings to be found in any video game.

Once Link has collected the eight Instruments of the Sirens, it is time for him to set forth and free the Wind Fish from its nightmares. He plays the melody that will awaken the fish, first on the ocarina and then on the other instruments, and an opening forms in the egg where the giant sleeps. To complete the adventure, it is essential that Link have completed the item trading quest—the only way to obtain the magnifying lens that he needs to decipher the book which reveals the path he must follow once inside the fish's lair. Having finally reached his destination, Link is quickly confronted with a new enemy: the Shadow Nightmares, a black shadow that can take on the appearance of its opponent's nightmares. It explains to our hero that in order to take control of the world, the forces of evil have put the Wind Fish into an endless slumber, to which the island of Koholint owes its very existence. A long battle begins, during which Link must confront his deepest worries and fears, represented by silhouettes of Agahnim and Ganon. Finally, the Nightmares collapse in defeat. The owl, who has been Link's faithful companion throughout the adventure, then arrives to reveal its true nature: it is in fact a part of the Wind Fish's spirit. From the very beginning, the Wind Fish had sought to help Link, whom it saw as an incarnation of hope. Now that its task is complete, the owl, guardian of the dream world, rejoins the spirit of the Wind Fish. Link then proceeds further into the heart of the giant egg, where he will finally meet its occupant face-to-face. The god appears in the form of an enormous whale of many colors, and tells Link of the origins of Koholint: in its dream, an egg appeared, followed by an island all around it. Animals and humans then appeared on the island as well. A world had been born. However, a terrible nightmare soon came to disturb this sweet dream. The Wind Fish knew all along that when it eventually woke up, Koholint would disappear. The god then tells Link that it wants the memory of the island to live on as a reality in the hearts of those who had the honor of walking its shores. Finally, the Wind Fish asks our hero to join it in awakening. The Song of Awakening sounds forth once more from Link's ocarina, and the world around them starts to disappear; the island and its inhabitants fade away, leaving only the ocean in their place. Link opens his eyes. He is alone at sea, floating amongst the wreckage of his ship, which was destroyed by the storm.

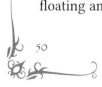

Raising his eyes to the sky, he sees the silhouette of the Wind Fish as it flies across the clouds. Was it all a dream? Confusion gives way to serenity. Link's face reflects a sense of inner peace. He smiles, visibly happy.

Dreams have been the subject of extensive study, but have not yet revealed all of their secrets. In what more fertile soil could Nintendo's designers have cultivated their chosen setting, a world of wonder and melancholy, than in the nightly theater of dreams? Choosing this unique theme allowed them to bring a real breath of fresh air to the *Zelda* saga. Playing skillfully with the confusion between dreams and reality, just as we experience it in our own lives, the Japanese publisher succeeded in breaking down barriers and creating a truly epic adventure for its portable console. In retrospect, the game seems like a dream that invites each player to give themselves over to its quiet flow—a chance to transcend their usual experience of a *Zelda* game.

The subject of dreams is a complex one, due to the many symbols that comprise its vocabulary. The allegories associated with dreams are multidimensional, and tied to both positive and negative meanings. For example, a cup placed on the ground can express a range of contradictory meanings, depending on whether it faces up towards the sky or down towards the ground. Dreams are always subject to interpretation. The epilogue to *Link's Awakening* provides the foundation on which we can base our study of the work as a whole, for that is where we find all the information we need to understand it. Starting from the clues left by Nintendo, we will now attempt to comprehend the meaning behind this one-of-a-kind adventure.

WAS IT REAL, OR JUST A DREAM?

In fact, the subject of dreams is evoked at many different times in the course of the adventure. First, let us note that Link is guided through the game by an owl, symbol of the night—the time when we are most likely to dream. The game's location and characters are also completely different from those that players had previously encountered in the *Zelda* series, which is a fairly strong hint in itself. The island of Koholint feels like a world unto itself, stripped of the fundamental reference points of Hyrule, Zelda and Ganon. The Triforce, that iconic symbol of the *Zelda* games, does not appear in *Link's Awakening*, except through a subtle implication in the words of the owl, who proclaims to Link at the end of the adventure that he was able to defeat the nightmare thanks to his strength, wisdom and courage—the three virtues associated with the divine object. There are many other references to dreams in the game, but one of the most intriguing is offered by the dream shrine. A small house in the north of Mabe Village, this refuge contains nothing more than a single bed. When Link lies down in it, he dreams of a new place in which progress depends on certain specific objects (the feather, then the boots), and in which monsters mimic his every action and gesture. At the end of his path lies a chest containing the ocarina. In other words, the saga's most iconic instrument cannot be found on Koholint itself. Only by passing through several layers of dreams is Link able to acquire the item and extract it from his dream. Attempting to interpret the many such details found in the game and tie them in to the theme of dreams is interesting enough in itself, but there are even more fascinating connections to be drawn. The overall quest in *Link's Awakening* echoes a more general theory of analytic psychology developed by the Swiss psychiatrist Carl Gustav Jung, who, like Sigmund Freud before him, saw dreams as the "royal road to the unconscious."

However, analytic psychology diverges from psychoanalysis, which interprets dreams as the simple expression of desires; for Jung, "The general function of dreams is to try to restore our psychological balance by producing dream material that re-establishes, in a subtle way, the total psychic balance" (*Man and His Symbols*, Pan Books, 1980, p. 34). In this way, dreams contribute to the construction of each individual's personality, even as they connect us to the vast reservoir of imagination known as the collective unconscious.

In *Link's Awakening*, the protagonist takes this "royal road" of dreams to develop aspects of his personality. Through the dream of his adventure on Koholint, he attempts to re-establish his own psychological balance. Recall that it was Link's doubts about his ability to protect Princess Zelda that led the young hero to embark on an adventure with the goal of becoming even stronger. Within the game, the owl would seem to represent Link's unconscious voice, guiding him on an initiate's pilgrimage through his own mind. From a Jungian perspective, dreams also have a collective aspect; in Link's psyche, this shared content appears in the form of norms already known to him. For players, this role is filled by gameplay mechanics that they have already experienced. This is how we can explain the presence in this game of routines similar to those in earlier *Zelda* games: the mimicry and borrowing of ideas from the third episode in the series are thus no more than the collected memories of the hero, getting mixed up with his own dream. The final enemy also bears a very powerful meaning. The Shadow Nightmares are presented to us as the nightmares of the Wind Fish. And yet, strangely enough, the shapes they take on are those of Link's past enemies. In this final battle, the hero of light confronts the essence of his own fears: Agahnim and Ganon. These dark obsessions are therefore not the product of the Wind Fish's nightmares, but of Link's. By defeating his enemies, Link also brings the Wind Fish's dream to an end; the hero's triumph over his repressed fears marks the completion of the dream, thus drawing the adventure to a close.

The final image of the closing cutscene reveals Link smiling and at peace, as though enchanted by his dream. By taking the "royal road" to his own unconscious, he has restored balance within himself. However, the end of the game still leaves certain questions open. When Link opens his eyes, we find him among the ruins of his boat; we are left to wonder if only a few minutes have actually passed since the boat was struck by lightning. And yet, Link sees the Wind Fish passing through the sky, thus obscuring the truth one last time. Link's time on Koholint could just as easily have really taken place as it could be a mere dream in the hero's mind. However, the clues suggesting that it really was a dream are too numerous to ignore. In *Link's Awakening*, a number of elements blend together and intermingle, just as in a dream. For example, Link confuses Marin and Zelda when he comes to his senses after the shipwreck. Other such mixtures address the player directly: for instance, the large number of references to other video games serve to blend the experience of the game in progress with that of other Nintendo titles. And there is no shortage of references for players to discover: the feather used for jumping, drawn from *Super Mario Kart*; game designer Will Wright, transformed into a character in the game, writing a love letter to his sweetheart as the theme to *SimCity* plays in the background; a Yoshi doll; monsters that look like Kirby; Goombas, the walking mushrooms from the world of *Mario*; and even Richard, a character from *Kaeru no Tame ni Kane wa Naru*, the game with which *Link's Awakening* shares its graphics engine. These amusing "cameos" can be explained by the central theme of the game—in a sense, they serve to break the fourth wall that separates video games from the real world. These elements continue to mix, right up to the last second of the adventure: As the closing credits begin and team members' names start rolling past, we hear the Song of Awakening arranged in skillful counterpoint against the saga's main theme, together giving rise to a beautiful new melody. A sense of ambivalence is maintained to the very end, and this dreamlike episode ends on an appropriately vague note.

Since the dawn of history, dreams have been an integral part of humanity's cultural heritage. Even the Greek pantheon includes Morpheus, the god of dreams, and in the Christian, Jewish, and Muslim religious traditions alike, God makes frequent use of dreams to communicate with men. Siberian peoples and shamanic societies reserve an essential place for dreams in their worldview. In the process of creating *Link's Awakening*, Nintendo's development team clearly did extensive research on the subject; it also seems likely that they explored a wide range of sources along the way. The game's story has certain commonalities with

an Australian myth known as "Dreamtime" or simply "the Dreaming." According to this myth, the world and its inhabitants were born of a god's dream; depending on the aboriginal tribe telling the tale, the god in question may or may not be equated with the "Rainbow Serpent," whose twists and turns are also said to be the source of Australia's rugged terrain and its rivers. When humans spread evil, this serpent god begins to have nightmares. Men's greatest fear, then, is that the Serpent will awaken from its bad dream, thereby destroying the universe in which they live. An island and a god haunted by nightmares, whose dreams are the basis of our world: each of these elements serves to connect the game to these aboriginal beliefs. Obviously, this is all mere speculation, since Nintendo has never confirmed anything about its sources of inspiration in the development of this episode of the *Zelda* series.

One point in which Nintendo's choice is clear, however, is the appearance of the Wind Fish. Although its name identifies it as a "fish," the physical form of this divine being is clearly that of a whale. What are the reasons for this choice? Since Nintendo was free to design this creature however it saw fit, this decision could not have been a mere matter of chance. Whales have a symbolic value in many cultures, and although the meanings linked to them are different from one tradition to the next, they nevertheless share certain essential features: the whale as bearer of the world, and as a symbol of life and resurrection. One of the most well-known myths associated with whales is that of the prophet Jonah. Having boarded a ship in an effort to escape from the mission that God had entrusted to him, he was thrown overboard by the crew in order to calm His divine wrath. The Bible and the Koran tell us that Jonah was swallowed by a great fish (which has traditionally been represented as a whale), then remained in the belly of the beast for three days and three nights, crying out to God the whole time, before being thrown up onto the shore. This tale, associated with Jonah's call, has been interpreted as a fairly obvious allegory for resurrection. We will return later to this very specific symbolism, which we will encounter in other episodes of the saga as well. Let us also note the undeniable parallels with Chapter XXXV of the *Adventures of Pinocchio*, in which the marionette is swallowed by a giant shark, again transformed into a whale in Walt Disney's 1940 film adaptation. The whale as a symbol, and dreams in the theories of Carl Jung, are both tied to the idea of a change of state, or an individual's passage from one mode of being to another. This is true of Link's experience in this episode as well: having "passed through" the Wind Fish, he finds himself changed.

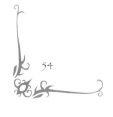

AN INCOMPLETE DIGRESSION

With a title that speaks volumes, and appears in retrospect to summarize the episode's plot in two short words, *Link's Awakening* seems to announce a pause for breath, a refuge, a place in which we discover a tale that is in fact much more astounding than we ever would have expected. With a taste for extremes, alternating between intimate moments and epic adventure, this episode of *Zelda* attempts to master innovation even as it harnesses tradition. And it was on the Game Boy that Nintendo chose to make this radical effort: a *Zelda* game with no Zelda and no Ganon. Despite its unique character, Link's nomadic voyage was a hit with the public, selling more than six million cartridges, including two million copies of the DX version alone. In the end, the aspects that made this game so different turned out to be its greatest strengths. Even as it built on the foundation of earlier installments, this episode was and remains an outlier within the series. As a result, it holds a special place in players' hearts to this day. *Link's Awakening* is no ugly duckling, but rather the culmination of all that had come before; Eiji Aonuma, the man in charge of the series today, once described it as "the quintessential 2D *Zelda* game." It is hardly surprising, then, that the approach taken by *Link's Awakening* would become the inspiration for an episode directed entirely by Aonuma, *The Legend of Zelda: Majora's Mask*—an equally strange episode that also lies at the outer fringes of the saga.

CHAPTER V
OCARINA OF TIME

t the dawn of time, when the surface of the world had not yet taken shape, three goddesses descended to Earth. The first, Din, goddess of power, cultivated the soil. The second, Nayru, goddess of wisdom, brought law and order to the world. Finally, Farore, goddess of courage, gave birth to all forms of life. Before returning to the heavens, the three goddesses left behind the Triforce as their gift to humanity and as proof of their existence. The magical object was kept safe in a sacred land while the Hylians took possession of their world. Hyrule was founded, and thanks to the Triforce, it lived in peace and abundance for many centuries.

Many more generations have passed, and today no proof remains of the three goddesses' existence. Only a single spirit, filled with wisdom and spirituality, still remembers how it all began: the venerable Deku Tree, located in the Kokiri forest, where he watches over the tribe of the same name. Every child in the forest is assigned a fairy at birth, whose job is to watch over the child. But there is one Kokiri who does not have his own guardian fairy. This young boy, named Link, is troubled in his sleep by a recurring nightmare. Aware of the boy's troubles, the Deku Tree sends him a fairy named Navi, and calls the boy before him. In his dream, Link sees a man by the name of Ganondorf who seeks to acquire the Triforce in order to plunge the world into darkness. This evil creature actually does exist, and already holds great power: the dark mage has cast a spell on the Deku Tree, which the great tree now asks Link to remove.

A brief adventure then ensues, ending with our young hero's return from deep inside the tree, after putting a stop to the evil that was consuming it from within. Finally at peace, the venerable Deku Tree nevertheless realizes that it is already too late for him. Knowing that he is close to death, he urges Link to visit Princess Zelda, the King of Hyrule's daughter. According to the prophecy, it is

she who will help the young hero to stop the evil wizard from seizing control of the Triforce. A long quest has just begun for Link.

A NEW DIMENSION

The Legend of Zelda: Ocarina of Time came out for the Nintendo 64 in November 1998. Its release had already been postponed several times, which only increased fans' eager anticipation. The first official presentation of the game had taken place in January 1997 at Shoshinkai (or Nintendo Space World), almost two years before the end of a marathon development process. However, an initial video had already been revealed when the Nintendo 64 was announced in December 1995, in which Link was seen battling a knight in dazzling chrome-plated armor.

As is often the case in the world of video games, and especially at Nintendo, the production of this *Zelda* game was subject to a number of changes, and even a few major upheavals. Even as Miyamoto and his team were still coming to grips with the design of a 3D world for *Super Mario 64*, the next *Zelda* game was already on everyone's mind. As the months went by, the development teams continued to grow in support of this enormous new project. The initial outlines were very different from the game we know today. At first, Miyamoto wanted the story to focus exclusively on Ganon's castle, with various levels inside of it as in the design of *Super Mario 64*. Later on, Miyamoto raised the idea of alternating between a first-person view like in an FPS for the exploration phases, and a side view for combat sequences, in which the player would finally get to see Link. Yoshiaki Koizumi, who collaborated with Shigeru Miyamoto, later admitted that he had never approved of this concept, unable to come to terms with the thought that the model he had created for Link would not be visible on screen at all times. The thought process then moved on to a new guiding principle: the inclusion of truly epic sword fights. To make these clashes exciting, it would have been hard to keep Link as a child—a ridiculously long sword might put him in danger when facing his enemies and make battles unnecessarily difficult. The character design therefore shifted towards the idea of a teenage Link.

As we can see, the gameplay was developed long before the story was written, as is often the case at Nintendo. So when Miyamoto declared after a year and a half of work that he missed his "cute" little Link, and preferred that he have a more childish appearance in the game, the entire development process was turned upside down! Willingly or not, the team submitted to Miyamoto's wishes, and the story was rewritten to allow Link to appear as a young child at first before growing into adolescence in the second part of the quest.

The production process was eventually drawn out to two and a half years—rather a long time for that era. During that time, the program migrated from the 64DD (a peripheral that allowed the Nintendo 64 to read and write data on a disk) to a cartridge format; the huge amount of content underlying Link's animations meant that the game couldn't function without constantly accessing the disk, which led to loading times that were not only too frequent, but more importantly, much too long.

When the game was released (in November 1998 in Japan and the United States, and a month later in Europe), it was received like the second coming of the Messiah. Professional reviewers and the general public alike insisted to anyone who would listen that the new game was the greatest of all time.

After a GameCube version (available on the bonus CD included with *The Wind Waker*), then another version for the virtual console (on the Wii), *Ocarina of Time* made its grand comeback in 2011 with an updated version for the 3DS. Developed by the Grezzo game studio under the direction of Koichii Ishii (previously a big name at Square), this version was adapted to incorporate stereoscopic 3D, but otherwise did not modify the original gameplay to any great extent. No significant additions, no extra dungeons or side quests—only a new "boss rush" mode and the Master Quest (a mirrored version of the original title), which players can only access after finishing the original game. The most important changes are on the technical side: presentation and interface. The environments and character models are truly impressive. The game is filled with bright colors, rich details and brilliant visual effects, and the fog of the N64 version has been lifted; in a word, the new version is sublime, and *Ocarina of Time* has never looked more beautiful. The animations for Link and the other main characters have also gotten a noticeable facelift. As for the 3D effect, which ought to have been the big attraction in this version, it is certainly pleasant enough, but falls far short of transcending the experience. With regard to the interface, players can now use the console's gyroscopic function to aim: they now have to physically move in order to shoot with the bow or the slingshot, using the console's screen as a sight. Finally, a few changes have been made to the game's difficulty level. For example, it is no longer necessary to finish off Stalfos with a bomb, and players can find the entrance to the forest temple without using music. In addition, Sheikah Stones have been scattered throughout Hyrule, allowing players who are having trouble with the game to access brief videos (presented as visions) that explain how to go about solving certain puzzles or defeating bosses.

THE DAWN OF THE 3D ERA

Most of the differences between this *Zelda 64* installment and its predecessors are due to the addition of 3D graphics. For Miyamoto and his team, the most important goal was to ensure that players could correctly come to grips with their environment, despite the new 3D format. At first, a jump action seemed unavoidable; how else could Link get around in a world made up of obstacles at different heights? One day, however, Miyamoto had a brilliant idea: to allow players to make their way around the world without complicating their task, why not make jumping automatic? As a result, when Link approaches a hole or a ledge, he automatically jumps to the other side. Exploration becomes easier, and less coordinated players are spared the frustration of struggling with a series of failed jumps.

Another problem remained to be dealt with: how would sword fights play out in 3D? The answer to this question turned up in a most unexpected place. One hot summer day, a few members of the Nintendo development team headed out to Toei Kyoto Studio Park, a theme park not far from their offices. To get out of the sun for a few minutes, they sat down in the shade to watch a ninja performance being put on for park visitors. After taking on multiple attackers, the hero of the show had to face an adversary armed with a sickle attached to a chain. To defend himself, the hero grabbed the end of the chain, which he then pulled taut so that he could circle around his opponent while controlling the distance between them. As the designers enjoyed the show, the idea of Z-targeting was born: with the press of a button, players could "lock on" to an enemy as though he and Link were joined by an invisible chain. In this way, players can move, dodge and attack without ever letting the enemy out of their sights. Link can counterattack easily without worrying that his attack will miss, and use his bow to fire off an arrow that is automatically aimed at his opponent. The problems that arise with judging distances along the x, y and z axes are thereby resolved.

In playing *Ocarina of Time*, one cannot help but notice how much thought the designers put into adjusting the controls to make life as easy as possible for the player. For example, the A button on the Nintendo 64 controller becomes a contextual action button—that is, its function changes constantly to adapt to the environment. For instance, if Link is in front of a door, pressing A will open it; near a ladder, A will trigger a climbing action; and when running, it allows him to roll. There is no longer any need to design for as many commands as there are possible actions, since the contextual action for the A button will always be shown on the screen. With the same eye toward comfort and practicality, when Link uses a weapon that has to be aimed (such as the bow or hookshot),

the camera switches to a first-person view, allowing the player to see through Link's eyes and thus to aim more effectively. All of this seems obvious today, but at the time, these were real innovations.

In the end, players can enjoy incredibly well-designed gameplay that allows for all the usual actions they expect in a *Zelda* game, without the slightest problem arising from the introduction of 3D graphics—a genuine accomplishment! And thanks to the third dimension and the power of the Nintendo 64, the designers were able to let their imaginations run wild. The level design in the dungeons is now more complex: each one is a real labyrinth, in which every room and every puzzle presents its own set of challenges. Exploring these places is more interesting than ever, constantly reigniting players' curiosity while putting their imagination and creativity to the test. Each level has its own unique features and its one crazy idea. For instance, it's a safe bet that anyone who has tried their hand at *Ocarina of Time* will remember the Water Temple quite clearly.

The raw power of Nintendo's new machine also made it possible to offer amazingly beautiful graphics, establishing the game's place among the classics of its era and allowing for a more realistic, less cartoon-like representation of Hyrule than in previous games. This emphasis on realism is also reflected in the way the game handles the passage of time: a day/night cycle has been put in place, the music changes based on the time of day, Link keeps his most recently used object in his hand, and so on. Overall, the game is much more immersive, especially when Link hops in the saddle to ride Epona. Although the horse was only added to the game quite late in the development process, the idea had been floating around since the days of *Super Mario 64*; Miyamoto was never shy about being a big fan of Westerns. Let us also note in passing that the name Epona is the same as that of the Gallic goddess of horses and fertility. Once the decision was made to give Link a steed, it was important to expand Hyrule's boundaries to create a vast territory to explore.

The last point we will discuss relates to Link's ocarina, the importance of which should be obvious from the game's subtitle. This instrument, with a name that means "little goose" in an Italian dialect, plays a critical role in the unfolding of the game's plot—Link receives the Ocarina of Time as a gift from Zelda, allowing him to gain access to the the Temple of Time—and confirms the central role played by music in the *Zelda* series. The flute is a recurring item in the hero's inventory across a number of episodes, but now players have to actually play the instrument themselves, with each button on the controller corresponding to a specific note.

HYRULE'S POPULATION GROWS

Not content to simply enrich *Zelda*'s gameplay with these technical improvements, *Ocarina of Time* also made major strides in fleshing out the saga's mythology. Hyrule's different species and tribes each acquired their own visual style. Already sketched out in earlier episodes in the form of generic enemies, the Zoras finally come into their own here: their people are fully characterized and acquire their "official" form. Also making an appearance are the Gerudos, a population of desert thieves consisting entirely of women (with one exception); the Gorons, skilled bomb-makers who live in the mountains; and finally, the Kokiri, small childlike beings who live in the forest and whose name is a play on 木こり (*kikori*), the Japanese word for lumberjack. As if to explain the hero's unique destiny, Link, who originally believes himself to be a simple Kokiri, is in fact revealed to be one of the mythical Hylian people. The backdrop of *Ocarina of Time*'s world is also presented in copious detail, in particular through a number of cutscenes that give the game a much more cinematic feel than its predecessors. Players learn the story of how the Triforce was created, and its nature as the legacy left to humanity by the three goddesses who first gave shape to the world.

The main plot of the game (Link's battle against Ganon) is also much more elaborate than usual, and includes a number of secondary characters: the mysterious Sheik, Darunia the Goron, little Saria, and others. Here again, this installment stands apart from the others—although it reflects a tendency that had already started to take shape in *Link's Awakening*. As a result, players' progression through the game becomes much more structured and dynamic, in an era when video games were making considerable advances in the realm of story and presentation (this was the same period when *Resident Evil 2* and *Final Fantasy VII* were released). An interesting anecdote: Miyamoto has said that he was inspired by *Twin Peaks* to include a variety of bizarre and mysterious characters in his story like the ones found in David Lynch's famous television drama.

THE PASSAGE OF TIME

In *A Link to the Past* and *Link's Awakening*, players traveled to parallel worlds and to a place beyond dreams. In *Ocarina of Time*, they are sent on a voyage through time—a subject that Nintendo is particularly fond of, and one that would return in several later installments of the series. In this first chapter to appear on the Nintendo 64, Link starts the adventure as a young boy, but falls asleep for seven long years in order to build up the strength he will need to battle Ganon and take on the threat facing Hyrule. In this way, *Ocarina of Time* presents the development of its iconic protagonist in accelerated form: in the blink of an eye, the adventure carries us off into the future. Much like Link himself, whose growth has allowed him to increase his abilities, the player also acquires new responsibilities. To be sure, other games had already explored the idea of characters' development through time; obvious examples include the *Phantasy Star* and *Dragon Quest* series, in which players can play as different generations in the same family. It is less common, however, to see a hero change radically over the course of a single adventure. In *Ocarina of Time*, people develop and grow. Like Link, Princess Zelda is also transformed here, taking on the identity of a Sheikah warrior. Hidden behind her identity as the Sheik, the young girl's innocence and fragility have given way to confidence and righteousness. The instant leap from childhood to adolescence is exhilarating in itself, but is also important to this episode's storyline.

But it's not only the player and the characters who have entered a new stage. With *Ocarina of Time*, the *Zelda* saga as a whole has expanded dramatically: the switch to 3D that became possible with the new N64 was a perfect occasion to bring a whole new level of detail to the series. Every aspect of the world is waiting to be rediscovered, and every second of the game is filled with wonder; players may find it difficult at times to tear themselves away from the sheer thrill of the new 3D perspective. The game truly comes to life, and immersion attains its greatest heights yet. Despite Link's silent demeanor, the look on his face can now communicate real emotions. More intense and better-paced, the battles now feel like truly epic challenges. Outside of the game itself, the Nintendo 64's one-of-a-kind controller makes the rest of the experience much more pleasant; being able to assign items freely to the three yellow buttons represents a real improvement, and a significantly more comfortable experience for the player. In addition, players can physically feel certain interactions with the game by attaching the optional Rumble Pak module, which makes the controller vibrate.

All in all, then, *Ocarina of Time* has crossed an important threshold not only in terms of its story and game design, but also in terms of the advances made possible by the console on which the adventure is played. With the Nintendo 64's improved hardware resources, which were quite impressive for the time, along with innovative game design and some creative story choices, players were thrilled with this unbelievable new episode and its rare ability to fulfill their grandest gaming fantasies.

63

JOINING THE PANTHEON OF VIDEO GAMES

Ocarina of Time made a major impression at the time of its release. As a follow-up to earlier episodes, Miyamoto's new project had been a long time coming—at a time when the Nintendo 64 still didn't have as wide a selection of available games as the PlayStation. Even as it followed in its predecessor's footsteps, this *Zelda 64* game boldly announced the saga's arrival in the age of 3D. The game become an instant classic, setting an almost impossibly high standard for later installments. It is also frequently cited as one of the best video games of all time.

Even today, *Ocarina of Time* is still as exciting a game as ever. The game may have aged, but only in terms of its graphics; a modified version released for the 3DS in June 2011 confidently brought the game's technical aspects up to 21st-century standards, while also making it easier to play. The new console's touch screen made inventory management easier, and its gyroscopic function meant that players could move the console to change the camera angle and aim more easily with the bow or the hookshot. *Ocarina of Time* is thus as breathtakingly modern as ever. Of course, with years of hindsight, and the subsequent release of many other titles offering more or less open worlds, it's hard to deny that Hyrule Field looks a little bit empty and overly clean. But no matter—this is a minor point with no effect on the overall experience.

Although *Ocarina of Time* remains a classic to this day, we must nevertheless admit that it is a fairly typical adventure in terms of its overall development, and that it does not offer as much substance or material for discussion as an earlier game like *Link's Awakening* or the episode that would follow it, *Majora's Mask*. None of that affects its quality, however; *Ocarina of Time* is definitely the perfect prototype of what a 3D *Zelda* game should be. Suffused with a mythical aura, this game is an ode to adventure and wonder.

Above all, the development of *Ocarina of Time* marked the arrival of Eiji Aonuma on the series. Originally tasked with designing the dungeons, enemies and boss fights, Aonuma was the man who would take control of the saga for the next episode—and he remains in charge to this day.

CHAPTER VI

MAJORA'S MASK

ink has defeated Ganon, the lord of evil, and saved Hyrule. The Triforce is no longer in danger, and Princess Zelda is safe and sound. The quest for which he had traveled seven years into the future and become the "hero of time" is now complete. The kingdom is well aware that it owes this boy a debt of gratitude. Appearing once again as a young boy, Link is celebrated as a hero, and has become a living legend throughout Hyrule.

But Link's heart is not at peace. Tired from his many battles, he is filled with a profound sense of dissatisfaction. He goes to see Princess Zelda, who immediately guesses what is troubling the boy. Link confirms her suspicions, and tells the princess that he has to leave. Where to? Nobody knows, not even our hero himself. And yet he feels that he must set out on a voyage that will soon become a quest to the very heart of his own being. He must first go looking for an "invaluable friend" that he had left behind after finishing his heroic quest. He says his farewells to the princess, who is filled with sadness but powerless to stop him. Astride his loyal steed Epona, Link rushes off into the forest. Time passes...

Several days of travel do not seem to have had the slightest effect on Link, who is still as agitated as ever. Two little fairies watch him from the edge of a clearing—a brother and sister named Tael and Tatl. These two fairies are accompanying a strange inhabitant of the woods, a member of the Skull Kids tribe. Their companion has just robbed a mask salesman, and has found an especially strange item in his haul: Majora's Mask. Always eager to play a trick or two, the Skull Kid asks the two fairies to give Epona a scare. The horse rears up, throwing its rider roughly to the ground. As Link lies stunned by his fall, the Skull Kid robs him of the Ocarina of Time that Zelda had given him, and that had been so essential in his fight against evil. When he comes to his senses a moment later, Link hurries after the Skull Kid, who has also managed to make off with Epona.

The thief has plunged into a gaping hole in the deepest heart of the forest, and our hero has no choice but to follow him. Surprised to find the young Hylian still hot on his heels, the Skull Kid casts a mysterious spell to transform Link into a Deku Scrub. The troublesome imp runs off, leaving the fairy Tatl behind. Abandoned, she realizes that her only chance of finding her brother again is to help Link. She leads him to a mysterious village known as Clock Town, nestled in the heart of the land of Termina. There, Link learns that the Skull Kid has unleashed a catastrophe: the moon will crash into the village in three days, bringing the world to a miserable end. Our hero has just seventy-two hours to head off this sinister fate.

A BOLD GAMBLE

After the impressive success of *Ocarina of Time*, Nintendo immediately decided to put out a direct sequel. By drawing new players in to the series, Link's fabulous 3D adventure on the Nintendo 64 had helped to further bolster the Japanese developer's considerable renown. To avoid losing this new audience, Nintendo had to dive into the development of this new episode without a moment's delay.

Nintendo has always been very tight-lipped about its productions, and prefers to keep the design of its games shrouded in mystery, rarely revealing the slightest detail. Nevertheless, rumor had it that *Majora's Mask* was the result of a bet between Miyamoto and Aonuma. With little interest in directing *Ura Zelda*, intended as a mere expansion of *Ocarina of Time*, Eiji Aonuma supposedly suggested that Nintendo create a whole new episode instead; Miyamoto only accepted on the condition that the game be developed as quickly as possible. This anecdote has proven extremely difficult to verify, however.

Originally referred to as *Zelda Gaiden* (which means *special edition* in Japanese), *Majora's Mask* received its official title in March 2000, only two months before its release for the Japanese market. However, the game did not come out in North America until October 26 of the same year. Directed by Eiji Aonuma and Yoshiaki Koizumi, *Majora's Mask* was still supervised by Miyamoto, who had started getting ready to pass the baton to other designers and step away from the franchise. In creating an all-new *Zelda* in less than two years, with gameplay mechanics not seen in earlier games, Aonuma and his team had pulled off a major accomplishment. However, they were only able to achieve this by reusing the graphics engine from *Ocarina of Time*. A few minor technical improvements were made with the help of the Expansion Pak, a small memory extension module for the Nintendo 64 which allowed for an increased draw distance, more characters on screen, and improved texture quality. By recycling the old graphics engine, the creators were able to put the technical phase behind them. This saved an enormous amount of work, allowing them to concentrate on the game's artistic dimension and spend as much time as possible on developing the world and atmosphere of the new *Zelda* episode.

The context in which *Majora's Mask* was developed had a major impact on the game's content: this installment was designed under stress in an anxiety-filled atmosphere amid the urgency of a looming deadline. Putting together a game of this size in just eighteen months is an extraordinary challenge. The difficult conditions and day-to-day pressure come through in even the tiniest details: from the overarching themes to the visual setting, everything about *Majora's Mask* reflects the great rush in which the game was developed. The threatening moon about to crash into the Earth is the perfect representation of this sense of impending doom.

Of all the *Zelda* games, *Majora's Mask* is surely the one that did the most to turn the saga's conventions on their head. In 2015, a 3D remake softened the experience by providing more guidance to new players in what was originally a somewhat surly episode. For example, to speed up or slow down the flow of time, players simply have to play each note twice in the song of time—a much simpler and more efficient method than the scarecrow's dance or Grandmother's stories! The save system was also revised to be more flexible. It is no longer necessary to restart the whole three-day cycle to save the game permanently. Unlike the original game, the owl statues in the remake (along with the new quill statues) also allow players to save their game without losing progress when they quit. Although it may be a questionable choice with regard to the game's overall philosophy, it is certainly understandable in light of the mobile 3DS platform and the new target audience for which the new version was intended. Inventory management was adapted for use with the touchscreen, and weapons could now be aimed with the help of the console's built-in gyroscope. Other changes in the name of accessibility included new hints and changes to a few puzzles; a Sheikah Stone was also placed in the Clock Town mill to provide less perceptive players with visual tips on beating the game's bosses.

Finally, let us consider the careful attention paid to the graphics. Without betraying the spirit of the original masterpiece, a wealth of details has been added to enrich the environment, the draw distance has been increased, and the colors no longer blur. A few new character animations have also been added.

THREE DAYS TO SAVE THE WORLD

In general, the gameplay in *Majora's Mask* remains true to the foundations laid by *Ocarina of Time*, so there is no need to describe it all again here. Three major innovations make their appearance, however, and help to give this episode its own unique character.

Atop the list of innovations are the timed progression and the three-day limit. Link has only seventy-two hours to save Termina. Since one hour in the game corresponds to about one minute in real time, the Game Over screen is obviously waiting just seventy-two minutes away from the start of the quest! The inexorable forward march of time, marked by a clock that is always on screen, puts the player in a state of ever-increasing stress: the end is near, even though Link is far from completing his mission. But just then, our hero gets his Ocarina of Time back, allowing him to rewind time to the beginning of the countdown whenever he likes. In the end, players have seventy-two minutes to get to the end of each dungeon or each side quest they accept, in exchange for having to see all of their accomplishments undone when they rewind time to prevent the catastrophe. Nevertheless, every time Link gets his hands on an item that is essential for the next step in the adventure (a new weapon, a mask, a melody learned on his ocarina), it is saved in the hero's inventory so that he can use it after he again rewinds to the beginning of the countdown. On the other hand, arrows, bombs and rupees collected along the way are lost forever. That being said, players can limit the impact by placing their rupees in the Clock Town bank, where they can be recovered after rewinding time. In addition, two melodies that Link learns on the ocarina allow him to affect the flow of time, in one case by slowing it down (giving Link more time to accomplish his mission), and in the other by speeding it up. To progress along the game's main path, players have to take all of these factors into account and master them quickly. The stress imposed by the constant presence of the clock may have bothered certain players and led to frustration. Still, for the first time, the game manages to communicate a real, physical emotion to the player at the same moment that the character is also experiencing that emotion.

The second major innovation in *Majora's Mask* proceeds directly from the first: the use of a notebook. The designers succeeded in creating a dense and realistic simulation of neighborhood life in the world of Termina. Since the whole quest occurs within a period of three days (even if you rewind time repeatedly, you always relive the same three days), every non-player character will also repeat the same actions throughout those three days, from the mailman and the mayor to the kid playing in the street. By watching each of them carefully to learn their routines, the player can work out a very precise schedule: on such-and-such a day at such-and-such a time, so-and-so will be carrying out a certain specific action. Link acquires a notebook very early in the adventure that allows players to record facts and actions for each of the characters. Naturally, this system is associated with a number of side quests that always lead to a reward for the player. The player therefore has to learn to observe the NPCs, understand their needs, and adapt to their schedule in order to help them get what they want. Often, Link has to show up at certain places at specific times in order to advance each character's story. If he misses the appointed hour, he will have to rewind time again and start over. This system leads to a considerable increase in the number of side quests and digressions within the game; but just as importantly, it allows the designers to simulate a real ecosystem in which each resident seems to be living their own life, independently of the player's actions.

The third and final major innovation in *Majora's Mask* relates, appropriately enough, to the use of masks. Sketched out in only the barest outlines in *Ocarina of Time*, the idea is presented here in a deeper and more interesting way. Twenty-four different masks are available, each providing the wearer with specific attributes that allow him to deal with a specific challenge. For example, the All-Night Mask allows Link to listen to all the stories told by a certain old lady without falling asleep, while the Bunny Hood increases his speed. Three of these masks (as well as a hidden fourth mask) turn out to be even more useful. Wearing them transforms Link into a Deku Scrub, a Goron or a Zora. Each transformation enables the player to perform a new range of actions. The Deku Scrub can fly, the Goron has great strength and can curl up in a ball to roll, the Zora can swim underwater indefinitely, and so on. These abilities are essential to the success of certain missions. Images published at an early stage of development show that each of these transformations was originally associated with a specific weapon—Goron Link used a hammer, for example—but this idea was eventually abandoned. In any case, this system of masks serves to add variety to the gameplay by providing Link with new options—not to mention the ways in which his interactions with different characters are affected by the change in the hero's appearance.

Beyond these notable innovations, *Majora's Mask* distinguishes itself from earlier *Zelda* games in a number of ways. First of all, progression through the game is based much more heavily around life in Termina and Clock Town (a fairly large city for a game of this era). There are only four dungeons, and they are no longer home to all the most essential moments in the adventure. In addition, there are far more side quests than usual, even within a dungeon, where Link is asked to gather a certain number of little fairies to acquire power-ups and magic. The sequences that players have to traverse between each dungeon have also been developed more fully. It's no longer sufficient to

simply visit the native village to gain access to the nearby temple. Players are required to make a much greater effort, and often have to deal with multiple characters along the way.

Progression within each dungeon still ends predictably enough with a fight against the local boss, and winning the battle may not necessarily require the use of an object discovered immediately beforehand. Nevertheless, these battles often turn out to be quite original. After each victory, the whole landscape and appearance of the surrounding environment will change. For example, once Link has completed his mission in the second dungeon, the sun returns, melting the snow which had covered the Goron village and the plateaus around it, and revealing the green grass beneath. In this way, the world of Termina turns out to be much more diverse than it first appears; exploring this world becomes a real pleasure, guided pleasantly along by the music of Koji Kondo. Although he reuses a number of compositions from the previous installment, Kondo introduces some lovely new melodies in this episode as well.

AN OPPRESSIVE ATMOSPHERE

Much of what distinguishes *Majora's Mask* from earlier *Zelda* games has to do with its dark and oppressive atmosphere. The end of the world is coming, and time is ticking away with no way to stop it. In the surrealist land of Termina, Link is the player's only point of reference to the classic Zelda saga. As in *Link's Awakening*, the hero is far from Hyrule and torn loose from his usual moorings.

But while the Game Boy adventure could be understood as a dream, here we seem to be dealing with a hallucination or a parallel world. There is no princess to be rescued, only a rather vague inner quest; although we are told at the start of the adventure that Link is looking for an "invaluable friend," this person is never explicitly mentioned by name. Since Zelda and Epona are present at the time, we might conclude that the friend in question must be Navi, the fairy that guided Link on his previous voyage. But his arrival in Termina seems to undermine this hypothesis. Reproducing the start of *Alice's Adventures in Wonderland* almost exactly (with the Skull Kid in the role of the white rabbit), the adventure sees Link tumbling down a bottomless pit, then transforming into a Deku Scrub. What if the person that Link is looking for in this episode is none other than Link himself? The off-kilter world of Termina would then be nothing but a "path" by which to find himself, a product of Link's tortured imagination in his quest for mental balance. If this were true, it would bring us back to the themes of *Link's Awakening* which (as the reader will surely recall) was Aonuma's favorite 2D *Zelda* game. Like a counterpart to

Ocarina of Time, Majora's Mask contrasts Link's classic heroic quest in Hyrule to a more inward-facing adventure, during which the character's faults and weaknesses begin to come out as he gets "farther away" from the princess and her kingdom.

This theory of inner conflict is supported by a look at Termina's population. It turns out that all of the characters that Link meets in this adventure were already in *Ocarina of Time*! As though Link were lying to himself by putting on a "play" directed by his subconscious, in an attempt at therapy intended to save him from depression... Of course, we can also find a more pragmatic explanation: reusing existing character models made the designers' job easier, given the intense time pressure on the project. Or it could be that by forcing them to reuse characters that Link had already met, these technical constraints gave Aonuma and Koizumi the idea for the overall theme of a parallel world. Let us also note that the idea of recycling "classic" Hyrule characters in a different role corresponds to a desire that Miyamoto had expressed in the past. He often regretted that players attached so much importance to the story and setting of his games, when he would have much preferred to reuse the same protagonists in a different role each time, like in the old Popeye cartoons he liked to watch. Was this off-kilter approach ultimately a result of the conditions under which the game was developed?

We need only consider the adventure's opening moments to realize that the hero is not his usual self. Slumped in the saddle, Link looks worn out, almost depressed. The start of this quest has an especially melancholy air. To be sure, earlier episodes generally started with a sense of misfortune. In *A Link to the Past*, Link sets out in the pouring rain, and soon discovers that his uncle has been gravely wounded; *Link's Awakening* starts with a shipwreck, and so on. But the tone here is much more pessimistic, because this time the hero is not merely confronted with external events. Rather, the problem seems to lie within himself.

The theme of death is also a major part of the adventure, which adopts a much more mature perspective than what players had been used to seeing in earlier *Zelda* games. For instance, the three characters that Link can "play" by putting on their masks are already deceased.

Both the old Goron, Darmani, and Mikau the Zora guitarist died trying to help their people; the Deku Scrub is less clearly identified, although there is reason to think he was the minister's son. When Link transforms, he screams in fear (in a rather disturbing scene), as if putting on a character's mask also filled our hero's mind with that character's anxiety and sadness. He therefore has to do whatever he can to tend to the suffering of these poor souls, even as he pursues his own quest.

This dark, even schizophrenic atmosphere (when Link resolves his avatar's problems, he is actually only pursuing his own goals) is reinforced by the moon's looming presence in the sky over Termina. Like an enormous sword of Damocles hanging over its inhabitants' heads, the moon is visible in every single scene. Even when Link is completing a "lighter" side quest in some quiet corner of Termina, a well-chosen camera angle serves to remind him of the presence of the celestial body falling irreversibly towards the Earth. To personify this threat while emphasizing its frightening nature, the moon has a face here—and quite a hostile one at that. Link also encounters a whole series of unhealthy personalities in the game, such as the mask salesman and the blacksmith's assistant. But none of them embody the darkness of this world as perfectly as the Skull Kid. At the end of the adventure, we learn that the Skull Kid is in fact the only character, other than Link and Epona, who appeared in *Ocarina of Time*—as himself, that is, rather than as one of the various recycled character models. This one-of-a-kind status, which relates him directly to the hero, makes him a unique character. The scarecrow-like Skull Kid used to live with others like him in the lost woods of Hyrule. According to legend, the Skull Kids were originally Kokiri who got lost in the woods and never found their way back to their village. As he approaches the land of Termina (in a rather mysterious interlude), Link finds the Skull Kid possessed by Majora's Mask, which has turned him into an evil being. Recall that Link had tried on different masks himself in the previous episode in the course of his struggle with Ganon. Another point the two have in common is that both Link and the Skull Kid come from Kokiri Forest and travel with fairies. Could Link's troubled mind have created a fictitious double, in the form of the Skull Kid, as he wandered lost and confused through the woods? As the story of *Majora's Mask* unfolds, we come to realize that the Skull Kid is completely under the mask's control, and that the reason it was able to corrupt his mind was because he felt so abandoned and alone. Believing that he had been abandoned by the four giants whom he considered his friends, the character seems to be a perfect incarnation of sadness, which corresponds exactly to our disoriented young Hylian's state of mind.

How can we explain Link's depression at the start of the game, knowing that he had just saved the world? In *Ocarina of Time*, Link jumps seven years into the future, and discovers the bitter reality of a world that has fallen under Ganon's control. Let us also note in passing that it was through Link's carelessness that the Lord of Evil was able to get his hands on the Triforce, and then use it to seize power. The young Hylian then witnesses the devastation caused by his actions. This vision of an apocalyptic future may have disturbed our hero after he went back to being a child. This destabilizing experience could well be the reason for

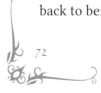

the doubts that Link is struggling with, to the point of losing confidence in his ability to maintain peace in Hyrule. In that case, couldn't the quest in *Majora's Mask* be interpreted as a concrete manifestation of that struggle—a symptom of the madness that is taking over Link's mind? As he questions his own status as a hero and his place in the kingdom, we are reminded of the opening moments of *Link's Awakening*, with depression taking on the same role here as the dream in that game. Attentive players will also have noticed a nod to the Game Boy installment: the hit song by the Zora group The Indigo-Go's, extremely popular in Termina, is entitled *Ballad of the Wind Fish*, based on the melody that Link has to play to complete his quest in *Link's Awakening*.

In *A Link to the Past* and *Ocarina of Time*, Link had to fight his way through two distinct worlds (with a split between the normal world and the dark world in the former, and the present versus the future in the latter); in *Majora's Mask*, however, the player has a constant feeling of being trapped in the "other world," or of being lost somewhere "through the looking-glass." This more mature, less "fairy-tale" tone provides *Majora's Mask* with some of the most dreamlike and poetic scenes to ever appear in an episode of *Zelda*.

THE NEVER-ENDING STORY

Ocarina of Time dealt with the passage of time in a fairly general way. *Majora's Mask* goes further with that theme by placing players in the role of a hero who looks like a child, but is tormented by adult worries. To fight the new threat that is about to destroy the world, he will have to travel through time once again. Link's childlike state and the issues related to it also find an echo in the side quest with Kafei. Kafei is an adult who has been trapped in a child's body by the Skull Kid. Ashamed of his new appearance, the man refuses to see his fiancée. With Link's help, however, Kafei comes to accept his condition, and finds the courage to meet with his beloved Anju. At the end of a long quest, and just a few minutes before the end of the third day, the couple is finally reunited. To complete this side mission, the player must commit to it completely, spending an entire cycle on resolving this one plot thread. The suspense remains high right down to the last second—Kafei is late to the rendezvous, even as the moon is about to crash into Termina. But for both Link and the player, any feeling of satisfaction is fleeting: once Link plays the Song of Time, a new three-day cycle begins, thereby returning both Kafei's situation and the player's back to their starting point. There are some obvious similarities between Link and Kafei. First of all, it is intriguing to note that Kafei is one of the few playable characters other than Link in the entire *Zelda* saga. In addition, Kafei's situation is strangely reminiscent of our hero's; he, too has been caught up in the Skull Kid's trickery. Link also notices that Kafei's situation is quite similar to the one that he experienced with Zelda in the course of his journey in *Ocarina of Time*: no sooner had the notes of the ocarina filled the air than the two of them were returned to childhood. But while Kafei will have no memory of what happened, despite having finally reached his goal at the end of those three days, Link remains fully aware of the events he has experienced—and those events will therefore remain a source of eternal frustration.

The obvious parallels between Link and Kafei provide a concise summary of how the subject of time is handled in *Majora's Mask*. Both characters are suffering from the same troubles, and without really knowing it, both are fighting the same demons. Through this touching story, Nintendo illustrates the game's vision of the passage of time with unusual subtlety and skill.

BACK TO ADULTHOOD

Ocarina of Time associated the end of childhood with the acquisition of new powers, along with new responsibilities. *Majora's Mask* returns to this theme, but with a greater emphasis this time on the idea of childhood as a prelude to life as an adult. Carefree but subject to influence, youth is at risk of corruption—but Link once again finds an astounding way to set himself apart.

At the end of *Majora's Mask*, we realize that the Skull Kid was a mere puppet controlled entirely by the will of the mask, which for its part was intent on doing evil. But the scene on the moon reveals that just like the Skull Kid, Majora is nothing more than a lonely child, rejected by the others, who refuses to grow up. Players who have explored all of *Majora's Mask* will be rewarded with a new mask after collecting the other twenty-four. Known as the Fierce Deity's Mask, it transforms little Link into a powerful and charming adult warrior. This mask is a fan favorite, and represents the ultimate incarnation of Link's adult form. This transformation gives Link a range of greatly improved abilities and powers which allow him to beat the various bosses without much effort, and easily put an end to Majora's ambitions. In other words, the player's ultimate reward for their efforts is to see Link reach adulthood, a transformation that was already sketched out in *Ocarina of Time* with Link's temporary stint as a teenager.

The influence, effects and different aspects of time: all of these diverse facets join to express an enduring message. Sometimes a source of fun, but often a dark obsession, time turns out to be one of Nintendo's preferred themes. The publisher has always emphasized the importance of gameplay, presented as the driving force behind its productions. But it's hard to imagine that the company

doesn't see the subject of time as equally essential, given the remarkably skillful and judicious treatment it receives, and the way in which it structures the themes of so many different *Zelda* games.

THE APOCALYPSE

In terms of both its gameplay and its major themes, *Majora's Mask* presents itself as a prelude to the apocalypse. The prospect of the end of the world looms constantly in the background of this adventure, represented on screen by the moon that grows larger each day in the skies over Termina. And an unspeakable melancholy fills the final moments before each "game over" screen, leaving little doubt as to how things will end. Concretely, this apocalyptic atmosphere is reflected in a dusky ambiance and in the choice of colors. Note also that it is rare to see every character in a game die at once; normally, "game over" applies only to the main character. When talking with the last remaining residents of Clock Town, we are also left with a sense of fatalism. The world in which they live also just so happens to be called Termina—probably from the Latin noun *terminus* (*boundary, limit*) or the imperative form of the verb *terminare*, namely *termina* (*stop! finish!*). Sacrifice is presented as a necessary part of the hero's success: Link goes through one three-day cycle after another to gather the information and items that he needs in order to save the world. During this time, however, he can only complete one side quest at a time (be it a dungeon or a favor for another character). He is thus forced to accept the fact that he must leave the others aside, even though it means losing the benefits of his actions once he returns to the beginning of the cycle. In fact, it is impossible to reach the end of the game having helped everyone who needed assistance.

A QUESTIONABLE CONVERGENCE

A strange coincidence? Or a genuine overlap of shared values? Three years before *Majora's Mask*, another landmark achievement in Japanese video game history, *Final Fantasy VII*, had addressed the end of the world in a rather similar way. In the RPG from Square, a meteor summoned by Sephiroth, a former soldier manipulated by larger forces, threatens to destroy the world. To defend itself, the planet awakens gigantic and powerful beings called Weapons. The storyline in *Majora's Mask* is similar in several ways: miserable and lonely, the Skull Kid is manipulated by Majora's Mask into summoning the moon to crash into Termina. To put a stop to his plans, Link must awaken four giants, the guardians of the world, so that they can stop the moon at the last moment before it collides with the surface. Although it is interesting to draw these parallels between two games set in such utterly different worlds, it is by no means proven that *Final Fantasy* was a source of inspiration for Aonuma.

AN ODE TO TERMINA

Much like previous episodes, this *Zelda* game brings substantial new depth to the saga's mythology. This time, the main focus is on the Dekus. While only a few members of the tribe appeared in *Ocarina of Time*, the Dekus finally get their fair share of attention here, like the Gorons and the Zoras in *Ocarina of Time*.

Let us emphasize once again that the action in *Majora's Mask* takes place outside of Hyrule. As in *Link's Awakening*, this new episode's setting steps off the beaten path and away from well-trodden fields to introduce us to Termina. And as in that Game Boy episode, the princess, the Triforce and Ganon are barely mentioned here. Nevertheless, Termina has a number of points in common with the Hyrule of *Ocarina of Time*, starting with the different characters that Link meets along the way. We have seen that a very likely explanation for this unexpected fact, at least originally, was the short development time available to the designers. But this sense of repetition, or of a sort of reinterpretation of *Ocarina of Time*, also plays a major role in the feeling that players get from this episode of discovering a parallel universe. Termina gradually acquires its legitimacy as a setting as players discover the culture and mythology attached to it. The four sleeping giants that must be awakened in order to stop the moon's descent, the mask salesman who seems to know a lot about the unfolding events, and the spirit of Majora: each of these elements adds to the coherence of this new world.

THE ROLE OF THE MASKS

They appear on the game's packaging, they are featured in its name, and they are a key part of the gameplay—even going so far as to push Ganon aside as the iconic villain of the series. The masks are an absolutely essential part of this new *Zelda* game. A powerful cultural symbol, the mask goes far beyond disguise; in the theaters of antiquity, it summarized a person's character in relation to their destiny, while for certain African peoples it symbolizes an ancestor's spirit or a force of nature. Much more than simply a means of hiding one's identity, the mask is reinvented to take on a new dimension in *Majora's Mask*.

Certain tribes use the mask as a mode of communication, rendering writing unnecessary. Their masks can be read like books, and the images, shapes and silhouettes are even more expressive and direct than words; among other functions, they serve to transmit a codified system of values and beliefs. In general, then, masks are a privileged method of communicating ideas and symbols. Nintendo is fond of this flexible form of visual expression, and uses it extensively in *Majora's Mask*: there is no lengthy verbal narration in this adventure, but rather a distinct preference for the immediacy and universality of images.

For the person who wears it, a mask is like a new face, designed to reveal their true essence. In Greek, the word πρόσωπον (*prósôpon*) is used for both faces and masks. In Latin, an actor's mask was called a *persona*, derived from the verb *personare* (for *resonate* or *resound*), in reference to the role that this type of mask played in amplifying actors' voices in the large open-air theaters of antiquity. As the reader will have guessed, *persona* is the ultimate source of the English word *person*, going back to the mask's role in antique theater as the representation of a character's essence. Carl Gustav Jung used this symbolism as the basis for his concept of the persona. For the Swiss psychologist, a persona is an archetype of social personality—that is, one of the various schemas that emerge from the collective unconscious to infuse each of our lives from childhood onward. Like actors, we change our masks in response to the roles we play in the different human relationships we take part in from one moment to the next. The persona represents conscious attitudes directed toward the outside world. We change masks as often as we change our role in society: in the course of a single day, a corporate employee becomes a mother, then a wife and a friend. For Jung, however, there is a certain danger in this reliance on personas. Generally, most people are not really aware that they are wearing masks. On this point, Jung commented that "the persona is that which in reality one is not, but which oneself as well as others think one is." Without even knowing it, we come to identify ourselves completely with a role, forgetting that it is never more than a tool that is meant to serve us. The persona then takes over and begins to control even our smallest decisions.

Majora's Mask seems to illustrate Jung's theory. The mask worn by the Skull Kid has completely taken over his individuality, and he has become its prisoner. The wearer is nothing more than an empty shell, unable to recognize his own friends, and his only desire is to obey the commands of *Majora's Mask*. Link, meanwhile, makes use of personas as a beneficial tool. Tormented by visions of the future he visited in *Ocarina of Time*, the young hero is despondent and

depressed. In reaction to his friend's disappearance (whoever that friend may be), and haunted by doubt even as he faces his destiny, Link puts on masks of Termina residents in the hopes of finding an answer in his quest for his own identity. The persona represents one's conscious identity, and Link plays with different personas to step into other people's roles. The idea of identifying with one's role is pushed to the limit in *Majora's Mask*, with masks allowing Link to completely change his appearance to that of a Deku, a Goron or a Zora. One by one, Link shares the suffering of these peoples, and thereby learns to better understand them. Learning about others is presented as a step in Link's reconstruction: he must understand his neighbors and the people around him before he can understand himself.

To complete our discussion of masks, let us consider the ways in which they shape the game as a whole. From Japanese Noh theater to African and Egyptian rites, not to mention ancient Greek and Roman cultures and Venetian Italy, masks have been subject to an enormous range of aesthetic influences. So it would certainly be pointless to try to identify just one precedent or inspiration for the unique character of *Majora's Mask*. Nevertheless, it is safe to conclude that one dominant influence was that of Mexican art. Positively bursting with color, the art direction in *Majora's Mask* has a clear predilection for the lively and evocative colors of Mexican tradition. *Majora's Mask* itself reflects this influence well, as do the game's bosses. The appearance of the first boss, in particular, seems to draw on Mesoamerican culture. Although Mexican art is certainly not the only influence seen in the game, that influence was most likely the inspiration for using masks in the first place. Beyond its penchant for certain specific colors and characteristic shapes, Mesoamerican and South American art return constantly to the theme of masks throughout their long history. Masks played an essential role in Mayan and Aztec culture, and were most often used to complete their death rituals. And death is a constantly recurring theme in *Majora's Mask*: the death of the characters whose appearance Link takes on by wearing the masks we discussed earlier, the impending end of the world, and so on. These references are the starting point for an influence that Nintendo and Aonuma would bring back for another episode later in the series, *Twilight Princess*—but also for a few much more subtle and discreet touches in *The Wind Waker*.

TOTALLY UNIQUE

Much like *Link's Awakening*, with which it has a number of key points in common, what distinguishes *Majora's Mask* from the four episodes before it is

its disorienting atmosphere. It stands out even more distinctly than its Game Boy counterpart thanks to its gameplay, based on a three-day cycle. This unique feature is at the heart of the most impressive and exciting entry in the whole series. Every detail in this chapter is designed to subvert fans' expectations of a *Zelda* game; every aspect of the game, right down to its game design, is bursting with originality and constantly catching the player off guard.

But although it is clear beyond a shadow of a doubt that *Majora's Mask* is one of the most original *Zelda* games ever, it nevertheless contradicted Nintendo's original intention to take advantage of the success of *Ocarina of Time*. In fact, *Majora's Mask* is more restrictive and much less accessible than its predecessor. The changes to its atmosphere and gameplay require a significant investment of effort from players, who have to quite literally get themselves organized in order to make their way around Termina efficiently. In terms of both the story and actual hands-on gameplay, the game's thoughtful approach to time is reflected in reality as players are encouraged to arrange and organize their time in order to better immerse themselves in the strange world of Termina. This is a huge difference from *Ocarina of Time*, and may explain the game's limited success; sales were barely over three million copies worldwide, making this the lowest-selling *Zelda* game (not counting the handheld titles). Even today, *Majora's Mask* is one of the series' most atypical experiences. Although the game certainly shows its age in terms of its graphics, the dark, mysterious and phantasmagorical soul of this episode will have no trouble touching the hearts of any player in the modern era.

CHAPTER VII

ORACLE OF AGES – ORACLE OF SEASONS

s Link enjoys his peaceful life in the land of Hyrule, the Triforce begins to pull the young Hylian associated with the triangle of courage irresistibly toward the Princess's castle. No sooner has Link arrived at his destination than the sacred object sends him off into another world, where his next mission is already waiting for him. Unconscious, Link has been picked up by a troupe of wandering artists. When he wakes up, he is immediately captivated by the beauty of one of the troupe's dancers. She introduces herself as Din, then welcomes Link to Holodrum and invites him to dance with her.

But suddenly, dark clouds appear overhead, and lightning strikes the camp. A sinister voice begins to speak: Onox, the evil General of Darkness, declares that he has finally found the Oracle of Seasons. At that moment, a tornado is unleashed, scattering everyone in the camp far and wide—including Link, who is unable to prevent Din from being kidnapped by this new enemy. Wielding formidable powers, Onox imprisons the young woman in a crystal, then submerges the Temple of Seasons in order to throw nature into chaos and eliminate all traces of life from Holodrum's surface. Soon after the temple disappears, chaos begins to spread as the cycle of seasons is disrupted. Link's new quest has begun: he must save both Din and Holodrum at the same time.

A CHASE THROUGH TIME

Immediately after saving the world of Holodrum, Link is transported to another unknown land. In the heart of a strange forest, he is awakened by nearby cries for help. The young Hylian rushes to help the stranger in distress. But when he gets there, he recognizes Impa, Princess Zelda's nursemaid, surrounded by a group of monsters that he is able to drive away easily. Still in shock, Impa struggles to regain her composure. She tells Link that she had come into this gloomy forest to find a singer named Nayru. The nursemaid implores him to help her in her search. Link agrees, and the two continue on their way. Pressing on ever deeper into the forest, Link and Impa finally manage to locate the singer. Suddenly, Impa bursts out unexpectedly in malevolent laughter as though possessed. A blinding light surges forth from her body, releasing a shadow in a strange curl of smoke: the sorceress Veran. She had taken possession of Impa's body in order to cross through the magical barriers that separated her from her real target: Nayru, the Oracle of Ages, who can control the flow of time in the land of Labrynna. Leaving Link no time to react, Veran rushes towards Nayru and takes possession of her body as with Impa's before her. Nayru's radiant and angelic face gives way to the witch's evil grin. Now in possession of Nayru's power, Veran seeks to return to the past to introduce a new era of chaos. And with these threats, the sorceress disappears. Link will have to chase her through the ages to prevent her from changing the present.

THE RETURN OF GANON

These two adventures appear to be independent, but in fact there is a dark connection between them. Off in the shadows, two sisters are pulling the strings. These twin witches belong to the legendary Gerudo tribe. All the trouble that the two of them have caused in Holodrum and Labrynna is aimed at completing a ritual intended to bring Ganon back from the dead. When she learned of this situation, Princess Zelda sent her loyal nursemaid Impa to save Din and Nayru. She had also dreamed of a young boy who would be able to restore peace to the lands of Holodrum and Labrynna.

OUTSOURCING ZELDA

In early 1999, Yoshiki Okamoto was the director of Flagship, a studio within Capcom that specialized in writing video game scripts. A huge fan of the *Zelda* series, he contacted Shigeru Miyamoto with the idea of remaking the first episode for the Game Boy Color.

Although it is difficult to know exactly how the negotiations went, the official story is that Miyamoto rejected Okamoto's offer at first, but soon changed his mind. The original plan was for Miyamoto to take on six projects, including two

based on previous episodes. The remake projects were quickly abandoned; for example, the first episode was seen as being too hard for children, who were Nintendo and Capcom's preferred audience. Intriguingly, though, players can still find a few artifacts of that remake's development in *Oracle of Seasons*. For instance, the geographical location of the first dungeon, as well as the boss inside it (a dragon), are similar to those in the first *Zelda* game. The creators ultimately decided to concentrate their efforts on a series of three brand-new episodes of the saga.

Whereas Miyamoto's usual approach to producing a new *Zelda* game was to start by thinking about gameplay, Capcom wanted to develop the script first, and delegated the job to Flagship. However, Miyamoto still kept an eye on the process, and he was even the one who suggested to Okamoto that each of the three games be associated with one of the values of the Triforce: courage, wisdom and power.

The first game was revealed at Nintendo Space World 1999 (a former trade show dedicated to Nintendo projects). This chapter focused on power. The press made sure to point out that the graphics engine was identical to the one used in *Zelda DX*, the "colorized" version of *Link's Awakening*. Entitled *The Legend of Zelda: The Acorn of the Mystery Tree: Tale of Power*, this version showed Princess Zelda being kidnapped by Ganon. The episode about power was supposed to build its puzzles around the theme of the seasons, while the wisdom episode focused on colors; the final episode, the one about courage, was going to concentrate on the passage of time in the course of a single day. Okamoto had also designed an original system that allowed the three titles to interact with one another. In the planned system, players could start with any one of the three games, then continue the adventure with one of the two others; the actions they took in the first installment could affect the plot in the second one, and so on. No fewer than ten Flagship scriptwriters were assigned to work on these stories. Okamoto originally planned to use a portable phone adapter to transfer data between games, but in the end, the connection was based on a system of passwords. Nevertheless, the limitations of this process and the difficulty of coordinating all three titles eventually led to the demise of one of the projects. Following Miyamoto's advice, Capcom decided to reduce its order to two episodes. *The Legend of Zelda: The Acorn of the Mystery Tree: Tale of Power* became the basis of the game that would eventually be called *Oracle of Seasons*, while *Tale of Wisdom* evolved into *Oracle of Ages*. Among the remaining traces of the original project, the reader may already have noticed that the names of the two oracles, Nayru and Din, are also the names of two of the three goddesses who created Hyrule and the Triforce: the goddess of wisdom and the goddess of power.

These problems in development led to a delay in the release of the two games, pushing it very close to the launch of Nintendo's new portable console, the Game Boy Advance. However, one last postponement of the console's release date allowed Capcom to put out its games on a more reasonable schedule—they came out in Japan on February 27, 2001—and to include a few little bonuses for anyone playing them on the GBA.

In a March 2013 interview with the gaming website *Polygon*, Miyamoto returned to the story of these two games and their original ambitions: "When we first released *The Legend of Zelda: Oracle of the Ages* and *Oracle of Seasons* on Game Boy Color many years ago, the original idea for those games was for them to be more episodic in content, and the development actually started with the notion of potentially trying to sell dungeons individually. At the time that we were working on the *Oracle* games, we felt that it just wasn't right to deliver the game in that fashion. But when we look at what we've done with the eShop and the possibilities that lie there, and particularly with the fact that we're now able to patch existing games that have already been released, that then opens up new possibilities for downloadable content."

MASTERY OF TIME AND SEASONS

Oracle of Time and *Oracle of Seasons* are largely based on the approach taken in *Link's Awakening*, since they did in fact inherit their graphics engine from that game. In terms of their overall look, the two titles strongly recall Link's first adventure on a portable console. However, the progression system in the two new games reflects a clear RPG influence. First of all, the story is richer and more complex than usual (although it never matches the complexity of the genre's biggest franchises), supported by a denser narrative using plenty of fixed images, which had previously been relegated to the very beginning and end of Link's adventures. In terms of gameplay, new items are introduced, like the rings that Link can collect by solving puzzles or doing favors for certain characters. Once they have been evaluated by a jeweler, Link can add them to his inventory, where they improve his abilities or even give him entirely new skills. These new aspects are somewhat reminiscent of classic roleplaying games—and to a lesser degree, of *Zelda II: The Adventure of Link*, which also had certain objects that could directly improve the main character's attributes. By encouraging the player to collect and exchange objects with villagers throughout the adventure, these two episodes reconnect with a principle that we saw in *Link's Awakening*, and that was somewhat hesitantly reintroduced in *Majora's Mask*. As for the hero's equipment, let us also note the addition of

seeds. These are divided into several different types—Ember Seeds, Mystery Seeds, Pegasus Seeds, and so on—each of which has its own specific effect, such as lighting fires, communicating with owl statues, or increasing Link's movement speed.

In addition, *Oracle of Ages* and *Oracle of Seasons* each have certain unique gameplay features that relate to their underlying storylines. In *Oracle of Ages*, for example, Link quickly acquires the Harp of Ages, which he can use to open portals that let him travel between the present day and a time four hundred years in the past. This allows players to discover the world of Labrynna from two very different perspectives, due to the immense changes that have taken place over the years. In *Oracle of Seasons*, meanwhile, Link controls the climate with the Rod of Seasons. At certain specific locations, our hero can use this tool to instantly change the weather around him. In autumn, the scenery takes on fall colors and the forest paths are lined with fallen leaves, while in winter, Link has to reckon with snow and ice. The change of seasons does not affect the overall look of the world to any great degree. Instead, Link calls upon the Rod of Seasons to solve specific problems. A certain dungeon can only be reached by climbing summertime ivy; a certain path becomes accessible in winter when rivers turn to ice. *Oracle of Seasons* also gives players the opportunity to explore the underground world of Subrosia. While it is certainly not as large a world as Holodrum, Link has occasion to return there many times over the course of his adventure.

While these two installments for Game Boy Color each have their own unique aspects, they also have certain new features in common, including animals that offer their help to Link. Three different companions will cross our hero's path: Ricky the kangaroo (who can box and jump over holes), Moosh the flying bear (able to glide before crashing to the ground with all his weight), and Dimitri the dinosaur (the only one who can swim in deep water). Link must put each animal's skills to good use in order to move forward with his quest. In order to summon one of these three animals when he needs it, Link must first acquire a special flute to call each of them.

One of the biggest innovations introduced by *Oracle of Ages* and *Oracle of Seasons* has to do with the connection between the two installments. After finishing one of the two adventures, players receive a code that lets them start the second quest by connecting the two storylines. As they move from one episode to the next, players will notice that the world has evolved, and that the story as a whole has maintained a welcome degree of consistency. Many characters will recognize Link, and even make comments relating to the previous adventure. To take another example, the player can name a newborn baby in one of the games, and meet it again in the second game—older this time, but still with the same name. And depending on which flute Link was holding at the end of the first game, the animal called by that flute will accompany him in the new adventure. Link also starts his second voyage with his wooden sword already in hand, and with one additional heart container. After Link has saved Princess Zelda as part of a side quest, she remains in the main village. Finally, and perhaps most interestingly, the link between the two games gives players access to a real conclusion to the story, in which Ganon is revived by the two witches.

Although each of the two installments includes certain exclusive original items, like the Magnetic Gloves in *Seasons* or the Roc's Feather in *Ages*, these differences are more aesthetic than functional in nature, since a counterpart to each of these items is found in a disguised form in the other installment. Overall, then, these two *Zelda* games offer fairly similar gameplay despite their distinct storylines. There is one inconsistency between the two games: whereas the Maku Tree is "female" in *Ages*, it is presented as "male" in *Seasons*. In any case, the connection between the games brings a clear added value to both of these *Zelda* episodes, even though each of them also stands up perfectly well on its own. And while the different versions of *Pokémon*, for example, were essentially multiple iterations of one and the same adventure, here we are definitely dealing with two distinct quests. To continue with the *Pokémon* comparison, we also note that the connection between these two *Zelda* games allows players to pass rings from one adventure to the next.

THE END OF TIME

Oracle of Seasons and *Oracle of Ages* represent the end of a cycle dedicated to the subject of time. After *Ocarina of Time* and its vision of childhood, then *Majora's Mask* with its look into everyday life, Capcom returns to this theme to consider the passage of seasons and centuries. This concrete manifestation of time finds an immediate echo in gameplay: players themselves are in direct control of the changing seasons and shifting eras. Although the theme of time would reappear in the form of brief references in later episodes, the gameplay mechanics would no longer depend upon it as they do here.

A UNIVERSAL HERO

Oracle of Seasons and *Oracle of Ages* mark the third time, after *Link's Awakening* and *Majora's Mask*, that the adventure unfolds outside of Hyrule. Unlike those

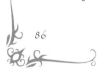

other two games, however, both of the *Oracle* games make explicit reference to the kingdom of Hyrule. In earlier games, Hyrule's extent and its place in the world were not entirely clear: was Hyrule the name of the entire world, or simply one kingdom among many? Starting with these installments, it seems clear that the world in which the *Zelda* series takes place is divided into a number of countries, one of which is Hyrule. Nevertheless, moving from one country to another seems to require passing through sacred barriers that only certain people can cross: Link is brought there by the Triforce, whereas Zelda is apparently able to move between the different regions at will. These details help to imbue our hero with a kind of universal character. His sense of duty and self-sacrifice are not limited to his own native land. He is a hero not only for Hyrule, but for everyone, and this perspective confers an even greater meaning on his many adventures.

DON'T MESS WITH SUCCESS?

An astute mix of the recipes used in earlier *Zelda* games (in both technical and gameplay terms), *Ages* and *Seasons* pluck different elements from here and there among the best episodes of the past, but without doing much to enhance them or add a real sense of personality. For example, the game puts an emphasis on time and musical instruments, but also recycles the cute, rounded graphics of *Link's Awakening*. Some characters are even taken over directly from *Ocarina of Time*, like Malon, Ingo and the Zoras in *Ages*, or the Gorons in *Seasons*. With their constant stream of references and familiar people and places, these two games ultimately fail to stand out in their own right. To be sure, the adventure is still a perfectly enjoyable and well-executed one, light and colorful as it is; but other than the animal companions and the interactivity between the two games, there is nothing much new to be found in these episodes. Even the games' interdependence turns out to be fairly limited in the end, and does not provide enough of a reward for the player who has bought and finished both quests. *Seasons* and *Ages* each have their own distinct storyline, a point for which Nintendo deserves credit; clearly, the publisher was not trying to sell the same thing twice to an eager public that would have been happy to buy any new *Zelda* game. Nevertheless, this pair of games, excellent though they may be in comparison to most other games for the Game Boy, makes for a rather timid addition to the series as a whole. They are both far too focused on diligently copying past glories, and miss their opportunity to enrich the saga by adding their own unique contribution.

As one might expect from Capcom's approach to production and the development of the two games, both installments certainly have a denser plot than their predecessors. But the way in which their stories are presented is ultimately a bit ham-fisted. The large number of secondary characters helps to add a certain weight to the tale, but too many artificial twists and turns make the plot feel more confusing than intriguing. And for the first time, a *Zelda* game falls victim to the curse of classic RPGs: at the start of the game, the player is forced to sit through lengthy exposition for minutes on end without touching the controls, unable to directly participate in the story. In short, the *Oracle* games had turned away from the simplicity and immediacy of what had made *Zelda* such a classic series. For the first time, the release of two *Zelda* games was not perceived as a big event. Many people consider them to be excellent games; although those people are not wrong, it turns out that excellence alone is not enough to ensure a memorable experience. In fact, this pair of *Zelda* games marks the beginning of a more watered-down and repetitive period for the series—a trend that would particularly affect the portable consoles, and one that we will discuss at greater length later on. The saga had started to feel a bit worn out, and while its formula was still as effective as ever, its freshness had started to fade. The two new games had checked all the boxes, but perhaps in too neat and tidy a way—and with a distinct lack of inspiration.

CHAPTER VIII

THE WIND WAKER

t is said that long ago, a kingdom had grown and prospered with the help of a magical object left to it by the gods—one that gave its bearers great power. The forces of evil had long coveted this divine object.

A demonic creature had tried to seize it for himself, but fortunately he was stopped by the efforts of a young boy. Hailed as a savior, the boy became known as the "Hero of Time." His story ultimately became the stuff of legend.

But alas, many years later, the evil creature that the Hero of Time had once defeated would return to seek the goddesses' power once more. His wicked shadow cast the kingdom into darkness. The people waited and hoped for the Hero of Time to return, but in vain; he never reappeared. No one knows what ultimately became of the once-prosperous kingdom.

The legend is still being passed down to this day. On Outset Island, however, it is a time for carefree celebration. According to custom, young boys on the island dress in green on their twelfth birthday to honor the Hero of Time's memory. Link is getting ready to celebrate this prestigious day with his grandmother and his sister Aryll. But before the main ceremony can begin, an enormous bird swoops over the island, clutching a little blond girl in its talons. The bird is being chased by a pirate ship that is firing on it with cannons, apparently in hopes of making it release the girl. With a few well-aimed shots, the creature loosens its grip, and the child falls into a forest on the island. Link goes to look for her, and finds her safe and sound. She introduces herself as Tetra, the captain of a band of pirates. As Tetra and Link walk back towards the village together, the giant bird reappears. This time, it snatches the boy's sister, Aryll, apparently confusing her with his earlier prey. Link decides to board Tetra's pirate ship immediately and start looking for his sister.

A BREATH OF FRESH AIR

The Wind Waker leaves behind the fear and excitement of a world wracked by constantly changing seasons and ages for the apparent tranquility of an immense and unchanging expanse of blue. But the sea will turn out to have its stormy side as well. This episode went into development immediately after *Majora's Mask* was completed, and Eiji Aonuma was once again in charge. At the time, Nintendo's flagship system was the GameCube. Faced with impressive competition from the warships sent forth by Sony and Microsoft, the Kyoto manufacturer's console had nevertheless managed to amaze and excite players with a technical demonstration that pitted Link against Ganon in a duel of astonishing realism. This video was the result of a series of tests and experiments carried out on the GameCube even before the development of *Majora's Mask* in 2000. And on August 23, 2001, Nintendo unveiled its official vision of the next generation of *Zelda* games... one that was completely at odds with the demonstration it had used to introduce its new console! Presenting Link as a child with a face that pushed the idea of *kawaii*-style cuteness to the point of caricature, the new video triggered an angry reaction from many fans of the series. Their noisy and impassioned reaction was understandable in light of the severe shock they'd been hit with. Not only was the unrealistic visual style used for this new chapter the furthest thing from epic, but it also went directly against players' expectations. The use of *toon-shading*, derived from *cel-shading*, offers a visual approach that makes the game look a lot like an animated film. This stylistic choice gave rise to fears that the new episode would be aimed exclusively at a very young audience.

But such fears are clearly misplaced for those who know Nintendo well; the new game would indeed be more accessible, but also far from simplistic. Aonuma had noticed that gamers were suffering from a certain degree of *Zelda* fatigue, and intended to bring new life to the series by pulling it out of the routine it had started to sink into. The fans were merciless, however; after catching a lot of heat over the first trailer for the new installment, we may assume that Aonuma decided to ease up a bit and moderate his ambitions. Be that as it may, Nintendo and Miyamoto still gave him free rein to give the series the breath of fresh air it needed. And so the game's world was born, dominated by the ocean and with wind as its central theme. This new chapter, christened *The Wind Waker*, also awakened an old desire of Miyamoto's: to represent wind in a game. Recall that the breeze was already blowing in certain *Super Mario* levels. But Miyamoto had to wait until computing power like that of the GameCube became available before he could finally see the wind come to life in one of his productions.

Released on North American shores in March 2003, *The Wind Waker* was sold in two distinct versions. The first, classic version included only the game itself, while the "collector's edition" also included a second disc containing *Ocarina of Time* and the notorious *Ura Zelda*, renamed as *Master Quest* for the occasion.

In late 2013, Nintendo published an HD version of *The Wind Waker* for its Wii U console. Already gorgeous on the GameCube, the cel shading in this HD version was positively sublime: the colors are brighter, lighting effects are even more polished, and details stand out more sharply than ever. But while the graphics had clearly improved, the biggest change was in the control scheme used on the GamePad. As with the 3DS version of *Ocarina of Time*, players could now use the controller's gyroscope to manipulate in-game objects. The view then changes to a first-person perspective, and the player has to physically move around in order to explore the world of *The Wind Waker* through the GamePad's screen. Those less enthralled with the idea of waving a controller around in their living room can still use the Pro controller for the same purpose, or even just the right thumbstick. Players can also use the GamePad's touch screen to select items, consult the map, or use the Wind Waker with just a few taps of the finger. The more comfortable control scheme helps to keep the adventure moving along at a steadier pace, especially in the somewhat sluggish segments where Link goes fishing for Triforce shards.

In the end, the updated version of *The Wind Waker* does not introduce any major shake-ups or substantial additions. It would have been nice to try out the two temples that were cut late in development to ensure that the game would come out on schedule for the GameCube, but players will have to settle for Hero Mode with its higher difficulty level, inherited directly from *Skyward Sword*, which can fortunately be switched off at any time.

AS DEEP AS THE OCEAN

Redefining its own codes seems to be a vast and ongoing project for the *Zelda* series. For its part, *The Wind Waker* breaks with a few of the saga's conventions—starting with its new aesthetic, to which we will return later—but never does anything to refresh the gameplay mechanics that players had grown accustomed to in previous games. Overall, then, the game is fairly similar to its predecessors. Nevertheless, a number of details clearly reflect the careful attention that the designers put into the game, as well as their desire to add something new to the series. For example, certain items that are essential to the quest are not found in dungeons, as had always been the case in earlier games, but are given to Link by different characters he meets. But in terms of

the link between gameplay and overarching themes, the focus of this episode's experimentation seems to lie in the choice of a new environment for Link to explore: the ocean. Hyrule has sunk almost entirely beneath the waves, and Link can no longer make his way across it on Epona's back. From now on, he will have to make use of a most unique vessel, a talking boat called the *King of Red Lions*. The immensity of the open sea is truly dizzying. From a glance at the world map, we see that each square on the map marks out a zone that will have to be explored in minute detail to find the island or islands within it. To gather vital information about the secrets hidden beneath the waves, Link has to talk to the Fishmen, cartographers who will draw the outlines of nearby lands on his map in exchange for a bit of food. This helps to make the young boy's voyage that much more exciting and addictive. In addition, the Fishmen will often volunteer clues, albeit incomplete ones, about where Link can find this or that treasure or secret—a way of piquing players' curiosity and encouraging their thirst for discovery.

This addiction to adventure is not limited to the vast ocean: the number of side quests and minigames on offer is itself enough to make players' heads spin. Rarely has a *Zelda* game provided players with so many things to do. Besides the usual search for Pieces of Heart, they will also have to go hunting for treasure maps lost in the briny depths, or collect items and letters left behind by defeated enemies and exchange them for impressive rewards. In exchange for ten Knight's Crests, for example, Link can learn an improved version of his spin attack. Or, if he gives forty Joy Pendants to Mrs. Marie, the boy will receive the Hero's Charm in exchange, allowing him to see his enemies' life meters— including those of bosses.

In all of these ways, the game makes plenty of room for exploration. As soon as Link acquires a sail for his boat, he is able to travel anywhere he likes on the map. However, this overdose of adventure is all too quickly limited by the lack of places to visit. To be sure, players are free to sail wherever they like, but once they drop anchor at an island, they will find that there is only a very limited amount of dry land to explore. That initial sense of freedom may start to seem like an illusion; punctuated only by a few dungeons and incidental side trips, sailing the seas ends up feeling like a long and boring process. For players with no interest in side quests and other optional parts of the adventure, the voyage thus boils down to an uninterrupted series of dungeons that soon turn into a mind-numbing chore. Of course, the notion of the voyage underlies and influences every aspect of *The Wind Waker*'s structure, and is inseparable from its ocean setting. Any player who turned their back on the travel elements would in effect be rejecting the most essential part of the adventure. On the other hand, players who are ready to get on board with this concept will find in it the true heart of this quest, one which will make up for the lack of pacing in the main plot and the rather formulaic storyline.

NEW POSSIBILITIES

The range of combat actions available to Link has been brought up to modern standards. More dynamic and better developed, these sequences draw the hero into a meticulous dance that will capture players' interest much more effectively than in the past, although their skill will not necessarily be tested any more than usual. For example, Link can snatch his adversaries' weapons away from them, either to slay them or to solve a puzzle. The rhythm of clashing swords brings new life to these altercations as well, with a different sound heard every time Link's weapon strikes home. In this respect, the similarity to games by Tetsuya Mizuguchi (like *Rez* or *Child of Eden*) is clearly a coincidence. Still, the fact remains that this rhythmic structure gives a real sense of weight to every battle in the game.

Despite the expanded range of options available to the player, the game remains intuitive and accessible. Without necessarily agreeing that this chapter is primarily aimed at children, as many of its detractors claim, we cannot deny that *The Wind Waker* is one of the easiest *Zelda* games. However, the two final dungeons turn out to be quite long and complex—enough to satisfy even the most fearless adventurer. They also introduce a system of cooperation with NPCs that was later recycled in another episode, *Spirit Tracks*. But frustration sets in with a detail that seems innocuous enough at first: the camera controls. The camera is completely free for the first time in the series, and is controlled with the right stick of the controller—but there is no option to invert its direction of rotation. In any case, just because a game is accessible doesn't mean it has to be boring, and *The Wind Waker* offers a playing field more extensive than anything seen in a *Zelda* game since *Majora's Mask*.

AN UNEXPECTED DESIGN

At a time when everyone was expecting a more realistic *Zelda* game with incredibly lifelike graphics that made full use of the GameCube's capabilities, Nintendo and the new head of the series, Eiji Aonuma, caught everyone off guard when they unveiled a new chapter rendered entirely in a cel shading style. Cel shading is a modeling technique that makes it possible to render three-dimensional objects in a style similar to that of a comic book or cartoon

(where *cel* refers to celluloid film), and bases its effect on patterns of light and shadow. Nintendo referred to this style as *toon shading* with regard to its use in *The Wind Waker*.

The general public's first exposure to the game was through its graphics, and the visual style of this new *Zelda* installment was a source of befuddlement and even anger for many fans. Miyamoto, on the other hand, was shocked by the reactions of the press, which had immediately categorized *The Wind Waker* as a children's game, interpreting its graphical approach as a marketing decision aimed specifically at kids. Nintendo's ambition was indeed to bring players together around a common experience—an accessible one, to be sure, but by no means exclusively for children. But the choice to use toon shading was intended first and foremost to bring new life to the series by returning to its origins in the earliest *Zelda* games. When the *Zelda* series first sprang forth from Miyamoto's mind, he wanted a feeling of freedom and adventure to be the guiding principle of the series—and it was precisely that feeling that *The Wind Waker* sought to bring back. So it is not surprising that the game's graphics, which used only solid colors and no textures, should evoke a fairy-tale world in much the same way as the first episode.

Although Miyamoto is not opposed to the use of photorealistic graphics, he has argued that they can never be convincing unless they are absolutely flawless. The little bugs that occasionally crop up on consoles—like a character who gets stuck in a wall, or climbs next to a ladder instead of on it—are much more distracting in games with a realistic look; the bug undermines the player's sense of immersion. This risk, often associated with the quest for hyperrealism in computer or robotic simulations, was dubbed the *uncanny valley* by the Japanese roboticist Masahiro Mori. This term refers to our feelings of discomfort or even repulsion when faced with a realistic humanoid robot. On the other hand, robots with a more obviously mechanical appearance do not trigger this sense of aversion, and may even evoke a feeling of goodwill, thanks to an appearance and range of actions which are not overly similar to those of human beings. Throughout the development of *The Wind Waker*, Miyamoto and Aonuma were guided by their desire to provide their characters with easily identifiable facial expressions. This makes the characters' reactions seem more plausible. Seen from this perspective, *The Wind Waker* is an extremely realistic game—not in terms of its similarity to the real world, perhaps, but in terms of the internal consistency of its own world. In order to make the most of these facial expressions, the team worked hard on the characters' eyes, and especially on their gaze. When certain objects attract Link's attention, players can see it on his face—and so their attention is drawn to those objects as well. Previously, Link had always had blue eyes, but for this installment they changed to a coal-black

color with a slight touch of green. The look of Link's eyes in this game was so important to Miyamoto that he nicknamed his hero "Cat-Eye Link."

The toon-shading technique also allowed Nintendo to bring a bit of stylistic consistency to the *Zelda* series. Miyamoto was pleased that the box art for *The Wind Waker* was finally a perfect representation of Link's look in the game. Before this installment, the different episodes in the series often had a completely different graphical style from one game to the next. In addition, Link's appearance on the game box was completely unrepresentative of how he was modeled in the game. Toon shading brought an end to these differences and gave the hero a consistent style, which was then reused in *The Minish Cap*, *Phantom Hourglass*, *Four Swords Adventures* and *Spirit Tracks*. In fact, thanks to the innovative graphics with their perfectly fluid animations, Link's own attitude in *The Wind Waker* gives rise to a kind of situational humor that had been impossible to capture in earlier games. In this new adventure, the hero can express his zest for life, his infectious joy, and his touching naiveté with a mischievous grin, a teasing glance, or any of a whole range of other hilarious expressions. The rest of the characters also benefit from this minute attention to detail—especially Link's enemies, who take on a comedic dimension not seen in earlier episodes. The relative simplicity of the design fits perfectly with the characters' naive attitudes.

No other *Zelda* game ever felt so alive. Packed with showy effects that will fill any player with a sense of childlike bliss, *The Wind Waker* still stands out today for its magnificent graphical style. The movement of the waves, the trails left by objects moving through water, and the grass blowing gently in the breeze (represented by simple lines that appear and fade in the sky) all help to create a unique and timeless fairy-tale atmosphere. Enemies give off a puff of smoke when they die; flaming arrows do damage that spreads to fabrics; in certain places, the heat from molten lava blurs the image on the screen; and clouds of ashes and particles blow towards the camera. Visual effects like these, some of them flashy and some more discreet, serve to transform an ordinary gaming session into a living experience. Players' concerns after seeing the earliest images of the game were understandable, but once those images were set in motion and the look had been polished, the visual consistency of the art design and its careful attention to detail ultimately won over even the most hesitant fans. While *Majora's Mask* had drawn players in with its rich and luxurious look, *Wind Waker* surprised them with its simple, almost austere tone. Toon shading is one of the rare graphics techniques that is truly timeless. The game still looks sublime in the age of high definition, and a slight blurriness caused by the migration to modern HD televisions was the one minor blemish on the game's visual purity—a problem that was resolved with the release of the 2013

remake. The overall look of *The Wind Waker* has certain aspects in common with the work of Hayao Miyazaki, co-founder of Studio Ghibli and a major star in the world of Japanese animation (known for directing *Princess Mononoke* and *Spirited Away*, among others). Nintendo's artists were raised on the director's work, and they don't try to hide it. Miyamoto has also cited Miyazaki many times in discussing the cartoon-like look of *The Wind Waker*. Players will notice certain elements borrowed from Miyazaki's productions—including *Future Boy Conan* (1978), set in a flooded world dotted with islands, but also the woodland spirits of *Princess Mononoke* that were clearly a source of inspiration for the diminutive Korok people in *The Wind Waker*. Those same characters also use leaves as parasols and umbrellas, much like the wood spirit in Miyazaki's 1988 film *My Neighbor Totoro*.

A REBOOT?

We have seen that even as this new *Zelda* game was revolutionizing the saga's look, it also aimed to take the series back to basics and inject new energy into the franchise. In short, the goal was to bring back the sense of freedom that had made the first episode so original and exciting. Although the overall ambition was therefore much the same as in the original *Zelda*, the core principles were applied in a very different way. Travel, discovery and exploration are indeed the guiding concepts in this episode, but this time around, the action takes place almost exclusively at sea. *The Wind Waker* puts a fresh coat of paint on the saga's slightly worn-out basic framework by introducing an all-new world and new gameplay mechanics, along with a boat and vast expanses of ocean to sail it on. In short, a new start to the series and a welcome change in orientation. Although the gameplay has not been entirely reinvented, the game feels fresh, authentic, and above all, unfamiliar.

Players can really feel the effort that Aonuma put into revitalizing some of the saga's core concepts. The changes show up in the first few seconds of the game: even before the start of the actual adventure, the art design presents us with a startling difference by showing little Link in his everyday clothes, not yet dressed in his iconic green outfit. Our hero has yet to become a hero. In this way, Aonuma encourages players to rethink the saga they have grown so attached to: if Link himself is no longer the same, then he is no longer the Hero of Time who saved Hyrule so long ago. Players will therefore have to relearn the basics of a saga that they have long taken for granted—and the following sequence confirms this. The game's opening moments unfold in a peaceful setting as Link slowly wakes up and starts getting ready for his

birthday celebration. This quiet atmosphere contrasts sharply with the high drama that marked the beginning of most earlier *Zelda* games. It is interesting to note that the subsequent installments (*The Minish Cap, Twilight Princess* and *Spirit Tracks*) also use this type of quiet, slow-paced prologue to start their respective adventures. *Phantom Hourglass* is the sole exception here, as the direct sequel to *The Wind Waker*.

A moment from early in the game provides a perfect illustration of this desire for transformation. Starting with the very first dungeon, the usual structure is set aside in favor of a challenge that turns its back on the saga's traditions to offer players an entirely new experience. Players must first make their way through a stealth sequence before the real action begins. Link rushes off toward the Forsaken Fortress where his sister is being held prisoner. But the boy in the green tunic is about to be tripped up by his innocence and lack of experience. No sooner does Link arrive at his destination than he loses his sword! With no weapon, he is forced to do whatever it takes to avoid being detected. The stealth section that follows is a concrete expression in this episode's game design of Nintendo's desire to make a break with other titles in the series. It also provides the opportunity for a few winking references to the *Metal Gear Solid* series: just like Snake, Link can now press himself against walls, hide in barrels, crawl along the ground, and even peek cautiously around corners. The boy will have to use all of these abilities, borrowed from Konami's classic series with an extra twist of humor, if he wants to get past the guards without being noticed—and thrown straight into jail.

This drive for renewal is also reflected in the range of objects Link collects in the course of his journey: the Telescope, the Deku Leaf, the Wind Waker, and of course his new mode of transportation, the boat. All of these new elements make their first appearance in the series here. The boy also acquires a very strange object that will provide the player, rather than this new Link, with the chance to reconnect with an old acquaintance. During his visit to Windfall Island, Link will encounter Tingle, the mischievous imp from *Majora's Mask*. After rescuing him, and then recovering a special item that looks like a Game Boy Advance, the player can count on getting help from the talkative little goofball in green. By connecting a GBA to their console, the player can get backup from a friend; the friend will see instructions on the portable console's screen to help them find hidden items. Tingle will also come back repeatedly to help Link, whether by giving him more hearts or more magic in critical situations, or even by throwing bombs at his enemies—all in exchange for a few rupees, of course.

In some ways, *The Wind Waker* almost seems like a reboot of the *Zelda* series. In the world of computers, a "reboot" implies stopping everything you've been doing and starting over from the system's initial state. Similarly, in video games, a reboot involves using a new episode as a chance to "start over" with a franchise, to give it a new look and perhaps to make some radical changes. In *The Wind Waker*, Aonuma is working with all of the typical ingredients for a reboot: a new hero, a new visual style, new gameplay mechanics, and so on. In hindsight, we can see that this episode is looking as much towards the past as towards the future. For the first time in a *Zelda* game, nostalgia is used as a source of emotional impact. The script for *The Wind Waker* evokes the events of *Ocarina of Time* by presenting them as an undying legend. Truly an homage to Miyamoto, *The Wind Waker* realizes Aonuma's vision for the series (over which he now has exclusive control) even as it shows his respect for the man who first gave him a chance to work on it.

THEMES AND INSPIRATIONS

Each and every *Zelda* game is packed with cultural references that helped to inspire its developers. With such a rich maritime theme to work with, it is hardly surprising that pirates and some of their codes are among those sources of inspiration. Going by the name of Tetra, Princess Zelda herself leads a crew of buccaneers in the game. Some of the other borrowed ideas here relate to the symbolism associated with Link's voyage. Stories in which legendary heroes explore the oceans and visit various islands to explore their different climates, landscapes and peoples are well-known from the literary adventures of Ulysses, Jason and Gulliver. Of course, *The Wind Waker* makes no claim to being a political, philosophical or social satire of our times like *Gulliver's Travels* by Jonathan Swift (who may himself have been inspired by Savinien Cyrano de Bergerac's *The Other World*, a predecessor to the modern genre of science fiction). Be that as it may, the game clearly drew inspiration from the emotions and sense of wonder felt by the legendary explorers in those classic adventures.

The theme of a great flood is also explicitly referenced. The reason that Hyrule now sleeps beneath the waves is because the gods sent down a deluge upon the kingdom long ago to put a stop to Ganon's evil plots. The myth of a great flood recurs in many different cultures. Texts from the Christian, Islamic, Mayan, Hindu, Scandinavian and Zoroastrian traditions, to name only a few, tell tales of torrential rains and floods that threatened to destroy all life. However, this fundamental, visceral fear of the end of humanity is not addressed in those terms in *The Wind Waker*. In contrast to the biblical tale of Noah, in which (aside from a handful of human beings) only one male and one female of each species are preserved, the entire population of Hyrule seems to have been

spared in *The Wind Waker*. Some groups have been changed by evolution—the Zoras have become the Rito, for example—while others, like the Gorons, have trouble finding their place in the ocean environment. But whether in ancient texts or in this new *Zelda* chapter, the great flood always represents the end of a cycle, as well as renewal.

THE BIRTH OF A PARALLEL WORLD

The introduction to *The Wind Waker* explains how, after the events of *Ocarina of Time*, Ganon returned from the dead to continue his quest for power. This time, however, Link did not stand in his way, and the dark lord was able to bring his evil plot to fruition. Just as Hyrule's fate appeared to be sealed, the king implored the gods to put a stop to Ganon's madness. His prayer was heard... but at what price? Much like Atlantis, the entire kingdom was swallowed up beneath the waves. Only a handful of chosen individuals were saved in order to found a new world on the few remaining bits of dry land.

With this new tale, *The Wind Waker* had just made a major addition to the mythology of the *Zelda* series. This was also the first time that an episode had made an explicit attempt to draw a connection to an earlier installment other than its immediate predecessor. Right at the start of the adventure, then, the player's epic adventure in *Ocarina of Time* is referred to directly: the search for the Triforce, the fight against Ganon, Link's victory and his status as the Hero of Time all serve as connections between the two stories. For the first time, there is no ambiguity about the fact that the Link we meet in *The Wind Waker* is a successor to the one from *Ocarina of Time*. This confirms that the hero of the *Zelda* saga is not necessarily the same person from one episode to the next, as some players had already concluded from the many inconsistencies between episodes. On the other hand, the story of the Hero of Time's exploits clearly indicates that even if the young Hylian that we control here is a kind of reincarnation of Link, the evil Ganon is still the same individual in both episodes—and therefore, most likely, throughout the entire series.

In interviews that he gave during the game's promotional phase, Eiji Aonuma went even further, stating that although the various *Zelda* games were related by a shared timeline, that timeline was divided into two distinct branches, each of which was associated with specific later episodes. The separation takes place at the end of *Ocarina of Time*, and is tied to Ganon's defeat at the hands of the grown-up Link. The first branch follows the consequences of that event, leading to the story of *The Wind Waker* a century later. The second branch, meanwhile, develops from events that take place after Link goes back to being a child.

The Link we meet in *The Wind Waker* lives on a small island with his grandmother and his sister Aryll. This is not the first time we have met the hero's family (he was living with his uncle in *A Link to the Past*), but never before have we gotten such a long look at them. The Link in this episode is simply an ordinary boy getting ready to celebrate his twelfth birthday with a ceremony in which he must don a green costume in honor of the legendary hero. Little does he know that he is about to become that hero's successor!

MAKE WAY FOR A NEW GENERATION

The ending of *The Wind Waker* resolves all the plotlines that are specific to this episode. In the background, however, we can also discern another faint message from the designers, and from Eiji Aonuma in particular—although it may or may not be intentional. For the first time ever, an episode of *Zelda* explicitly refers to one of its predecessors in order to draw a connection between the two stories. At the very end of the game, the king of old Hyrule (which therefore represents the world of the past) expresses his deepest regrets to Link and Tetra: he and others like him led the world to destruction, leaving nothing to later generations but a largely uninhabitable seascape. We can interpret this speech from an environmentalist perspective: the rising sea levels could be a reference to the world of today, and to the disasters being predicted as the results of global warming—thus evoking yet again some of the heavy subject matter we find in Miyazaki's work. But there is another perfectly reasonable interpretation: the speech might really be Aonuma's plea on behalf of his creation, urging his audience not to give in to nostalgia, and to give new generations a chance to express themselves. On this view, old Hyrule and its kind represent the saga's past, which culminated with *Ocarina of Time*; Link and Tetra, symbols of renewal and a world in the process of rebuilding itself, would then represent Aonuma as he defends his own vision of the series. Aonuma even has one of his characters say that the future may not necessarily be amazing, but it deserves to be given a chance. *The Wind Waker* thus turns out to be a turning point in the saga. With its deeply respectful references to *Ocarina of Time* (which treat that game's story as positively sacrosanct, as in the scene where Link first discovers the flooded world), this new episode evokes the past in an obvious way, even as it works to surpass its glorious ancestor. It encourages players not to get caught up in nostalgia, but to accept the idea of moving on to new gaming experiences.

REFRESHING AND ALWAYS RELEVANT

We have seen that even before its release, *The Wind Waker* had drawn fire from a certain subset of players who were unhappy with the direction that the creators of the series had chosen to take it in. In the end, however, the game was well-received by critics and the general public alike. Even though it turned out to be among the weakest-selling episodes in the series, it has always maintained a unique status at the heart of the debate between fans and detractors of the saga's new direction.

Let us begin by noting that *The Wind Waker* is both an excellent game and a very good entry in the *Zelda* series. With an incredible atmosphere that is further enhanced by its captivating visual style, this installment has an aura of freshness about it that is as new and exciting today as the day it came out. Thanks to its use of cel shading, it's probably safe to assume that this episode will age more gracefully than any other 3D *Zelda* game. Nevertheless, we must admit that the game's efforts to make a sharp break with its predecessors also led to some unpleasant side effects.

The choice of an ocean-based world in which Link travels by boat means that getting around in the game is somewhat laborious and repetitive. Each sea crossing can take several long minutes to complete, even though the authors made some effort to make these trips more exciting (with monsters to attack, marked paths to follow, and so on), and even provided a way to teleport to certain places on the map through the use of tornadoes. However, it is important to understand the designers' intentions: this game is meant as an ode to freedom, and aims to engage the player's taste for exploration. The length of the boat expeditions was an intentional choice that serves to emphasize the feeling of getting away from the rest of the world. According to Aonuma, making these sequences shorter would have made them feel incidental—in direct contradiction to the project's original goals. As it turns out, not only are players able to turn aside from the main quest, but they are actively encouraged to do so, chasing adventure wherever it leads as they explore the many islands scattered across the ocean.

Although we have argued that the sailing segments do not necessarily deserve all the criticism that has been leveled at them, we must still admit that this episode is not quite as epic as it might have been. The quest as a whole is somewhat less structured than usual, especially in the quest for the Triforce fragments towards the end. The main issue is that players lack an incentive to keep them moving forward, as the story and short-term goals are not especially clear. The adventure is a lightweight one, then, in line with the new direction chosen by Nintendo. The dungeons are more open, less "claustrophobic"—and

contrary to popular opinion, there are just as many of them here as in other *Zelda* games, and they're not necessarily any easier. Gameplay is also more tolerant and permissive: a new move allows Link to unleash a devastating counterattack, enemy attacks do less damage, and visual hints show where to throw the hookshot or boomerang.

After all this discussion, and despite all the effort put into this installment, we still have to wonder whether the *Zelda* formula might be starting to lose steam. Although the games' quality is still impressive, their constant reuse of the same elements inevitably limits the sense of surprise. More specifically, the village-dungeon-boss cycle is unchanged, the majority of the objects that Link collects are the same as ever, and the adventure ends up feeling self-referential in the extreme as players once again pick up the Master Sword, visit the Deku Tree and Jabu-Jabu the giant fish, collect three artifacts at the start of their adventure, and so on.

However, it would be unfair to direct all of these criticisms at *Wind Waker* alone; after all, this episode tried out its fair share of new elements. We meet new tribes, and Link can acquire important objects outside of the usual dungeons; indeed, although the heart of the game remained unchanged, *The Wind Waker* is the one *Zelda* that made the most changes to the original formula that was established by the first episode and refined in *A Link to the Past*. It takes a different path than its predecessors, allowing players to pursue the adventure at their own pace.

CHAPTER IX

THE MINISH CAP

any years ago, the kingdom of Hyrule was invaded by evil spirits. Just when it seemed that all was lost, a mysterious race of tiny creatures known as the Minish descended from the skies and gave a sword and a golden light to one courageous young boy. With these weapons to help him, the boy was able to drive back the demons and restore peace to Hyrule.

With the passage of time, the existence of the Minish came to be considered a mere legend. Nevertheless, the inhabitants of Hyrule continue to organize a ceremony each year to celebrate the little creatures that were said to have saved them from the forces of evil. Princess Zelda asks her childhood friend Link to accompany her to the one-hundredth annual celebration. Legend has it that on this special occasion, a secret doorway will open to allow the Minish to return to the kingdom.

The king has organized a grand tournament for the one-hundredth anniversary of the festival honoring the Minish. The winner will be allowed the rare honor of touching the legendary sword. Easily defeating all of his opponents, a sorcerer by the name of Vaati is declared the winner. Link and Zelda take part in the ceremony, during which Vaati uses his powers to break the Minish sword and open the chest that it had kept sealed, thereby releasing the many monsters inside. When Princess Zelda tries to intervene, Vaati uses his magic to turn her into a statue. To remove this curse, Link has no choice but to find the Minish and ask them to reforge the broken blade.

SMALL, SMALLER, SMALLEST

The Minish Cap puts the power of the Game Boy Advance to good use and has a very polished look. Taking the same approach in its art design as *The Wind Waker* (from the look of the characters to the special effects), this title is the first on a handheld platform to distinguish itself visually from *Link's Awakening* and *A Link to the Past.* As in the episodes for home consoles, and the GBA port of the third *Zelda* game, Link has a voice in this game, but only for a few interjections. The young hero even has a few moves not previously seen in a handheld game, like the roll. Although it borrows a number of recurring elements from earlier *Zelda* games (including many character models drawn from *The Wind Waker*), this episode, developed by Capcom, also makes an effort to innovate. The classic bow, bomb and Roc's Cape are back, of course, but other objects are strikingly new—like the Mole Mitts, for example, which allow Link to dig, the Cane of Pacci that flips objects over, and the Gust Jar that sucks up dust and spider webs.

Without a doubt, the most unique new element in *The Minish Cap* is the character Ezlo. Besides his habit of pestering Link, this cap in the shape of a talking bird allows the hero to change size. With his help, Link can shrink down to the size of a Minish. Although the change in scale caused by this transformation is amusing enough in itself (in this minuscule world, a simple drop of water takes on terrifying proportions), it still doesn't change a thing about the saga's classic gameplay mechanics. Once Link has progressed to a certain point, he acquires a new sword. When infused with the power of the elements, this sword gives him a new ability: to make copies of himself. Little by little, Link's power grows. He can only create a single copy at first, but over time he gains the ability to create two and even three copies of himself. This exciting skill opens the door to some very well-designed new puzzles.

Finally, on the sidelines of the main adventure, the player can also go on a quest for Kinstones. He finds these medallion pieces during his travels, and must compare them with other pieces held by inhabitants of Hyrule. When two pieces fit together, a new marker appears on the map: a cave entrance, a new character or enemy, and so on. A most enjoyable new feature. Besides these fragments, players can also collect Mysterious Shells that can be exchanged for figurines of different characters in the game, much as in *The Wind Waker.*

BIRTH OF A TRILOGY

The Minish Cap appears to be somewhat set apart from the other episodes. Even as it develops a previously unknown background story, the game introduces an all-new enemy: Vaati the sorcerer. This episode is also the first in a trilogy that pits Link against this wicked creature—to be followed by *Four Swords* and *Four Swords Adventures*, which we will discuss in the next chapter. In addition, *The Minish Cap* presents the origins of the *Four Sword* (the basis of the multiplayer mode in *Four Swords*) by explaining how Link helped to reforge the blade in this episode.

As its title indicates, *The Minish Cap* puts its primary focus on the newly introduced Minish people. These tiny creatures—whose ancestors were apparently gods, and who had entrusted the Triforce to one of Link's forefathers—would never really be used again in the franchise. In addition, just to scramble the chronology of the different episodes in the series a little more, we learn in this episode that Link and Zelda already know each other, and are even childhood friends. Nor does Link start out with his familiar appearance from other installments; he only acquires his famous green hat a few minutes into the adventure.

Released in North America in January 2005, *The Minish Cap* was an enjoyable game if not a brilliant one, and it successfully won over the audiences of the time. With this episode, Capcom had put together a genuinely fun and entertaining adventure. Joining new elements (an innovative graphics engine, new items) and familiar ones (classic gameplay mechanics), this was an excellent episode that was nevertheless not especially memorable. Like its immediate predecessors, *The Minish Cap* was a solid application of a well-established formula, but stopped short of expressing any strong personality of its own. Many players also criticized its somewhat limited world, its short play time, and its low level of difficulty. Meanwhile, the idea of shrinking Link down to a tiny size ultimately went no further in the series. There was a clear sense that rather than trying to make fundamental changes to the core structure of the series, the developers were now content to come up with just one unique element for each episode—the boat in *The Wind Waker*, Link's transformation into a wolf in *Twilight Princess*, and so on. Although the series was still serving up delicious fare, many players were starting to feel they had eaten their fill.

CHAPTER X

FOUR SWORDS
FOUR SWORDS ADVENTURES

our *Swords Adventures* follows up on the events of *The Minish Cap*. Vaati, the devious Wind Mage, manages to escape from the jail where Link had imprisoned him with the help of the Four Sword, the extraordinary blade that gave him the power to split himself into four nearly identical copies. To take revenge on his adversary, Vaati kidnaps six young girls—and Zelda as well. Lashing out at Link's childhood friend like this carries a risk, as Vaati soon discovers. He becomes the target of Link's wrath as the young Hylian, bent on saving Hyrule from tyranny, again takes up the Four Sword to face the evil Wind Mage.

CONNECTING THE GAMECUBE AND GAME BOY ADVANCE

To maximize the GameCube's chances of success, Nintendo had been working on ways to connect it to the immensely popular Game Boy Advance since the earliest stages of its design. This idea would eventually be implemented with a cable to connect the two machines, allowing for exciting new multiplatform experiences. Unfortunately, few games of this type managed to spark much interest among players; *Final Fantasy Crystal Chronicles* and *Pac-Man Vs.* are often cited as the best representatives of this new category of games, but *Zelda: Four Swords Adventures* is also a member of this elite club.

The project originated as a bonus mode entitled *Four Swords*, added by Capcom in conjunction with its Game Boy Advance port of *A Link to the Past*. For the first time in the series, more than one player could take part in the adventure, which offered a mix of cooperation and competition among four players. This extra game mode was based on the same art design as *The Wind Waker*, in line with Miyamoto's desire to keep Link's appearance the same across episodes.

The end result was highly polished and very successful—and so well-received among players that it became the basis of the *Four Swords Adventures* project for the GameCube.

Nintendo's original idea was to release multiple *Zelda* installments that would highlight the compatibility between the GameCube and the Game Boy Advance. In the end, the Japanese version of *Four Swords Adventures* would include all three games designed for this project. However, the European and North American versions omitted one of the games, *Navi Trackers*, in which the player has to find members of Tetra's crew who are trapped in a labyrinth. That game was the first in the *Zelda* series in which Tetra's character was fully voiced. Ultimately, the versions sold outside of Japan and Korea kept only two of the games: *Four Swords Adventures* and *Shadow Battle* (a smaller, competitive multiplayer mode in which the different Links fight one another). In Europe, the release of *Four Swords Adventures* was pushed back to January 2005 to avoid any ill-timed competition with *The Minish Cap*. As a result, the title was not available there until the very end of the GameCube's life cycle.

REVISITING AN OLD PRINCIPLE

Due to the multiplayer orientation of *Four Swords Adventures*, certain changes were to be expected in the saga's traditional formula. For the first time, players progress through the game one level at a time. Rather than exploring an open world, they have to get to the end of the current level before moving on to the next one, much like in an arcade game. The adventure has eight different levels, each made up of three sections—enough to ensure a solid amount of play time. Each level also includes one of Tingle's minigames, such as a horse race. Unlike the *Four Swords* mode on the Game Boy Advance, *Four Swords Adventures* can be played by a single player; in this case, the player directly controls all four Links on the screen. Clearly, though, the game is at its most exciting when multiple players jump in, given that its gameplay is designed around equal parts of cooperation and competition. One to four players must work together to solve different puzzles and defeat enemies. When it comes to collecting objects and bonuses, however, it's every Link for himself, and players' scores are displayed at the end of each level to let everyone know who came out on top. This encourages players to master the art of dirty tricks. For example, just after defeating a boss, a chest full of rewards appears—the perfect moment for one player to grab hold of his friend (and rival!) and throw him out of the way to get first crack at the treasure. The treasure includes typical items from the *Zelda* series: the bow, Fire Rod, bombs, etc. However, each player can only hold

one object in addition to their sword; to pick up a new one, they must give up the one they have.

Besides this progression system, which is quite unusual for the series, *Four Swords Adventures* also makes use of a unique control scheme. Except for the host player, who can use a GameCube controller, each of the other players uses a Game Boy Advance connected to the GameCube by a cable. Most of the action takes place on the TV, but if one of the players decides to go into a cave or a house without the others, their view of the game will continue on the screen of their Game Boy Advance to avoid interrupting their partners' progress. This approach turns out to be highly effective; above all, it perfectly captures the in-game dichotomy between cooperation and competition.

HOW THE MIGHTY HAVE FALLEN

With these games, Nintendo continued its tradition of high-quality games in which every detail is perfectly polished. One of the developer's great strengths is the unwavering respect it shows to its customers by holding each of its productions to the same high standard of quality. But Nintendo has also been known to misuse its creations, tarnishing its most iconic characters by recycling them for purposes outside of their original mission. While multiplayer versions of franchises like *Mario* have always existed, they were always based in gameplay that had nothing to do with the original game. For example, our mustachioed plumber friend has been spotted playing tennis and golf or racing go-karts in various individual games, clearly distinct from genuine platformers. Only much later, on the DS, would a "canonical" Mario game (*New Super Mario Bros.*) offer a multiplayer mode. So it was in fact Link in *Four Swords* who would be the first to make the leap. He had become the standard-bearer for a new technology—connectivity between the GameCube and Game Boy Advance— and the tradition of quality associated with the character was being used as a tool to promote a product that had not yet proven itself. Although this approach did produce a high-quality game, it nevertheless also played a role in "desecrating" the saga, or at least bringing it down from its pedestal. Sadly, this was only the first step in the recycling of *Zelda*. In later years, Nintendo would go so far as to transform its iconic character into little more than window dressing for another game with no pretensions to greatness: *Link's Crossbow Training*, to which we will return later.

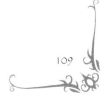

UNCOMFORTABLY FUN

Four Swords Adventures can be a chore to play alone, and its true value as a game becomes clear only when multiple players get in on the action. Admittedly, setting up a four-player game can be awkward, as it requires at least three Game Boy Advance consoles and a connector cable for each of them. But the result is thrilling all the same. *Four Swords* and *Four Swords Adventures* are a real pleasure to play, a journey of laughter and tears that whipsaws from the joy of swiping a friend's rupees to the pain of being cheated by that same friend just moments later. Nothing is certain until the very last second! This battle among brothers achieves moments of true glory in the heat of real gameplay, providing a perfect mix of two approaches that at first seem incompatible: competition and cooperation. Both innovative and extremely well-designed, the *Four Swords* games still shine brightly enough today to convert four intrepid players to the subtle joys of the *Zelda* series. In light of more recent technological developments, however, it is hard to see this use of the Game Boy Advance as a game controller, and especially its use as an additional control screen, as anything more than a first draft of the concept that would come to life six years later as the WiiU in 2011.

CHAPTER XI

TWILIGHT PRINCESS

hen the three goddesses created the world of Hyrule, they left behind the four Spirits of Light to watch over the new kingdom. Today, life here is peaceful, in places like Ordon Village where Link passes quiet days with his childhood friend Ilia. An outstanding rider and cowherd, the young man is respected by the other villagers and adored by the local children. Recently, however, an unexplained surge in the number of monsters has begun to disturb the peace in Faron Woods near the village. A new danger seems to be threatening the village's residents.

As Link is getting ready to travel to Hyrule Castle to present the royal family with the gift of a prestigious sword, he is interrupted by the arrival of a gang of horrible creatures. These monsters belong to the world of Twilight, a sort of parallel universe existing alongside the world of Light that is home to Hyrule, and they kidnap Ilia and the children of Ordon Village. As he rushes to save them, Link finds his way blocked by an apparently impenetrable supernatural barrier. Suddenly, enormous arms burst through the wall and drag Link through to the other side, into the world of the Twilight. Almost immediately, the sign of the Triforce on Link's hand begins to glow, and within moments he has transformed into a wolf. Link learns that he is the chosen one, the only person who can stop Zant, King of Twilight, and his ambitions of invading the world of Light. While the inhabitants of Hyrule appear in a disembodied form under the oppressive power of the Twilight, Link intends to use his new form as a wolf to save the four Spirits of Light, who will then drive the darkness from the kingdom. Along the way, he will be helped by Midna, a mysterious inhabitant of the Twilight Realm who decides to join forces with him. But Midna will not agree to help him without compensation: in exchange for her knowledge, she asks Link to collect a number of Shadow Crystals.

A DREAM COME TRUE

The "grown-up" *Zelda* episode that many fans had been dreaming of since *Ocarina of Time* was announced at E3 in 2004. In his first outing as a spokesman for the company, Reginald "Reggie" Fils-Aimé excitedly announced one last surprise at the end of Nintendo's press conference. A trailer started to play, and within seconds it had swept up the entire audience in a wave of epic excitement. Heart-pounding, breathtaking and highly cinematic in tone, especially in terms of its musical soundtrack, the video showed a grown-up Link in a realistic graphical style, riding on Epona's back to face a horde of dark enemies. While some in attendance were stunned into silence, others began applauding wildly, entranced. And when the trailer's final image faded to that of Nintendo's most famous designer, Shigeru Miyamoto, armed with a sword and shield as the hero of the Triforce, the journalists' excitement turned to rapture. Later communications about the project were more restrained, releasing information no more than a drop at a time. First a few images, and then a subtitle: *Twilight Princess.* It soon turned out that Nintendo also had another, less pleasant surprise for its fans: the game's release would be delayed due to the upcoming launch of the Wii console, the anointed successor to the GameCube. In 2006, an official announcement confirmed that *Twilight Princess* would be released for the GameCube, while also revealing that the Wii version would have its own control scheme for the Wiimote. Interestingly enough, the Wii version of the game is almost identical to the GameCube version, except for one visual detail: the on-screen image is inverted so that Link, who is normally left-handed, can brandish his sword with his right hand—the one that most players would use to hold their Wiimote. Because the Wiimote reacts to the player's movements, it would have been strange and confusing for players to act out a sword stroke with their right hand, then see that action play out on screen as a movement of the hero's left arm.

As more information trickled out about the game, players learned that they would not only be controlling Link in his humanoid form, but that their hero would also transform into a wolf for certain parts of the adventure. What were the reasons for this choice? As usual, the Nintendo team in charge of this *Zelda* project had focused on gameplay first and foremost: Aonuma wanted to shake up the game's routines by giving players a chance to experience the hero's quest from the perspective of a four-legged avatar. Only later did he decide to make that animal a wolf. Aonuma associated wolves with a divine image, and the wolf has an inner strength that, in the designer's mind, was much like Link's own. However, having carried out a few tests with the hero in his quadruped form, Miyamoto quickly realized that playing as a wolf with its back always to

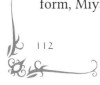

the camera might lose its charm for the player rather quickly. Something was missing... It was then that the designers decided to create a second character who would ride on the wolf's back. The idea was that this humanoid character (who would eventually become Midna) would be a kind of reference point for players, with recognizable facial expressions that would add a more attractive element to the rear view of the running wolf. It is interesting to note that if this game design decision had never been made, players of the new *Zelda* game would have missed out on one of the most fascinating and endearing characters in the entire series.

Twilight Princess ultimately became the launch title for the Wii. This was a bold decision on Nintendo's part. To say the least, the *Zelda* series does not seem to reflect the type of family game that the new console's target audience would be interested in. In terms of their length and their complexity, their detailed gameplay and their polished graphics, the *Zelda* games are a far cry from the sparse, simplified look of the Miis and games like *Wii Sports*, which were also associated with the console's launch. Later developments would confirm that delaying the release of *Twilight Princess* to coincide with that of the Wii was indeed the cornerstone of a new strategy to conquer the market with an effective console launch.

REFINED MECHANICS

Now comfortable in its 3D skin, the new entry in the *Zelda* series continues to refine the basic formula introduced in *Ocarina of Time*. From this point of view, there are no major surprises, as *Twilight Princess* remains extremely faithful to the structure and gameplay of its predecessors.

The main innovation therefore lies in Link's transformation into a wolf at the beginning of the story. The character gains new abilities from his new form: he can dig in the ground, detect smells (which appear on-screen in a visual form for the player), and jump on his enemies to bite them. In general, Link's abilities as a wolf are fairly true to reality; we never see him fighting with a sword in his mouth like in *Kingdom Hearts II* or *Ōkami*. After *Twilight Princess* was introduced at E3, many people pointed out the obvious similarities with Capcom's *Ōkami*—although it is only fair to point out that the gameplay in that game was itself inspired by the *Zelda* series as a whole, and that its atmosphere was reminiscent of the light tone of *The Wind Waker*. In the end, the presence of a canine hero and a few artistic similarities are merely superficial details. We must simply admit that the two games were developed in parallel, and conclude that their similarities reflect a convergence of ideas rather than plagiarism in either direction. Indeed, Ōkami is widely seen as one of the greatest homages ever made to Miyamoto and Aonuma's classic saga.

We mentioned before that Link can count on Midna's help during his time as a wolf. Riding on the animal's back, the young resident of the Twilight Realm can assist him in several ways. When climbing, she helps Link get to hard-to-reach places; in battles, she allows the hero to lock on to multiple enemies at once, then take them out in one continuous chain—which turns out to be the only technique that is effective against the Shadow Beasts.

Twilight Princess also adds another innovation to the usual structure of a Zelda game. In the first part of the adventure, when Link is in wolf form, he must drive the shadows from Hyrule by breaking the Twilight's grip on occupied areas. To do so, he must find and destroy Shadow Insects in order to collect enough Tears of Light to fill the corresponding Vessel of Light. This is the only way to free the good spirits in each area who can drive away the darkness. By introducing a mission that breaks out of the usual village-dungeon-boss cycle, these enjoyable sequences provide a bit of diversity, while also extending the length of the game considerably.

Besides these new features, there are also a few new items in Link's inventory, as expected. These include the Clawshot, the Dominion Rod (which allows Link to bring statues to life and control them), the Ball and Chain, and the Spinner (a floating vehicle shaped like a gear). It's even possible to combine items now: for example, combining the bow with bombs allows Link to fire explosive arrows. All in all, this game certainly has a wider variety of objects than any other in the series, which fits nicely with the length of the quest and the large number of dungeons. Finally, let us note that Link is able to ride Epona right from the beginning of the game this time, and that he can now use his sword from the saddle—lending an appropriately epic dimension to certain sequences in which Link takes on a group of orcs. The range of attacks available to the hero is expanded still further when he learns new techniques from an old knight.

As mentioned earlier, the quest in Twilight Princess clearly evokes the one in Ocarina of Time. As in that game, and A Link to the Past before it, the structure of the adventure is clearly divided into two sequences. In the first one, Link must gather the Shadow Crystals, while in the second, he must collect Mirror Shards. Only in this second part is Link able to change into a wolf whenever he likes, teleport to different places on the map, and freely visit all the different regions in the kingdom of Hyrule—far vaster here than in earlier installments. However, unlike the Link in Ocarina of Time and a number of other Zelda games, the young Hylian we meet in this episode no longer carries a musical instrument—although he can still howl when in wolf form, and use certain herbs found along the roadside to whistle a few tunes.

Twilight Princess is unique in that it was designed for both the GameCube and the Wii. A few slight differences can be observed between the two versions. On the Wii, the gameplay takes the special features of the Wiimote into account. For example, players shake the controller to use the sword—a bit more immersive, but less precise. In addition, players aim the bow and the clawshot by pointing the controller directly at the screen, which turns out to be a much more pleasant system now that aiming is no longer from a first-person perspective, but from a point of view behind Link's shoulder. The Wii's other control accessory, the Nunchuk, is used to manipulate the shield: shaking it makes Link thrust the shield forward to block projectiles. Players have to learn all these skills at the beginning of the game in a relatively long prologue—as befits the length of the quest that awaits them. The GameCube version, on the other hand, allows the player to move the camera around freely with the second analogue stick.

THE AGE OF REASON

Ever since the 2001 video that showed an adult Link battling Ganon, and the disappointment that some fans felt when the visual style of *The Wind Waker* was revealed, many players had been waiting for a return to a more mature and realistic style in later *Zelda* episodes. It was in order to please these fans that the decision-makers at Nintendo chose to produce *Twilight Princess*, whose mission was to transform the saga without denying its past. That goal looked like quite a gamble, or even a pipe dream, but Aonuma nevertheless succeeded in bringing it to life.

How does one go about improving *Zelda's* gameplay? The impressive design of the series' gameplay system had always required top-notch work, with each detail sculpted in careful and minute detail, but with plenty of creativity too. Raising this level of excellence even higher seemed like an impossible challenge, perhaps more of a fantasy than a reasonable goal. And yet, by reworking the proven system of *Ocarina of Time*, *Twilight Princess* managed to transcend the saga's unshakable traditions. The usual village-dungeon sequence is preserved, but broken up by a number of interludes, as well as the exciting sequences in which Link transforms into a wolf. The game also presents a number of scripted sequences that brilliantly highlight certain key moments of the adventure, including Link's unforgettable duel on the bridge with King Bulblin, or the sequence where he escorts a carriage through a horde of bloodthirsty enemies. These moments of valor are presented in a highly cinematic style, and the saga's epic character has never been so effectively emphasized. More than a mere imitation of film techniques, and going beyond the different conventions and connections supposedly shared between video games and cinema, these sequences are at their most exciting when they are entirely interactive. The grandiose Hollywood style on display here, with its thundering soundtrack and dramatic use of slow motion, builds on gameplay mechanics that are rightly considered as setting a standard for future games. At long last, this adventure brings a fresh look to the series—and avoids mechanically recycling a proven formula, as certain earlier episodes had perhaps begun to do. The interludes between the various dungeons no longer feel like mere distractions that serve only to pad out the length of the game. On the contrary, they make a genuine narrative contribution and enrich the overall cohesiveness of the series in important ways, making the world of Hyrule feel like a real place.

As we consider the fruit of two decades of magnificent and inspired creations, one key point we must address is the subject of *Zelda*'s dungeons. In *Twilight Princess*, these essential sequences that have been so typical of the saga are transformed into true monuments of game design, each associated with a full-fledged story of its own. Although they contain the same keys, compasses and maps as ever, the dungeons in this game are unquestionably the most memorable in the entire series for both their size and their content. The maturity achieved here in terms of level design is positively breathtaking. Inventive and original, and each built around its own exquisitely unique aesthetic, these dungeons will enchant players while putting their logical skills to the ultimate test. In each of the dungeons, the actions to be taken are essentially the same: pushing stone blocks, jumping, turning a wheel, and so on. But this apparent simplicity is only an illusion, because the larger problems to be solved could not be more different. Each designed around a single coherent theme, the dungeons draw on the characteristics of a specific element (e.g. ice, fire or wind) or environment (e.g. sky, mountains or ocean) to test the player's memory and sense of space. They are also the longest and most challenging dungeons in the series.

But the satisfaction of overcoming a different test each time is as thrilling as ever—from swinging with the monkeys in the Forest Temple to a floating labyrinth in the City in the Sky. After so many *Zelda* episodes, *Twilight Princess* deserves a lot of credit for accomplishing this *tour de force*.

BETWEEN LIGHT AND SHADOW

Twilight Princess has one of the most fully-developed stories of the entire series. Although its chosen starting point is the simple, classic opposition between light and shadow, the story nevertheless unfolds in a highly interesting way. More serious in its tone and reflective of a greater maturity, the script is more ambitious and more carefully crafted than in earlier episodes. For example, it is not uncommon this time to see a friend suffer, or to see an enemy's cruelty on display. Certain strange and dreamlike scenes evoke the sometimes twisted atmosphere of *Majora's Mask*. This evolution is clearly related to the changes made here in terms of art design, and to this episode's far more realistic tone. But although the story is unusually ambitious for a *Zelda* game, with a number of dramatic twists, we must acknowledge that its basic themes and development are still very much based in a classic structure (e.g. it turns out that the bad guy is being manipulated by an even greater evil). The story in this episode is hardly among the greatest in video game history, although that's obviously not the goal in a *Zelda* game. Still, the effort that went into giving this adventure a richer, more complex and more interesting story is clearly felt throughout the game.

One of the most successfully executed aspects of *Twilight Princess*'s script is the character of Midna. Although we saw earlier that she was originally added to the game in response to a purely technical problem, the designers at Nintendo showed great skill in integrating her character into the storyline. Midna spends plenty of time teasing Link at the start of the adventure, but she gradually comes to terms with our hero and starts to form a closer friendship with him... without ever losing her edge. This character turns out to be not only funny, but extremely talkative. Midna also acts as an "interpreter" for Link, allowing him to communicate with other characters and move the story forward. She even gives him tips when he has trouble making progress. In addition, Midna is the only character in this game who has a voice. Even though the language she uses is incomprehensible and sounds more like high-pitched burbling, this addition helps to establish her personality and increases the player's sympathy towards the character. Zelda's character seems ill-defined or even downright dull in comparison. All in all, Midna is one of the most enjoyable aspects of this episode.

A QUEST FOR REALISM

For the most part, the *Zelda* series had evolved in a fairly straight line through its earliest episodes, but all that changed when Aonuma was chosen to direct the saga. Starting with *Majora's Mask*, the new leading architect of Nintendo's adventure games enthusiastically got to work shaking up the series' well-established traditions. But even with Aonuma in charge, Miyamoto was never too far away, and his presence was still felt throughout the series. Aonuma liked to say that his job was to build the table, and Miyamoto's job was to clean it— or to flip it over, an allusion to Miyamoto's well-known willingness to send

a project back to the drawing board even when its design was well underway. For every episode that went into development, the two master artists found a way to re-examine the foundations of the series, then improve them by adding new elements—which nevertheless had to stay true to *Zelda*'s essence. In short, keeping the player's experience fresh while making sure to respect tradition has always been an absolute imperative. In this light, we can better appreciate the full weight of the decision to change from a more childlike style to a realistic style in *Twilight Princess*. The fact that this episode is set in a darker, more serious landscape can also be interpreted as a step into maturity for the series. As we have seen, that maturity is also reflected in changes to the gameplay and the design of the dungeons. After trying on a realistic style in *Ocarina of Time* and toon shading in *The Wind Waker*, the look of the world and its hero undergo another radical transformation in *Twilight Priness*, marking a sharp break with Miyamoto's plan to standardize the saga's look within the cartoon-like aesthetic introduced not long before. Was this merely a brief aside, or the achievement of true stylistic maturity? In either case, *Twilight Princess* marks a decisive change in the look of the *Zelda* series.

The use of realistic 3D graphics makes the world of *Twilight Princess* feel like a more coherent and believable whole. Characters' faces look more human, as do the proportions of their limbs. The design of interactive objects also reflects this more realistic tendency. Doors no longer open themselves, objects look like they really work, and the vases and other pottery blend in with the rest of the art design. From the textures and the menu system to the dialogue boxes and the design of the world map, every aspect of the game's look has been worked out in meticulous detail. The comedic aspect of the enemies in *The Wind Waker* is gone, replaced by monsters with the scary appearances and attitudes we would expect from "real" orcs or spiders.

This realistic approach extends to the entire world of this new *Zelda* game— including the kingdom's plains and fields, which now show more variety than ever, and the game's more natural and authentic animations. Combat has also been affected by this change. At their core, fights are no more difficult than before, but they are no longer presented in the somewhat childish way we saw in *The Wind Waker*. They are more violent now as well, especially when it comes to Link's finishing moves. The only missed opportunity here is that *Twilight Princess* does not introduce recorded voices for its characters. Nintendo did make the effort to animate characters' lips when they talk, however—but this only serves to further highlight the lack of audio. At a time when all the other big series had taken the plunge, starting with *Final Fantasy*, this detail locks the *Zelda* series into what seems like an unexpectedly conservative approach. The absence of recorded voices feels like a real defect in the game, and can even

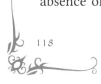

break the player's immersion at times, reminding them all too clearly that the dreamlike world of Hyrule is really just a video game.

A GAME OF EPIC PROPORTIONS

When asked about his inspirations, Eiji Aonuma tends to be very evasive and reserved in his answers, even rejecting the question to insist that he is actually not inspired by any culture or work in particular. This reserved response may be intended to keep fans focused on the true essence of the *Zelda* saga: its gameplay. But this doesn't change the fact that any creative endeavor will reflect the cultural heritage of its creator. *Twilight Princess* is no exception to this rule, and we can find places here and there where it has borrowed from other works and other cultures.

Right from its opening moments, the first trailer for *Twilight Princess* clearly drew inspiration from a source that was very much in vogue in 2004: the *Lord of the Rings* movies. Link is seen galloping towards a group of orcs, then confronts an intimidating boss that looks like a cross between a troll and a Balrog in Peter Jackson's cinematic interpretation of the classic Tolkien novels. Not until much later would Aonuma acknowledge the New Zealand director's influence on *Twilight Princess*—although that influence would have been difficult to deny, given the epic proportions of both the overall setting and certain specific scenes.

The immense size of the game's bosses also recalls the creations of another big name in video games: Fumito Ueda. Of course, the *Zelda* series has always included huge monsters, often several feet taller than Link, but never before had our hero had to actually climb up onto them in order to slay them as he does in *Twilight Princess*. At two different points (underwater and in the desert), Link has to find a way to clamber up on the behemoths he encounters in order to defeat them—a technique first introduced in *Shadow of the Colossus*, published by Sony Japan for the PlayStation 2.

As for the similarities to *Ōkami*, we are dealing more with artistic convergence here than with real influences, just as with the gameplay. Still, the aesthetic parallels between the two games are fairly striking—for instance, the patterns of lines on the Light Spirits' bodies in *Twilight Princess* closely resemble those seen on the gods in the Clover Studio production. This detail, part of the drive for visual purity in this new *Zelda* chapter, once again confirms Miyazaki's influence as a major source of inspiration. To take another example: in the secret lands of Faron, where Link goes to retrieve the Master Sword, he finds knights guarding the entrance to the sacred site. In both their slender and luminous appearance and their attitudes, they clearly evoke the very similar-looking soldiers in Miyazaki's animated film *Castle in the Sky*. There is a certain overall sense of spirituality in the themes of *Twilight Princess*: the strong presence of the animal kingdom (wolf, eagle, boar, etc.) and the anger of gods and spirits recall the frequent use of those same themes by the master of Japanese animation.

Beyond the cultural borrowings from a variety of different ethnic traditions—the costumes worn by the residents of Ordon Village, for example, which were clearly inspired by traditional Mongolian attire—the visual identity of *Twilight Princess* most clearly reflects the aesthetic influence of Mesoamerican and South American cultures, which we had previously glimpsed in *Majora's Mask* and *The Wind Waker*. The most obvious examples are the inhabitants of the Twilight Realm, starting with Midna, Zant and the Shadow Beasts. Midna's mask, in particular, seems to evoke the symbols on the stone tablets discovered in Guatemala at the Kaminaljuyu archeological site. The tablets in question include a sculpture of a character wearing a mask with a snake on it. Although its style is different from that of Midna's mask, this type of headdress still represents an important code (a reference to the creator god in Mayan culture) that the designers of *Twilight Princess* were able to build upon. On the other hand, the characteristic line style used in the game seems to draw more heavily from Inca culture. For example, the motifs on Midna's mask evoke those found on vases from the pre-Incan civilization at Tiahuanaco (with their traditional abstract and decorative geometric patterns) and the Ica and Chincha valleys in Peru. Recent research has begun to examine these signs, associated with certain types of glyphs that were used to decorate Inca fabrics. These include the tocapu, a horizontal band filled with geometric forms—one of which, the square spiral, is again found among the patterns on Midna's mask. Based on the evidence collected thus far, it seems that the tocapu's function cannot be reduced to a merely ornamental one; rather, these geometric forms appear to represent a kind of written code. Nintendo probably didn't go quite this far in its iconographic research, however. As one final possible source of inspiration for the patterns on Midna's mask, let us consider the statues at Tihuanaco, notably the Ponce monolith at the center of the Temple of Kalasasaya, or the monolith known as El Fraile. Its dark color, somewhere between black and brown with an occasional hint of green, is another attribute that evokes Inca culture. Finally, the stone-like textures used to model the masks worn by Midna, Zant and the Shadow Beasts are also reminiscent of the huge blocks at Cuzco and the Sacsayhuamán fortress with their unmistakable look.

While *Twilight Princess* draws a part of its unique character from the cultural and mythological heritage that seems to have inspired it, the game also stands out for its anachronistic representation of the Twilight Realm. While the game as a whole has a highly realistic aesthetic, this *Zelda* chapter depicts its parallel universe with simple, modern geometric shapes in bright fluorescent colors—a far cry from the architecture seen elsewhere in the game. The vortex-like Twilight Portals through which the Shadow Beasts descend from the sky are represented by black pixels and brightly colored energy lines.

From the world of the movies to Amerindian cultures, *Twilight Princess* draws freely from a vast range of influences, making use of ancient and modern art forms alike to establish a sense of massive scale and epic adventure. Of course, this approach makes perfect sense here: since the gameplay in this episode is more expertly polished than ever, and the adventure is longer and the plot more ambitious than any other in the series, the art design had to be monumental as well.

THE BEST IN ITS GENRE

Brilliant craftsmen that they are, Miyamoto and Aonuma applied their meticulous techniques to shape a perfectly formed jewel for Nintendo. Their accomplishment was not a matter of revolutionizing the gameplay mechanics of *Ocarina of Time*, but of transcending them. The adventure is perfectly paced, and each sequence—whether a dungeon, a section where Link takes on his wolf form, or an interlude—flows smoothly into the next. Steering nimbly between the twin dangers of frustration and boredom, the overall result is simply perfect. More impressive still is the fact that the game's precise construction does not falter even once in the forty hours it takes to complete the adventure.

Twilight Princess borrows freely from its predecessors—a tendency that could be annoying to some players. But it does so with such virtuosity and skill that those players will be having too much fun to waste time sulking. The gameplay and dungeon design work together like a well-oiled machine. Within the parameters of its own simple logic, *Twilight Princess* provides an impressive range of possible interactions, and ties it all together in a system of exemplary clarity. In just the time that it takes to get used to the controls and the unfamiliar new Wii controller, players are swept away by the magic of the game—almost by surprise. And so begins the latest fable of our favorite swordsman in green, with all the panache we expect from a *Zelda* game, but this time with a darker and more ambitious story than we're used to. Even today, this adventure which marked the twilight years of the GameCube and the dawn of the Wii era is as enjoyable as ever. Nintendo's famous purple Cube may be over fifteen years old, but its graphics are still high-quality. *Twilight Princess* is a landmark achievement, the answer to a dream that players indulge in with delight and abandon, and an endless source of pleasure. A dense and masterful chapter in which the action reinforces the game's larger themes, and which has remained a fond memory for fans ever since.

Like *The Wind Waker* before it, *Twilight Princess* was also ported to the Wii U in HD. The remastered graphics make a slight but welcome difference for players who didn't have the chance to enjoy the game on the GameCube or the Wii. *Twilight Princess HD* was released on March 4, 2016. Also released on the same day was a bundle including the game, the original soundtrack and a new Wolf Link Amiibo (a Nintendo figurine with a built-in NFC chip). The figurine serves as a key to access a new dungeon called the "Cave of Shadows," and older Amiibos associated with the series can be used as well. The Link and Toon Link figurines allow the user to refill their empty quiver with arrows, while the Zelda and Sheik Amiibos refill the hero's health meter, and the Ganondorf figurine increases the game's difficulty.

CHAPTER XII
PHANTOM HOURGLASS
SPIRIT TRACKS

fter defeating Ganon, Link and Tetra (who was revealed to be the reincarnation of Princess Zelda) can now live their lives in peace. Or can they? Sailing off cheerfully into the unknown on Tetra's pirate ship, the two heroes crisscross the seas in search of adventure, and seeking the "World of the Ocean King."

But before long, the crew crosses paths with a legendary ghost ship, shrouded in mist. There is said to be a fabulous treasure on board. Curious to find out the truth of the matter, Tetra decides to board the abandoned ship. But no sooner has she stepped aboard when lightning splits the sky! A cry rings out: the princess must be in danger! As the ghost ship starts to sail away, Link summons his courage and jumps towards the ship in hopes of boarding it as well—but he only just manages to get a grip on the railing. Unable to hold on, he falls into the water below.

The boy wakes up on the beach on a small island, where he is greeted by a fairy named Ciela. She explains that she had found refuge on the island after losing her memory, and asks Link what brought him there. Once Link has told her his story, Ciela takes him to see Captain Linebeck, a sailor with a reputation as a bold adventurer. That reputation turns out to be little more than a front; Linebeck is a coward whose only interest is in acquiring the legendary treasure said to be carried by the ghost ship. But for him, that's a good enough reason to let Link come aboard. The two set out to search for Tetra.

After a long series of adventures, Link and Tetra ultimately succeed in defeating the evil Bellum and saving the World of the Ocean King. Many years pass.

ONE HUNDRED YEARS LATER

Legend has it that at the beginning of time, when the gods reigned over a world at peace, a demon king named Malladus launched a devastating attack on the world. For centuries, a bitter struggle pitted the gods against the king of demons, and Malladus was ultimately defeated. But the gods had lost their omnipotence as a result of the long battle. With what little strength remained to them, they imprisoned the demon in a deep abyss, and built a tower to keep him trapped inside. His prison was shut tight with divine seals that surrounded the entire planet. One after another, the generations passed in peace. Rising high above the center of the world, the Tower of Spirits protected the four kingdoms that were criss-crossed by these divine tracks, now used as train tracks by the people living there. The most important function of these railway lines was to direct energy from the four sacred temples to the tower in order to keep Malladus sealed away in his prison. One day, however, the seals put in place by the gods mysteriously disappeared. After years of peace, the world was in danger once again.

A servant of the demon king named Cole had hatched a scheme to set his master free. His plan was to destroy the sacred tracks in order to weaken the magical barrier and the Tower of the Gods that were holding Malladus prisoner. All the demon king needed now to assume physical form once more was the body of someone from Hyrule's royal family. Having successfully disguised himself as a human being, Cole had managed to infiltrate the palace. Through subterfuge and perseverance, he eventually climbed to the rank of chancellor, where he was then able to use his position to achieve his goals. It is revealed that Cole was behind the recent events, and finally he attacks the princess directly. He separates Zelda's spirit from her body, intending to present her body to his master Malladus so that he can use it to take physical form. Young Link, a railway engineer in training, is present when Zelda is kidnapped. So begins Link's quest: he must save the princess and restore the sacred tracks to put a stop to Malladus and Cole's evil schemes. Zelda's spirit travels with Link and helps him throughout the adventure.

AN INSEPARABLE PAIR

After a number of games on various versions of the Game Boy, Link's adventures had finally arrived on the Nintendo DS. With a microphone and two screens, one of them a touchscreen, this portable console had several revolutionary features that boded well for the series. By the very nature of the console itself,

this new *Zelda* episode was sure to be something special. It was at the 2006 edition of the Game Developers Conference—when everyone was waiting for news about *Twilight Princess*, still in development at the time—that Nintendo chose to reveal the *Phantom Hourglass* project. Denying the rumors about a possible DS adaptation of *Four Swords*, Nintendo instead presented their official announcement of a new chapter that was a direct sequel to *The Wind Waker*, the seafaring odyssey with its "toon shading" style that had come out for the GameCube. The first *Zelda* game for the DS allowed Nintendo to recycle a wide range of elements that it was eager to use again. The technical possibilities offered by the console breathed new life into those elements, and served as the central axis around which Aonuma designed the entire game. His initial ambition was to allow all of Link's actions to be carried out with the stylus. In this way, *Phantom Hourglass* would help to associate the *Zelda* tradition with the cutting-edge new console, with the goal of attracting an even larger audience. Touch controls, more intuitive "for women and children" (in Aonuma's words), provided an opening for this move when the first *Zelda* game for the DS came out in 2007.

But Miyamoto still thought that the game was too complex. Improving gameplay to appeal to a wider audience was once again the center of a lively debate. Nintendo then decided to develop a sequel to *Phantom Hourglass*, based on the same game engine, in hopes of making the series more accessible to everyone.

In 2009, *Spirit Tracks* was revealed at the Game Developers Conference, as its older brother had been three years earlier. This time, Link would leave behind the ocean waves and return to dry land. Much to everyone's surprise, the little green elf had traded his boat for a locomotive! Although this mode of transportation was a surprising choice, it turned out to be an essential part of Eiji Aonuma's creative vision for the game. Describing the choice of railway travel as the most critical aspect of the game's design, the *Zelda* producer acknowledged having taken an entire year to decide on his gameplay ideas for the travel sequences. The creative teams tackled this thorny question every day, but couldn't come up with an acceptable response. And since the development of the game took only a bit more than a year—*Spirit Tracks* was able to come out quickly because two different teams had been working in parallel on two episodes of the saga, one for the Wii and one for the DS—that meant that Aonuma had only made his decision at the very end of the project, when the rest of the game was already finished! But the game's development had to come to an end at some point, so the team mustered up their courage and presented a train sequence to Miyamoto. Up to that point, no one had dared to show him any of the previous versions. Miyamoto played for a few minutes before announcing that he was satisfied with the result. Aonuma insisted that he test the game a bit more before approving it, but the creator of Link stuck with his decision and confirmed that he was happy with things as they were.

The second essential point for Aonuma in *Spirit Tracks* was Zelda's constant presence at Link's side. Because the princess had been robbed of her bodily form, only her spirit could interact with the hero. Aonuma had therefore placed Zelda in a unique position, comparable to that of Navi the fairy in *Ocarina of Time*. The goal was to give players a chance to get to know this character, one of the most important in the entire series—but paradoxically enough, one that players had scarcely spent any time with so far. In placing the princess in the role of Link's partner, Aonuma hoped that players would form a deeper attachment to a character who was often seen as little more than window dressing. The second reason for Princess Zelda's appearance in this particular form was a much more pragmatic one, tied directly to gameplay. *Spirit Tracks* used Zelda's spirit to introduce a new gameplay system—cooperation between two heroes controlled by the player—which had been sketched out in earlier episodes, but which took on a whole new dimension here. The game ultimately came out in 2009, in the same year when it was presented for the very first time.

BUTTONS VS. STYLUS

Phantom Hourglass follows up on the events of *The Wind Waker*. Not content to merely continue Link's adventures with Tetra, it also reuses the same art design approach as the earlier GameCube episode. The same was true for *Spirit Tracks* as well, proving (along with *The Minish Cap*) that all of the handheld titles in the series would continue to strive for a uniform look. Of course, since the DS could never compete with the GameCube in terms of power, a less spectacular level of production was to be expected. Nevertheless, the 3D effects are charming here, based on a three-quarter perspective sometimes referred to as isometric 3D. The overall effect is a very pleasant one.

The first key step in the *Zelda* saga's arrival on the DS involved adjusting to the console's new features. Entirely touch-based, the control scheme requires extensive use of the stylus. Of course, a few shortcuts are provided (such as a button to open a menu) to let players switch more quickly among functions in the heat of the action with no loss of precision or control. To move, the player simply points the stylus in the desired direction, and Link will head there on his own. Attacking an enemy also requires a tap with the stylus to send our hero into action. It is also possible to attack by "drawing" a line from Link to an

enemy, although this movement leads to a slight loss of precision. In general, the player no longer has to memorize which buttons are associated with which actions; everything works intuitively and transparently, although movement commands and sword attacks can occasionally get confused. In *Phantom Hourglass* and *Spirit Tracks*, the choice of items available for Link's inventory was based on their suitability for a touch-based control scheme. To throw the boomerang, for example, the player must draw the desired trajectory on the screen before releasing it. Due to this constraint, the available items are not especially original, nor are there very many of them. Still, it's worth noting that for the very first time in a *Zelda* game, access to the inventory and switching between items are managed in real time! Players must learn to switch skillfully between in-game actions and menu navigation in order to defeat their enemies.

The DS was a success in the handheld console market because of its originality and many unique abilities. Nintendo's teams took advantage of those abilities to incorporate a series of cleverly-designed puzzles into the game. Players have to use the microphone (by blowing into it, they can blow out a candle), the dual screen (to "stamp" a seal on a map), and the touch screen. Taking notes turns out to be very important when it comes to dealing with the secret mechanisms in the dungeons. Players frequently have to add notes to the map in order to remember combinations, precise paths they have to follow, specific symbols, and so on.

The dungeons are also shorter than usual, less complex in their layout, and only a few levels deep. Nor is there any need to go looking for a map or a compass: everything is already shown on the screen. Only the boss key returns here, but now Link has to actually hold it in order to open the door—and is thus at the mercy of his enemies while his hands are occupied with the key. Each dungeon ends in the usual way, with a fight against the local boss, and many of these confrontations are quite original and well-staged. One of the dungeons in *Phantom Hourglass* was particularly memorable for players. A central element of the plot, the Temple of the Ocean King requires players to return to it several times; each time, an hourglass counts down the time they have left to find the object they are looking for. Getting through these areas depends much more on stealth than usual, since the guards patrolling the temple are invulnerable phantoms. These phantoms also appear on the map, where they are indicated as colored cones. If an enemy manages to catch Link, he will lose precious time. Much like in *Metal Gear Solid*, players have to move through the dungeon without being seen. Each time they finish one of the classic dungeons, players have to come back to the ocean temple to find a map which they can then use to explore new lands. And for every boss they defeat, more sand is added to the hourglass, thereby increasing the time available for exploration. With more time, Link is able to make his way down to ever-deeper levels of the dungeon. Each time he returns, he has to explore the dungeon all over again and repeat the same sequences as before, although acquiring certain items sometimes opens up shortcuts. The idea behind this dungeon looks good on paper; unfortunately, it doesn't work out so well in the actual game. Stressful, repetitive and rather tiresome, Link's repeated visits to this temple quickly become a source of frustration.

The classic alternation between villages and dungeons is once again broken up by voyages on the sea. Unlike the one in *The Wind Waker*, Link's boat has a paddle wheel this time, freeing him from his reliance on the wind. The player sets their course by drawing a path on the touch screen, and can then focus their attention on keeping enemies at a safe distance with the help of the ship's cannon. Players can also acquire new items to make improvements to the boat; for example, adding a salvage arm allows Link to go hunting for undersea treasure in an enjoyable minigame.

TWO HEADS ARE BETTER THAN ONE

Spirit Tracks follows closely in the wake of *Phantom Hourglass*: its stylus-based controls and colorful graphics, along with the overall structure of the adventure, are clearly reminiscent of Link's previous adventure. This new iteration for the DS revisits and improves upon some of the major ideas from *Phantom Hourglass*, including its main dungeon. In contrast to the Temple of the Ocean King, however, the recurring dungeon in *Spirit Tracks* does not impose a time limit—and more importantly, each visit is different from the ones before it. Once they release the energy of the sacred tracks, Link and Zelda must make their way to the Tower of Spirits, where they will discover a new symbol to unlock the next section of the world map. Each symbol is hidden in one of the four levels of the central tower, which Link can get to by climbing a spiral staircase. Much less punishing than its ocean counterpart, this dungeon serves primarily as a way for Nintendo to introduce a new gameplay system based on cooperation. Each floor of the tower is a sort of mini-dungeon containing just a few rooms, where Link is faced with walking suits of armor that seem invincible at first glance. After collecting three Tears of Light, however, our young hero is able to stop the iron giants temporarily with a simple stroke of his sword, and Zelda's disembodied spirit can then take possession of the armor. By drawing a line on the touch screen, the player can then order the princess to carry out certain specific tasks such as fighting, pressing a switch, protecting Link or even carrying him. The image of a frail person's spirit

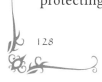

occupying a heavy suit of armor is somewhat reminiscent of Alphonse Elric's situation in the manga series *Fullmetal Alchemist*. Could that be where this *Zelda* episode took its inspiration from? Regardless, this type of cooperative gameplay, already sketched out in *The Wind Waker* with the Command Melody, is a source of refreshing new puzzles that highlight Princess Zelda's tough character, even though her moment of independence has not yet arrived. Still, there is no denying that this was the first episode to put such a strong focus on this funny, mischievous and touching personality. Together, she and Link make an explosive pair.

Nothing better evokes the idea of getting away from it all than the ocean. How could this game hope to give the player a greater sense of freedom than in *Phantom Hourglass*? In fact, the decision to build the game around train travel seemed as questionable as it was surprising: by definition, following fixed rails is incompatible with any real freedom of movement. Fans of the intrepid Hylian hero didn't hesitate to express their doubts and concerns about the prospect of an all-too-linear *Zelda* game. Be that as it may, Nintendo made every effort to make the train trips as interesting and dynamic as possible. It's true that there's not exactly a vast range of available actions once Link climbs inside the locomotive; the options are limited to forward and backward movement, a button to change tracks, and a cord to blow the whistle. But once a few elements have been added to the basic setup, the possibilities expand accordingly. Transporting passengers while respecting the railway code, avoiding sheep sleeping on the tracks, even taking down nearby enemies and stopping explosive locomotives: tasks and side quests like these provide structure to the train trips, and help to turn them into impressive and sometimes highly memorable experiences. While these railway escapades are an enjoyable way to explore the countryside, the all-too-frequent back-and-forth trips and added excursions required by the main storyline end up slowing down what is already a fairly moderately-paced game. Still, the world as a whole is a pleasure to explore. Players may be surprised to catch themselves slowing down to appreciate the warm, soothing colors of the landscape as they work to complete a side quest or two, in an atmosphere that feels more like a laid-back expedition than a legendary quest to save the world.

This chapter has more depth to it than *Phantom Hourglass*, thanks to its larger number of side quests. These optional challenges are intriguingly varied: help a customer with his everyday troubles, catch rabbits for a reward, collect stamps from different stations for Niko—but there are no side missions involving Pieces of Heart.

Finally, these two DS installments are notable for the addition of multiplayer modes. In *Phantom Hourglass*, one player controls Link in a battle against a second player who controls a group of Phantoms from the Temple of the Ocean King. The player in charge of Link has to move Force Gems around while the other player tries to stop them. This game mode can also be played online, although it ultimately feels more like a small added bonus than an attraction in its own right like *Four Swords*. In *Spirit Tracks*, meanwhile, the multiplayer mode is limited to arena battles in which up to four Links try to gather as many power gems as they can. Enjoyable enough, but hardly thrilling, this bonus mode can be played locally by up to four players on the same cartridge, but with no online option—a disappointing omission, given that *Phantom Hourglass* had offered online play two years earlier.

TOWARDS A NEW WORLD

The adventure in *Phantom Hourglass* follows up directly on that of *The Wind Waker*. We therefore encounter a number of familiar characters right away: Link, obviously, but also Tetra, as well as various members of her crew. However, the new quest leaves the flooded lands of Hyrule behind for a new kingdom: the World of the Ocean King. One unfortunate difference is that even though the ocean setting remains at the heart of the adventure, the area available for exploration is much smaller than in *The Wind Waker*. The handful of islands that are scattered across this new kingdom seem downright tiny, and the villages are made up of just a few houses each. The new kingdom is faced with a new threat: Ganon is nowhere to be found, so his role is filled by a substitute bad guy named Bellum (Latin for *war*—the name says it all). Also new in this game is the Anouki tribe, an Inuit-like group that Link finds living not far from the Gorons. Despite the reduced scale of the world, our hero's voyage will lead him to discover a whole series of distinct islands and societies (some apparently inspired by African tribes)—a kind of miniature world tour.

Alongside these new elements, the game also introduces Linebeck, an important supporting character who will accompany Link throughout his voyage. This cowardly, treasure-loving sailor stands out immediately with his colorful personality and consistently bad mood. His presence leads to a number of comedic scenes in which Link, even more expressive here than in other games, takes on an unaccustomed role as the whipping boy. This comic duo guides players through the adventure, bringing a welcome touch of humor to the proceedings.

Spirit Tracks is more than happy to follow in the footsteps of *Phantom Hourglass*. However, since this adventure takes place about a century after the events of the preceding game, we meet a few descendants of the heroes from those earlier days: Link and Zelda, of course, but also Niko, the hero's grandfather and a descendant of a long line of pirates, one of whom had joined Tetra on her adventures. We even run into a young sailor named Linebeck III. A new tribe appears to help Link: the Lokomos, guardians of the ancient spirits, each of whom plays a unique musical instrument.

INNOVATIVE, YET SIMILAR

Phantom Hourglass and *Spirit Tracks* both have the typical features of *Zelda* games designed for handheld consoles. These adventures are less ambitious than the ones produced for home consoles, but they are still serious, well-designed games. These two installments are not particularly bold in creative terms; if anything, the tone feels a bit like "My First Book of Zelda." Nevertheless, they deserve credit for a genuine innovation on the formal side: the touch-based control scheme is deployed perfectly here, seamlessly integrated with a gameplay system in which everything is carefully thought out and adapted to the console's design. Both titles are very interactive, then, in the original sense of the word. From this perspective, Nintendo's efforts at innovation are clear. Looking beyond the control scheme, the games get a few welcome updates to their structure, with puzzles and little details that take advantage of the DS's features: its dual screen, microphone, and so on.

Both of these *Zelda* games have a bit of a "goody two-shoes" vibe: the quest lacks any real dramatic tension, the bad guy doesn't seem all that bad, and there is no strong sense of pressure to move quickly through the game. Everything that we have just seen confirms Nintendo's hope that these two games would make the saga more accessible to the wider audience that had flocked to the DS and made it the top-selling handheld console to date. With their childlike tone, these episodes are accessible to everyone, and of course they are every bit as polished as players had come to expect from the *Zelda* series. Objectively speaking, these two adventures are virtually flawless, although they are missing some of the magic of earlier games. Viewed on their own, each of these games looks like a solid success, but fans who had been buying all the *Zelda* games as they came out could hardly be blamed for feeling a bit bored with these two, considering that both games are based on the same template.

CHAPTER XIII

SKYWARD SWORD

 long time ago, the legend goes, a terrible battle took place. Pouring forth from the bowels of the earth, evil creatures set the world on fire, sowing destruction in their wake. These foul monsters sought to acquire the source of ultimate power, the Triforce, which could make any wish or prayer come true. This power had been left to the goddess Hylia by her divine ancestors. In order to protect the last surviving humans, the goddess sent them and the Triforce into the skies by raising a part of the earth above the sea of clouds and beyond evil's reach. She then put her life in danger to fight and contain that evil. Once again, the world was at peace.

Passed down from generation to generation, the legend gradually changed over time. In this age of happiness, the inhabitants of the floating island of Skyloft no longer have much interest in myths and stories of ancient times. They have forgotten everything about that era—the existence of the earth below the clouds, the ultimate power, the forces of evil—except for the goddess Hylia. An imposing statue in her image towers proudly above the northern end of the village, reminding everyone of the worship that is due to her.

Zelda is the daughter of Gaepora, the leader of Skyloft—and she has been feeling troubled lately. She has been hearing voices, and she's beginning to wonder: could there be another world below the clouds? But this is no time for questions. Today is the day of the Wing Ceremony, a hotly contested race for students about to graduate from the Knight Academy. This year's event is even grander than usual. It is the twenty-fifth anniversary of this ceremony dedicated to the goddess Hylia, and Zelda will play the role of the protector of Skyloft, presenting the winner with a gift of her own making. She hopes that Link, her childhood friend for whom she has grown to have certain feelings, will win the competition. So he'd better not miss his practice run! She sends her Loftwing to bring him a message, suspecting that Link must still be asleep.

And indeed, the young man is dozing in his room. But his sleep is disturbed by strange nightmares, in which he sees an enormous and frightening dark beast beginning to stir. Just then, the noise made by Zelda's bird jolts Link awake. He reads the letter addressed to him: his friend wants to meet with him.

Link goes to see Zelda immediately, and she encourages him to start training more intensely. But his Loftwing has disappeared. These giant birds have a symbiotic relationship with the people of Skyloft. Each of the island's residents has their own animal assigned to them as a kind of alter ego. Link shares a very close bond with his Loftwing, which is especially unique in that it belongs to a race of crimson-colored Loftwings that had long been thought extinct. Link finally finds out that his bird has been captured by Groose and his henchmen, the terrors of the school. Behind his tough-guy exterior, Groose is secretly in love with Zelda, and can't stand seeing her interested in anyone other than him. After getting his Loftwing back and teaching Groose a lesson, Link settles the score with his classmate during the Wing Ceremony. He grabs the Bird Statue before anyone else can get to it, thereby winning the race.

Zelda and Link meet for the ceremony on the palm of the goddess's statue. She gives him the sailcloth that was promised to the winner. At the end of the celebration, Link and Zelda go for a walk, both hoping to make the moment last a little longer. Mounted on their winged steeds, the two lovebirds take flight together. Just as Zelda is getting ready to tell Link how she feels about him, she is suddenly interrupted: a black tornado heads straight for them, and the girl is carried away by the powerful winds. Link, meanwhile, is knocked out instantly.

He regains consciousness a few hours later, after another strange dream about the same monstrous creature that had appeared in his other recent nightmares. This time, however, he also saw a curious young woman with a supernatural but soothing appearance. Recovering from his emotions, Link realizes that while he was unconscious, his bird has brought him back to the Knight Academy. He tells his story to Gaepora, who is sick with worry over his daughter but nevertheless does his best to appear reassuring. Link then returns to his home. Before long, Link's attention is drawn to noises coming from the hall. To his astonishment, he finds the mysterious woman from his dream floating in the air right in front of him, seemingly inviting him to follow her. The young man agrees to her request. The mysterious and ethereal creature then leads him to the Goddess Statue. Inside, Link discovers the divine sword embedded in a stone. The strange young woman introduces herself to him as Fi. Created by the goddess, she lives within the sword he sees before him. She explains that Zelda is still alive, and that Link must go looking for her "below the clouds" in order to fulfill his destiny. She gives him a tablet that can be used to activate the Goddess Statue and break the barrier that Hylia had put in place to prevent anyone from ever crossing through the clouds. Link takes hold of the divine sword and heads out to search for his friend.

A PAINSTAKING CREATIVE PROCESS

The Legend of Zelda: Skyward Sword made its first appearance at E3 in June 2010. However, an early piece of artwork had already been revealed the year before, showing Link alongside a mysterious female character who would later turn out to be Fi. And for good reason! This time, the designers knew exactly where they wanted to go next with the series: *Skyward Sword* was intended as a prequel to *Ocarina of Time*, and would tell the story of how the Master Sword, our hero's faithful blade, was first created.

While still under the supervision of Eiji Aonuma, this new episode was entrusted to new director Hidemaro Fujibayashi, who had already worked as an associate director on *Phantom Hourglass*. The freshly promoted designer has since acknowledged feeling a certain amount of pressure. Since this was his first game for a home console, he didn't hesitate to ask for plenty of advice from the guardians of the temple, the venerable Miyamoto and Tezuka.

Despite their help, the creation of *Skyward Sword* turned out to be a truly laborious process. Development on the game dragged on for five full years, two of which were entirely dedicated to experimentation. The point that raised the most questions was the integration of "motion gaming." The first *Zelda* episode to appear on the Wii was *Twilight Princess*, which was a simple port of an existing GameCube adventure. As we have seen, that game made only modest use of the Wiimote's unique capabilities. Since that time, Nintendo had improved its controller's performance with the help of an optional add-on peripheral. Called the Wii Motion Plus (WMP), this new accessory found a perfect showcase in *Wii Sports Resort*, released in July 2009 to show off the new device's abilities.

THE POWER OF MOTION GAMING

The *Zelda* franchise represents the pinnacle of Nintendo's achievements in creating the ideal gaming experience. A series with such high ambitions cannot afford half-measures. In that sense, it was obvious that gameplay in the new episode would have to incorporate the use of the Wii Motion Plus. The team's first challenge was to learn how to use the device. Everyone took their turn at playing *Wii Sports Resort* to explore the new possibilities opened up by the

accessory... as well as its limits, which became obvious in short order. In this simple demo game, every challenge is based in a single type of gameplay—sword fighting, archery, throwing a Frisbee, and so on. But in a *Zelda* game, the player must be able to combine all of these actions! A second obstacle had to do with the fact that *Wii Sports Resort* uses highly simplified 'Mii' avatars to represent the player. But those simple, low-detail shapes are vastly simpler to manage than a more realistic-looking Link would be. To spare his team an exhausting ordeal, Aonuma decided to abandon the idea of integrating the Wii Motion Plus into the new *Zelda* game. And so they went back to the drawing board for the classic combination of Wiimote and Nunchuk, as in *Twilight Princess*. But at Nintendo, things are never really that simple. Aonuma faced daily taunts from his colleagues, who pressured him to explain why he had abandoned the WMP. Unsurprisingly, one of those colleagues was the producer of *Wii Sports Resort*, Katsuya Eguchi—working as a kind of secret agent for Miyamoto, who was little inclined to see Aonuma give up the fight. Ultimately, the *Zelda* producer gave in to the pressure. The team went back to square one, throwing all their existing work on the scrap heap.

MIYAMOTO'S BRIGHT IDEA

Unlike the characters in *Wii Sports Resort*, Link would have to hold his sword with confidence and class. The legendary hero certainly couldn't be allowed to look like a mere Sunday morning swordsman! And so the creators of *Skyward Sword* spent countless hours studying the detailed anatomy of the human shoulder joint. Of course, their initial idea was to represent their hero's movements in a realistic way. Given that Link is a humanoid character with normal human proportions, that seemed like the most logical approach. But even after many hours of work, the result fell short of expectations. The team would have to cheat a bit, bending Link's shape slightly beyond the usual norms to make certain details and positions work more effectively. One night while the team was enjoying a rare chance to get a good night's sleep, a few of its members were surprised to receive a call from Shigeru Miyamoto himself. The master designer had come up with a new insight: If Link's movements were going to be realistic, then the character should certainly be able to interrupt an action at any time of the player's choosing. In other words, the sword stroke should not be carried out until the player completes the corresponding action. So they would have to be able to stop Link's actions at will! Miyamoto then followed up on his own idea with another one that he had been working on for a while: when the player lifted the sword over their head, Link would charge up energy before releasing a deadly blast towards his enemies, in much the same way as he did in the first episode on the NES when his health meter was full. It was at that exact moment that the team first had the idea for the subtitle *Skyward Sword*.

INTERFACE AND WII MOTION PLUS

The decision to incorporate the WMP had two immediate repercussions. First, the combat system would no longer focus on timing as in most other games in the series, but on the precision of Link's attacks and their execution. Second, the A button, which had normally been reserved for sword attacks, was now freed up for another use. The team took advantage of this to add a new action: sprinting. When Link is running, pressing A makes him run faster for a short time. This was also an opportunity to add new, more dynamic movements: for example, if Link runs towards a wall when sprinting, he can run along it vertically for a few feet. In this way, Link keeps moving as he explores and never has to stop, unlike in earlier episodes where the character would come to a screeching halt if he ran into a tree at top speed. In much the same way, adding the WMP also influenced the development of the user interface. For instance, a new system allows Link to quickly select objects from his inventory with no need to interrupt the action by opening a traditional menu. Players have Fujibayashi to thank for this very helpful addition to the game. Link's inventory items are presented in a circular menu, as in *Twilight Princess*; once a player has learned the location of each item, they can select the one they want with a quick, reflexive action. An early version of this system required players to turn their wrist (as if turning a dial) to select the desired object, but this approach was imprecise and was limited to just one hundred and twenty degrees of rotation. It was quickly replaced by a simple tilt of the Wiimote. Players no longer even need to look at the screen, since the pointer is not used here as it is when shooting with the bow. The WMP does all the work. Similarly, Link consumes health potions in real time, even while he's running! The cutscenes that showed him stopping to drink are gone.

For once, the story in this episode was written in advance, and explains the saga's origins and the creation of the Master Sword. It is interesting to see how this story is paired in the finished game with a new kind of gameplay that also focuses on the sword.

CONCRETE APPLICATIONS

The addition of the WMP also affects how weapons are managed in the game. The only truly new weapon is the remote-controlled Beetle. Although it was originally intended to be a simple boomerang, the movement options that the designers had in mind for it went beyond what a boomerang could do. The weapon therefore became a kind of "rocket fist"; older readers may have nostalgic memories of a similar weapon from the *Tranzor Z* cartoon series. In this case, it functions as a remote-controlled hand, with the ability to grab and bring back objects when thrown. In the end, the designers decided to make it look like a beetle. But they were then faced with a problem: wouldn't players use this new item to explore ahead in a level, and discover things that they weren't yet supposed to have access to? Another concern was that the item's mechanical aspect didn't seem to fit with the world usually presented in the *Zelda* series. Rather than redesigning the weapon, the development team added new elements to the plot in order to justify the Beetle's existence. This became the inspiration for the ancient civilization with its advanced technology. Once again, it was the gameplay and the player's needs that would shape this episode's plot and backstory. This may not be the most "romantic" way to write a video game script, but it certainly led to a more enjoyable game overall.

Certain other items in Link's inventory went through some twists and turns in their development as well. One of these was the Gust Bellows, which had already appeared in *The Minish Cap*. In addition to blowing out a gust of air, it was originally supposed to suck up items too. There was even a plan to give the Gust Bellows a kind of "mouth" that would allow the player to adjust the rate of airflow. The problem was that since Link is always seen from the back, the "vacuum bellows" was hidden by his body; the resulting effect looked rather bizarre on screen, and didn't clearly show how the item worked. The idea was ultimately dropped, leaving the bellows with only the blowing ability. As for the whip, which had first been introduced in *Spirit Tracks*, the team had designed it without really knowing whether it would be kept in the final version of the game. But when they showed the game to Iwata right before the E3 conference in June 2010, he adored the new weapon, and the team decided to keep it and refine its control scheme. Finally, let us point out that both the Gust Bellows and the whip, along with the Mole Mitts, are more closely associated with handheld *Zelda* titles than with episodes for home consoles. This might have been due to director Fujibayashi's earlier experience with installments for Nintendo's portable consoles.

THE STRUCTURE OF THE GAME

With its new combat system designed entirely around "motion gaming" (to which we will return later on), *Skyward Sword* seemed destined to bring change to the series. But the designers didn't stop there: they even decided to reshape the very structure of the game. As any *Zelda* fan can tell you, the cycle from village to dungeon to boss is a constant feature of the series. When Link leaves a village, he soon comes to a dungeon entrance, marking his passage from an area made for exploration (or even just hanging out) to a much more action-oriented section filled with puzzles. The creators of *Skyward Sword* had the idea to remove the boundary between these two components, or at least to blur the lines a bit. Puzzles would no longer be confined to dungeons, but scattered across the entire world map. Taking the opposite tack from *Twilight Princess* (with its large world to explore and equally huge dungeons), the temples here are more compact; now that they no longer have a monopoly on puzzle sequences, the dungeons don't have to be as big.

THE STRUCTURE OF THE WORLD

The team's desire to make the game's world more compact was no empty promise. It became a guiding principle, a mantra that Miyamoto emphasized to Aonuma again and again: "If the game is too spread out, the adventure becomes a bore and ends up going on too long." This choice runs counter to the wishes of most Western designers (and gamers) nowadays, who tend to favor vast open worlds where there is always something new to discover—as in *Skyrim*, the fifth episode of the *Elder Scrolls* saga, which came out at the same time as *Skyward Sword* in November 2011 and was an enormous success. For this episode of *Zelda*, the designers decided to limit the world to three regions (woods, volcano and desert), and to have the player go through each of them several times. This certainly seems like a small number, especially considering that all of these regions were designed to be quite compact, but they also turn out to be very dense and rich. Each time a player returns to a region they have already visited, new surprises and unexpected changes help to make the experience feel fresh again. The layout of the woods changes, and the volcano section uses a different kind of gameplay with each new visit; the desert undergoes its own transformations, and is home to three clearly distinct regions (as we will discuss in the section on gameplay mechanics).

At a certain point in the adventure, Link has to search for Sacred Tears in a special zone called the Silent Realm, cut off from the rest of the world. Here, the designers clearly took their inspiration from the segments in *Phantom Hourglass* and *Spirit Tracks* in which players had to make their way through a dungeon filled with invincible phantoms, with no choice but to run away from enemies or outsmart them. Inspired by the children's game of tag, these sections in *Skyward Sword* block the hero from using his weapons. Originally intended to take place in the dungeons, these sequences instead unfold in places that players have already explored and become familiar with—the idea being to give them an advantage over their enemies.

THE CASTLE IN THE SKY

Including these three dense and highly distinct zones led to a new difficulty: how to connect them to one another? By adding a vast field to tie the three regions together? The producer had no interest in such a solution. Once again, he favored a simpler approach and a more compact world. Instead of connecting them, which Aonuma thought would be too complicated, the team would have to come up with a "Plan B." He and Fujibayashi thought back to their time playing *Mario Bros.* and its level selection screen: a flat, static map with direct access to the levels in question. But it would be difficult to make that approach work in the same form in a *Zelda* game. Instead, they imagined a starting point high up in the sky; Link could jump down from there and land in any of the different zones! That way, no roads or connections would be needed. Bingo! Their first idea along these lines involved climbing a gigantic tower. Link would then leap down from the top of it. But then Fujibayashi had another idea, inspired by his love of skydiving: a world floating in the sky!

It was at this point that Daiki Iwamoto, the director of *Spirit Tracks*, joined the *Skyward Sword* development team after finishing his own game. Fujibayashi soon promoted him to the role of "gang leader" for the sky section—that is, the person tasked with designing and setting up this floating level. At the time, the idea was still to have an island floating in the sky from which the player would jump down through holes in the clouds to reach different regions of the world below. It then occurred to Iwamoto that what Link needed was a means of transportation—and that a bird would be the perfect way to connect earth and sky, bringing our hero through those holes in the clouds from his floating island high above. Jumping directly from the island would have given the impression that the three zones on the ground were relatively close together. The bird seemed like a good compromise, providing a way to move quickly from one sector to another while maintaining the idea of a cohesive world. To add a bit more variety, Iwamoto later added a number of smaller islands in the sky.

And that's how the world of Skyloft was born. Fujibayashi describes how he developed this new world: "I worked on Skyloft's design. When I create a house, I start by asking whether it's made of wood, bricks or some other material. [Skyloft] is a piece of the earth that's floating in the sky, so it would be strange to see a lot of trees growing there—the wind is strong, so they wouldn't be able to grow very tall. That would make trees a precious resource for the inhabitants, so they wouldn't use a lot of wood as a construction material. The designers and I imagined some different things, and we finally decided: 'The houses should be made of dirt!'" From there, the world continued to evolve and more details were filled in (the Wing Ceremony, the dormitory, etc.), but early tests were not very encouraging. Since Skyloft is where the adventure starts, the events that take place there have to grab the player's attention immediately. Since Iwamoto was busy, Aonuma himself had to roll up his sleeves and personally take care of making this location more exciting! Once again, Miyamoto's presence made itself felt in Aonuma's work—after all, he had always insisted that the beginning of a game had to be especially well-executed!

POPULATING THE WORLD

Of course, this world would need equally well-designed characters to live in it. It was particularly important that the game's antagonist, Ghirahim, should hit all the right notes. The designers imagined him as a sort of anti-Ganon. Whereas the *Zelda* saga's most iconic bad guy had always been very brutal and masculine, the team wanted to try out the opposite approach this time. Above all, they didn't want to make him into a Ganon clone, as if to camouflage the absence of Link's longtime adversary. The character designers chose to start from a diamond shape as the basis for Ghirahim's appearance, arguing that "a character symbolized by a shape would make a stronger impression." The diamond shape was therefore a key element not only in his costume, but in the special effects associated with his attacks. Finally, one of the designers wanted Ghirahim's tongue to "wriggle like a snake's"—and in the end, it was integrated directly into his skeletal structure!

As for Zelda, the idea was to bind her more closely to Link. In this game, her own adventures were planned out in advance for a change. As a result, we can easily keep track of Zelda's path as it evolves in parallel with Link's adventure. And finally, the appearance of the robots from the ancient civilization was inspired by Japanese clay figurines and terra cotta pottery from the Jōmon period; the idea was to make them look "soft," rather than metallic and hard as one would normally expect from a machine. New tribes were also created to populate the game's various regions.

In the end, the design team succeeded in establishing a unique atmosphere and providing a solid characterization of the different inhabitants of the new *Zelda* game's world, thereby earning Miyamoto's all-important endorsement. But not without one final piece of advice: he thought that the game contained "too much text!"

A PAINTERLY EFFORT

Let us now turn to what was surely the most hotly debated aspect of the game from its initial announcement up to its release: its graphical style. In the beginning, the designers had attempted an entirely new approach: applying a watercolor effect to the backgrounds and characters. Unfortunately, the enemies blended in with the environment instead of standing out from it. This even inhibited players' progression through the game, since it was difficult to see where they had to go. The team then decided to apply a cel-shading treatment, similar to the one used in *The Wind Waker*, for the characters and certain elements of the game to make them stand out. They then had to carry out some final checks, fine-tune the colors and brightness, and change the pastel colors in the backgrounds, the lighting, and so on.

A GREAT ZELDA GAME?

After a complicated five-year development process, Nintendo finally released a *Zelda* game that Aonuma described as both "simple and rich." The number of people involved in the creation of this episode was much larger than any other project at the company, which speaks to the unique status of this *Zelda* episode. Ten employees were assigned to the sound component alone (including the actual composition and the creation of sound effects). The adventure eventually included more than two hours of cutscenes, and Nintendo declared itself very satisfied with the result. Aonuma even went so far as to predict that it would be very difficult for future episodes to return to a traditional button-based control scheme (i.e. one not based on motion controls). Overall, critics were ecstatic, as usual for a *Zelda* game. But the game was not universally well-received among players. Released in November 2011, *Skyward Sword* saw its sales figures climb to 3.4 million copies by the end of that year. The marketing campaign even brought in actor Robin Williams and his daughter Zelda—who was named after the series, a favorite of her father's.

THE SOURCE OF THE MYTH

As a prequel to the entire series, *Skyward Sword* is presented as the very first chapter of the Legend of Zelda in chronological order. As we will see in Chapter XVI, untangling the knots in this timeline turns out to be fairly complicated, but *Skyward Sword's* intentions are very clear. Obviously, players shouldn't expect an entirely surprising story that would shake the very foundations of the saga's founding myth. In any case, this episode presents its story in a highly effective way.

The game's first defining aspect is of course the Link-Zelda-Ganon triad and the relationships that guide it. A creature called Demise has attacked the world in order to seize the source of ultimate power. It's not completely clear from the game's introduction that the item in question is the Triforce, but that is never really in doubt. The goddess Hylia (who has evidently given her name to Zelda's world once again) was able to weaken her opponent enough to lock him away in the Sealed Grounds. Trapped in a monstrous form known as the Imprisoned, Demise might have stayed a prisoner forever. But having suffered a number of wounds during the battle, the goddess was forced to abandon her divine form and transfer her soul into a human body. Knowing that this would weaken the seal and that the Imprisoned would resurface again one day, but that she could do nothing about it now that she was mortal, Hylia created the divine sword and gave it a soul, Fi, whose destiny was to guide the Chosen One—the only one who would be able to destroy Evil once and for all.

We learn that Zelda is none other than the reincarnation of the goddess Hylia, and that Link, her knight, is the bearer of the Triforce. Aware of Zelda's divine ancestry, Ghirahim captures the young woman and travels back into the past. By sacrificing the princess, he intends to awaken Demise—for Ghirahim, like Fi, is the spirit of his master's sword. His sole mission is to bring his master back to the world of the living, even if it means his own destruction.

When Demise awakens, he is surprised to find himself facing a human opponent; he had considered that species weak, since none of its members had dared to oppose him in his previous incarnation. Nevertheless, he is defeated by young Link. Before dying, he intones a curse: "My hatred... The curse of the Demon Tribe... It is born anew in a cycle with no end! [...] Do not forget it! History will repeat itself. Those like you... Those who share the blood of the goddess and the spirit of the hero... They are eternally bound to this curse. An incarnation of my hatred shall ever follow your kind, dooming them to wander a blood-soaked sea of darkness for all time!" Here we have a clear prediction of a future incarnation of this evil. The birth of Ganon in the Gerudo tribe provides this hatred with a new vessel, a bearer of hate that will never stop pursuing its enemies, the heirs of Link and Zelda, who will have to rise up again in every generation to continue the fight against Ganon. It is here that the triad's never-ending battle first begins. This clarifies an idea that we have already encountered: while Ganon remains the same in every *Zelda* episode, Link and the princess are new, contemporary incarnations of the two heroes in *Skyward Sword* and the heirs to their eternal struggle. We do not learn any new information from this moment in the game, other than the demonic origin of the evil later reincarnated as Ganon, and the idea of a curse as the starting point of the story. Although Nintendo avoided taking any risks in this regard—the sequence of events remains more or less the same as in previous games—the way in which the story unfolds still feels like a success.

But *Skyward Sword* doesn't stop there. The most important part of its mythology lies in the story of how the Master Sword, the iconic sword referred to here as the Goddess Sword, was first created. Originally, it was a divine sword created by the goddess Hylia to defend against Evil's eventual return. To guide the Chosen One who would be able to wield it, she even gave the blade a spirit: Fi. Once the sword is in Link's possession, it must go through two additional steps before becoming the Master Sword. It must be purified by three sacred flames, then blessed directly by the goddess herself—when Link returns to the past and finds Zelda. Once Demise has been destroyed, the sword absorbs what remains of its spirit, and serves as a seal that keeps evil imprisoned. Link's mission comes to an end, and with it, Fi's as well. She then asks her master to place the sword back in its stone, where she enters a long slumber. The sword will now await the next incarnation of the hero of legend. Although the Master Sword's creation myth is nothing exceptional in itself, it gave fans a chance to see previous Zelda episodes from a different perspective, and to better understand what this weapon truly represents. Finally, on a more anecdotal level, we also learn in Skyward Sword that the Sheikah tribe (of which Impa is the only known representative) was entrusted by the goddess herself with watching over the legendary sword and preventing the forces of evil from returning, while also ensuring that the reincarnation of the goddess remained safe.

A UNIQUE VISUAL STYLE

Skyward Sword first caught the public's attention with its highly distinctive visual style. While the art direction in recent *Zelda* games had oscillated between realism (*Twilight Princess*) and toon shading (*The Wind Waker*), everyone could see that this episode had chosen a compromise between the two. The human

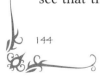

characters have realistic proportions, but the images have a distinctly cartoon-like style. Although there is no denying that the close-ups on the heroes are staggeringly beautiful, the environments seem to have suffered in the new approach. Nintendo took its inspiration straight from Impressionism here, and even from Pointillism in certain places. The first of these artistic movements, which arose in the second half of the 19th century, is characterized in part by a softening of the opposition between foreground and background. It was led by artists like Monet, Cézanne, Pissaro and Manet. Pointillism, on the other hand, was a direct descendant of that early trend, and is sometimes referred to as Neo-Impressionism. It is defined by its method of juxtaposing small dots of color in primary and complementary colors.

Zelda thus joins the ranks of video game works inspired by the visual arts, alongside the woodcuts in *Ōkami* and the India ink in *Vib-Ribbon*, among others. Nintendo would continue on this path with *New Super Mario Bros.* U, which included a level heavily inspired by Van Gogh's painting *The Starry Night.* Where *Twilight Princess* emphasized visual sophistication (an abundance of details and decorations on characters' costumes, for example), *Skyward Sword* chose to return to a much simpler, cleaner style, but without going as far as the semi-abstract forms of *The Wind Waker.* In principle, this was an interesting and promising choice, but it was ultimately disappointing in practice.

In 2011, when a large part of the gaming population already had high-definition televisions, the graphics in this *Zelda* episode were rendered poorly on the new screens. Despite the high quality of the 3D character models, the game has its share of jagged edges caused by aliasing, and the impressionistic style of the backgrounds looks more like a visual artifact of poorly compressed video. Unfortunately, then, the end result does not do justice to the development team's efforts.

Despite a somewhat shaky result, this style helps to establish an enchanting atmosphere. The characters have expressive faces, although their lack of voices is as regrettable as ever—especially in the scene where Link gestures wildly, a stunned look on his face, in a ridiculous attempt to explain to Gaepora what happened to Zelda. Even so, the relationship between Zelda and her childhood friend is represented brilliantly. The young woman's appearance in this episode is a particular high point: she has never looked more radiant. The genuinely touching story of newfound love between the two youngsters is presented without much ambiguity this time; the designers seem to have mustered up their courage for this aspect, although the game as a whole is very dark. Director Hidemaro Fujibayashi was especially insistent that Zelda should play more than a purely cosmetic role in this episode. That was why she and Link were now presented as childhood friends, but it also explains the constant references to her presence throughout the adventure: different people that Link meets mention that they just saw her go by, or that she's right behind a nearby door, and so on. Fujibayashi wanted to player to have a real motivation to go and save the young woman, rather than using her character as a mere plot device. All in all, a particularly successful take on the princess.

Unfortunately, the same cannot be said of Fi. This character acts as a guide, and serves as the interface between the player and the designers, between Link and the world around him, much like Navi in *Ocarina of Time*. Sadly, the spirit of the Master Sword never really manages to move us, and turns out to be more annoying than truly useful in the long run. Her advice, repeated *ad nauseam*, along with her cold and rational personality, make her a somewhat tiresome ally. To be sure, this was exactly the personality that the designers wanted her to have. But given that there is no way to make her an enjoyable character, we can simply add her name to the long list of annoying sidekicks that are forced on the player, inevitably spoiling the fun a bit—an old tradition in the world of video games.

MOTION CONTROLS WITH MIXED RESULTS

As we explained at the start of this chapter, *Skyward Sword* uses the Wii Motion Plus to faithfully reproduce the player's arm movements in the game. In line with the "new way to play" that Nintendo had pitched for its new console, the idea was to strengthen the sense of immersion by "acting out" what Link would do in real life. The hero would then reproduce the player's actions exactly—a feat that *Twilight Princess* had only been able to achieve in a very limited form five years earlier. It was an admirable goal.

The guiding principle of the Wii, beyond the desire to open the wonderful world of video games to a wider audience who were put off by complex controllers with a huge number of buttons, was increased immersion: "I'm not just pretending to be an orchestra conductor, I *am* one." With an on-screen avatar that reproduced the player's own gestures "exactly," the sense of identification would be strengthened. Although the approach in *Twilight Princess* was a rudimentary one (a simple shake of the Wiimote would make Link swing his sword), the effect was convincing and the player felt physically involved. This sense of increased immersion was seen by most critics and players as giving the Wii version of the game a distinct advantage over the GameCube version. With the Wii Motion Plus, the developers at Nintendo wanted to go even further, removing any last remaining barriers to provide—at long last!—the "Wii experience" that had originally been promised to players.

In practice, however, the results were mixed. From a technical point of view, the overall approach certainly works fairly well, aside from a few occasional hiccups. Certain battles even reach exciting new heights, most notably the superb fight against Demise in which the player must raise their sword to the sky to bring down a bolt of lightning upon their enemy. Every stroke of the sword is made from whatever angle and direction the player chooses. In fact, all of the gameplay in this episode is built around this concept. If a man-eating plant opens its jaws horizontally, then a movement along that same axis can be used to slice it in two. If a spider web blocks Link's path, he can cut it at certain strategic points to clear the way. The same principle applies to the hero's other tools and accessories: players aim with the bow by moving the Wiimote, control the Beetle by tilting the controller in various directions, and put up their shield with a shake of the Nunchuk.

It's simple: in *Twilight Princess*, a rough approximation of each movement was enough to make the character perform a more complete version of that action on-screen. The system worked. Nintendo's approach came down to asking, "How can we make sword fights more immersive by bringing them closer to reality?" and looking to the controller for answers. In *Skyward Sword*, the thought process seems to have gone the other way around: "We've got the Wii Motion Plus, now how can we build a game around it?" In any case, the realism of Link's sword attacks, which faithfully reproduce the player's movements, is a far cry from his enemies' fighting style. As they approach Link, the enemies go into a fixed pose. They don't try to attack, but instead adopt one defensive pose, then another and yet another, before finally launching their attack. Each time they drop their guard, a single specific opening appears, allowing Link to attack from a single specific angle. And then there's the three-headed sand worm; although its multiple heads are in constant motion, it seems to be going out of its way to line them up as often as possible so that Link can attack. This kind of unnatural and implausible enemy behavior sticks out like a sore thumb, as if our opponents in each battle were taking us by the hand to explain the best way to attack them. And even so, it's not always easy to execute the desired movement on the first try. Could the Wii Motion Plus simply be too sensitive? Some might argue—and perhaps correctly—that in real life, any of us would need a few tries in order to throw a bomb into a small hole thirty feet away, for example. From that perspective, there's nothing unusual with failing a few times, since everyone knows that it takes several attempts to get it right. Be that as it may, the end result is the same: Frustration! Paradoxically, players no longer feel that they "are" Link, battling enemies to save Zelda. Instead, *Skyward Sword* constantly reminds them that they're playing a game with a Wii Motion Plus, and the sense of immersion is reduced. In addition, the pairing of the Wiimote with the Nunchuk means that there is no second analogue stick, and therefore no fine control of the camera—not to mention that players have to stop regularly to recalibrate the WMP. Taken together, these minor annoyances start to put a certain strain on players' enjoyment of the game itself. When players struggle to throw a bomb by tilting the controller and shaking it, knowing that earlier games had allowed them to do the same thing more easily and intuitively—oh, the irony!—by simply pressing a button, it seems safe to say that there's a problem with the game.

As interesting as motion-controlled gaming may seem, a clever and amusing approach when used occasionally for certain functions, the idea of building the entire game around it may not have been so wise. Not to mention that the player has to stay constantly on their toes in front of the screen and have enough free space around them, and that they can't even sit down on the couch without limiting their mobility. While motion gaming did work admirably for certain "simple" games like *Wii Sports Resort*, was it really a good idea to use it as the basis of a *Zelda* game that requires the player to engage in over forty hours of physical activity? Wouldn't the *Twilight Princess* approach have made more sense? After all, that was Aonuma's original preference... *Skyward Sword* and *Red Steel 2* are the only games that really offered the "full Wii experience" with 1:1 motion controls (in which movements are reproduced immediately and in their entirety) as Nintendo had promised when the console first came out. In hindsight, doesn't this seem to imply that the concept itself was a failure? After all these years of motion gaming, including Microsoft and Sony's contributions to the field, no game has really revolutionized the way we play games and convinced us to throw our traditional controllers away once and for all. Isn't it fair to conclude that motion control was a technological dead end, doomed from the beginning?

A NEW KIND OF STRUCTURE

The control scheme was not the only aspect of this new episode in which Aonuma and his team wanted to make changes. In fact, the whole structure of the adventure was in for some fundamental changes as well. At its core, the sacrosanct cycle from village to dungeon to boss has been preserved, except that Skyloft is the only town where Link will meet other people and find shops. Outside of this floating island, the world "below the clouds" is comprised of three independent regions, as we have seen: Faron Woods, Eldin Volcano, and Lanayru Desert. Each is inhabited by a native species never encountered before in the *Zelda* series: the Kikwis, the Mogmas and the Ancient Robots. It's always fun to meet new people! Unfortunately, the absence of a "playing field" to connect these different territories leads to an unpleasant lack of cohesion in the game's world. Although the designers did their best to explain this decision, the result is still regrettable. The team chose to compensate for the small number of environments by making them "evolve" over time. Players are required to pass through each of these zones at least three times, giving them the chance to experience those changes: the forest is flooded, the desert changes into an ocean, and so on. But even that isn't enough to eliminate a certain sense of monotony and claustrophobia. On the other hand, the blurring of the line between dungeons (where battles and puzzles are found) and the different environments (dedicated more to contemplation and exploration) is much more effective. For example, it is not uncommon for Link to have to solve several puzzles before he can even enter the local dungeon. In addition, the dungeons are no longer the only place where Link can acquire new items. But even here, it's too bad that the designers didn't go a bit further with their ideas.

Finally, the repetitive nature of certain sequences undermines the fun of the game. A good example of this is when Link has to locate a specific character he's looking for. Fi gives his sword a kind of "radar" function. By switching to a first-person perspective (a new option in this installment), the player sees an indicator that tells Link what direction to search in, and a beep tells him how far away his target is. While the first sequences of this type are exciting because of their novelty, they lose their interest quickly through constant repetition. Flying on a Loftwing's back soon turns disappointing as well, due to the small area available to explore (the area around Skyloft) and the limited number of related activities.

AN RPG DIMENSION

Frequently criticized for its resistance to change, the *Zelda* series manages to make some progress in *Skyward Sword* with regard to how the character and his equipment are managed. Although the naysayers would see these changes as baby steps, the fact remains that in a series as rigidly committed to specific codes as the *Zelda* saga, even the slightest advancement is worth celebrating. *Skyward Sword* adds a slight touch of RPG: Link's inventory now includes a pouch in which he can carry a certain number of items (potions, shield, etc.). As the pouch is upgraded, it can carry more and more items throughout the game. Link has to decide which items he needs, and leave the rest at the Item Check in Skyloft. Another boutique allows the hero to upgrade items or have them repaired. In this episode, certain items can actually wear out over time through use in battle. The shield, in particular, has to be repaired regularly, or Link runs the risk of losing it in the middle of a fight. He can also choose to reinforce it, as long as he has the necessary raw materials. In general, any piece of the hero's equipment can have its properties improved; this applies to potions as well, which are more abundant this time and have a variety of effects including health and stamina boosts, repair and protection. Note also that, even though the adventure is not especially difficult, Link takes it on with six hearts in his health meter, rather than the usual three. This new RPG component may be insignificant compared to the leading names in the genre. Still, it adds an enjoyable element to the game, and one that most players wouldn't necessarily have expected.

A CONTENTIOUS GAME

No other *Zelda* game had ever seemed so redundant. The items and accessories are the same as usual. There's no real difference in the player's progression through the game. Link returns to the same environments over and over. Even *Majora's Mask* with its four dungeons offered more variety. These shortcomings are surely attributable to the length of the development process, and to the trial and error of its early years, which clearly didn't do anything to improve the game. There is far too much back-and-forth trekking for no apparent purpose, other than to artificially extend the length of this episode. And throughout the first section of the game, there is nothing to counter this feeling of déjà vu. Fortunately, the second part starts out by raising the bar significantly. This more extensive section is built around a number of quests embedded one inside the other. At this point, players' enthusiasm surges to new heights. But they'll soon come back down to earth as they realize that the trip through time they were promised is not actually going to happen. Just when it seemed like the adventure was about to take off, it turns out to still be idling on the runway.

Of course, this may seem like a very harsh review of an episode that was actually trying to innovate for once. Unfortunately, the fact is that not all of the few new features introduced in this episode are especially interesting. Even worse, they ironically end up emphasizing the larger lack of innovation overall. Despite all that, this installment has the qualities of a solid *Zelda* game: the dungeons are inventive (especially the last one), the progression system is well-designed (although this is hardly shocking after twenty-five years with the same set of items), and the adventure has its share of powerful, touching and heroic moments. Finally, although the WMP is of questionable value for combat sequences, it allows for a number of very well-designed puzzles, especially the one in which Link has to distract an enemy by "catching its eye" (so to speak). The world is also enriched by the addition of new tribes with a pleasant look and enough personality to ensure a few smiles. And yet, in this *Zelda* episode, the story never really takes off. Although it is supposed to explain the origins of the saga, it unfolds too similarly to other games in the series. Perhaps the main reason why this repetitive structure drew few complaints in the past is that the gameplay was always brilliant enough to make up for the script's shortcomings. But as soon as that gameplay loses some of its shine, as it does here due to the use of motion controls, the illusion is broken, revealing mechanics that have been used a few too many times. *Skyward Sword's* biggest success was in reconnecting with its hero's humanity: Link no longer seems like an empty shell, and we finally get to see him fall in love. The hero and the series have matured, which is a good thing—but still the least that we'd expect after twenty-five years of *Zelda*! Besides that, the handful of innovations and the introduction of a "New Game+" mode were minor improvements at best.

Much like *Twilight Princess*, this episode feels like it's caught in the middle: the earlier game was merely a port of a GameCube project that arrived too early to deliver on all the promises that had been made for the Wii, while *Skyward Sword* came out too late, after the motion gaming fad had already passed, and at a time when the console's technical shortcomings compared to its rivals were becoming too big to ignore. In the end, the Wii never got the benefit of a real *Zelda* game at the right time.

CHAPTER XIV
A LINK BETWEEN WORLDS

legacy from the gods, the Triforce is the guardian of prosperity in the kingdom of Hyrule. According to legend, it has the power to grant the wishes of anyone who touches it. But not everyone has noble motives. Some corrupted souls sought to use it for their own wicked ends, plunging the kingdom into endless war. Troubled by these perpetual conflicts, the royal family called for a meeting of the Seven Sages. Together, they developed a plan to hide the Triforce in a sacred land. But alas, a thief with a dark reputation, the infamous Ganondorf, managed to discover the Triforce's resting place, and to seize it for himself. Now known as Ganon, the Lord of Evil, he turned his new powers against the kingdom of Hyrule. It was during this dark period that the hero awakened, guided by the princess. Taking up the purifying blade, the sword of legend, he was able to trap Ganon in a place that was then sealed with the magic of the Seven Sages. After the hero's victory, the Triforce broke into three fragments before falling into a deep slumber. The first of those fragments remained with Ganon, the second with the royal family, and the third became a part of the hero's very soul. Even today, the people of Hyrule continue to pass this legend down from generation to generation. But the legends have faded over the years. These tales are still well-known, albeit in an altered form, but they are now considered to be nothing more than fairy tales. And yet...

It's a sunny morning like any other. Young Link is rudely awakened by his friend Gulley, the blacksmith's son, who urges him to go and see his father at the forge as quickly as possible. Once again, Link has gotten lost in his dreams, and forgotten to wake up and head to the workshop where he is finishing his training as a blacksmith. Just as his teacher is getting ready to lecture him yet again, he notices that his most recent customer, the captain of the guard, has forgotten his sword at the workshop. Before receiving the punishment he deserves, Link will have to take the sword back to the captain. The young apprentice tracks the confused customer to the Sanctuary, but suddenly a scream rings out, breaking the silence in this place of contemplation—the voice of Sister Seres! A magician named Yuga has just used his unique powers to transform her into a painting! Summoning up his courage, young Link tries to confront the mysterious figure—but in vain. Yuga dodges his attack by melting into the wall like a painting, then escapes.

Since last night, strange murals have appeared on the walls around Hyrule Castle, almost like a curious echo of the magician's power. That mysterious Yuga is probably up to something... Before long, Princess Zelda will be the one in danger.

THREE LONE MEN

In late 2009, a large part of the *Spirit Tracks* team joined the development effort for *Skyward Sword*. Under the guidance of Eiji Aonuma, meanwhile, Hiromasa Shikata (director), Shiro Mouri (assistant director and lead programmer), and another programmer started considering the options for a new episode on the successor to the Nintendo DS: the 3DS. The three of them worked together on the project for an entire year. They tested and experimented while their colleagues were focused on *Skyward Sword*. The project was still only vaguely defined, and the three men's efforts were still somewhat scattered. For the first six months, their ideas were all over the place: the trio had plenty of concepts, but none of them were truly convincing. To force themselves to make progress, they decided to present a more concrete project to Shigeru Miyamoto. There was no plan at the time to create a sequel to *A Link to the Past*; rather, their idea was to build the game around the idea of "communication." But Miyamoto shut them down, displeased with what he called a "twenty-year-old concept"! Being rejected by the father of the *Zelda* series was a crushing blow to the designers tasked with creating the new installment. Naturally, they felt compelled to rethink all of their plans to that point from the ground up. At some point during this period of reflection, Shikata blurted out in a meeting: "What if Link could just merge into walls?" The director instantly regretted his outburst, and had no confidence in his own idea. But Mouri thought the idea was "brilliant," and the programmer even called it "fantastic." Still, Shikata squirmed and hesitated... Mouri jumped in and exclaimed, "I'll build a prototype!" What would have normally taken a full week of work was finished in a single day, thanks to the assistant director's boundless energy. The next morning, he presented his prototype. Shikata was immediately convinced. Seeing Link switch from 3D to 2D in the blink of an eye, blending into the background, negotiating different angles and going to

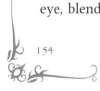

places he never could have reached before suddenly gave the three creators any number of new ideas: new puzzles, new game mechanics, and more. Link's new life as a painting had opened a whole new range of gameplay possibilities. But what really made the trio happy was getting Miyamoto's approval after he tried out the prototype.

Despite this validation from Miyamoto, development on the game was suspended in late 2010 so that the small 3DS team could help their colleagues with the launch titles for Nintendo's new home console, the Wii U. When the trio broke up, Shikata started to lose hope; after all, he was well aware that once a project is interrupted, it rarely starts up again. Hoping to break the curse, the 3DS project team gave Miyamoto, Tezuka and Aonuma a 3DS with a sticker bearing the code name of the new *Zelda* game—to make sure that they wouldn't forget about it.

A NEW TRIO

Shikata's little gift had the desired effect: while his small team tackled the Wii U titles, Aonuma decided to continue work on the suspended 3DS project. He felt that it was important to get the project underway, and to move it along quickly to ensure a 2013 release date. Aonuma formed a new group, temporarily assigning Tominaga to Shikata's role and asking a programmer to continue refining Mouri's prototype in which Link could merge into the walls. This new team developed a few dungeons, then presented them to Miyamoto. Proud of his team's work, Tominaga bragged to the "big boss" that he could create another fifty dungeons if he liked the first batch. But as one might expect, Miyamoto was none too happy with that suggestion. But he did more than simply criticize—he pointed them in a new direction. Like so many times before, a simple request or suggestion from the great Miyamoto was enough to turn the original plan completely upside-down. His suggestion this time was to emulate the style of one of the saga's key turning points: *A Link to the Past* for the Super Nintendo. At the time, Aonuma was giving a lot of thought to the future of the *Zelda* series (the big question was whether to produce a remake of *Majora's Mask* or to create an all-new episode). Following Miyamoto's advice, he decided to combine the idea of Link as a living mural with the style of *A Link to the Past*.

Miyamoto had previously asked Aonuma to direct a *Zelda* game for the 3DS—similar to *A Link to the Past*, but in stereoscopic 3D. Aonuma listened to his boss's advice, but for him, the idea of doing a 3D remake of a 2D game didn't hold much interest. The prototype that showcased Shikata's idea of "Link the painting" was brilliant, but the three-quarter perspective (like in *Phantom Hourglass* and *Spirit Tracks*) didn't fit with the concept. With an overhead perspective, on the other hand, the effect was striking. And since Miyamoto had asked Aonuma to convert a 2D title to 3D, making the 3DS game a sequel to *A Link to the Past* fulfilled all the terms of the contract. Rather than starting over from scratch with the world, Aonuma decided to reuse the terrain from the Super Nintendo hit. But the producer still worried that the public would see this game as a simple remake. His own teams were rather skeptical as well, which only added to his concern. Aonuma then used an in-house production tool to prepare a 3D rendition of *A Link to the Past* in just under a week, with the specific goal of convincing his colleagues... and his plan worked! Even Miyamoto gave the idea his seal of approval.

Once *Skyward Sword* was released, the production of the new 3DS episode could continue with help from all of its teams. They went to work on designing the dungeons, building on the central idea of wall paintings. But the overhead perspective was not quite ready yet. Due to the camera's position above Link's head, it was hard to see the hero properly when he moved in certain directions; in particular, when he moved towards the bottom of the screen, only his pointed hat was visible. The team would have to simulate the desired perspective rather than copying it exactly. They achieved the illusion by tilting every element of the game towards the back, including Link. The resulting perspective was much clearer and easier to understand. It may not have been realistic, but the effect was perfect. It was also critical to ensure that the game could run at a steady sixty frames per second, in order to maximize the stability of the stereoscopic 3D view. That stability also made it possible to use the stylus to select items, a technique that required a high frame rate.

BEYOND ALL CONVENTIONS

For its creators, one of the main goals of this new *Zelda* game was to offer players a renewed sense of freedom. A kind of freedom that had truly never been seen in the series. A freedom that would shake up the firmly established traditions that every *Zelda* game had followed over the years. With this perspective in mind, the team decided that players would be allowed to explore the dungeons in any order they liked, and that items would not necessarily be acquired in the usual way; instead, Link could buy or rent them directly from shops. Shikata, the director of this episode, had been working on the saga for fifteen years. And for fifteen years, he had been hearing his friends complain with every new episode that they had gotten stuck at this or that point in the

adventure—an incredibly frustrating experience for the creator. The problem is that in a *Zelda* game, if you can't make progress in a given dungeon, you have no choice but to keep thinking about how to get out; there's simply no other solution. Providing players with new options was therefore a guiding principle for the 3DS title. The players can choose to visit any of the seven dungeons in the second half of the game at any time. No longer were they forced to go through the dungeons in a predetermined order. Obviously, this was a major shift in the saga's traditional formula, and created a few problems as well; nevertheless, it was precisely these constraints that would force the designers to rethink the classic structure and bring change to the series.

The new episode was officially announced on April 17, 2013, in a Nintendo Direct presentation. Viewers learned that the game would be called *Triforce of the Gods 2* in Japan—indicating its direct line of descent from *A Link to the Past*, which was called *Triforce of the Gods* in that country. The creators even considered naming this episode *The New Legend of Zelda*, a bit like the *New Super Mario* games. Outside of Japan, on the other hand, the game would be called *A Link Between Worlds*, in reference to the parallel world that exists alongside Hyrule: Lorule, the new game's cleverly-named counterpart to the Dark World of *A Link to the Past*.

THE BEST OF BOTH WORLDS

A Link Between Worlds brings out the skill, the philosophy and the charm of both the 2D Zelda episodes from the NES – Super NES era and the 3D episodes for the DS that followed in *The Wind Waker's* footsteps (though not those associated with *Ocarina of Time*). The result was a *tour de force* that combined nostalgic charm with a sense of wonder and renewal. Of course, the big pixels we remember from Link's days of pink hair are not seen here, but other elements do return to remind us of old times. For example, *A Link Between Worlds* reuses the map from the third *Zelda* game, along with its top-down perspective. In fact, the entire structure of the Super NES game returns here as well, offering players another two-part adventure: the quest for the legendary sword, and exploration of the parallel world. As a result, this 3DS episode struggles to step out of its predecessor's long shadow. For players looking for something new, this was all the more frustrating given that the two *Zelda* games before this one were only ported versions: *Ocarina of Time* for the 3DS, and *The Wind Waker* for the Wii U. And yet...

A SCRIBBLE ON THE WALL

The big surprise in this episode, and indeed its most striking aspect, is its gameplay. The core mechanic in *A Link Between Worlds*, the one that distinguishes it so clearly from its predecessors, is Link's ability to merge into a flat surface in the form of an animated painting. In controlling their character in an environment reduced to two dimensions, players are forced to see space in a totally different way. Link can merge into any wall that has a flat vertical surface, allowing him to discover items that are hidden by the usual perspective and to cross chasms or grab on to moving blocks. By using the walls around him like this, Link can cleverly make his way around all sorts of traps that he would otherwise never be able to pass—but the player still has to remember to make use of this new option. Even when we know that any wall can be explored in this way, both in dungeons and in the outside world, it's easy to walk past this or that secret simply because we're not used to testing the limits of the wall-painting mechanic whenever the opportunity arises. But once this skill has been mastered, exploration takes on an unexpected new sense of depth, especially once the player discovers that Link can enter cracks in the walls to switch over to another world. This new functionality alone offers a vast range of possibilities in terms of puzzles and exploration.

THE LAUNCH TITLE

As showcases for new technology, messengers for a whole console generation, and representatives of a specific audience segment, the video games released in support of Nintendo's new consoles have always played an important role throughout the company's history. Nintendo has consistently released its own launch titles to support each console's new features: In 1986, there was *Duck Hunt* for the NES and its laser pistol; in 1990, *F-Zero* for the Super Nintendo and its mind-blowing Mode 7; in 1996, *Mario 64* for the N64, with its full 3D world; and in 2001, the GameCube and... its revolutionary new controller! The Wii and Wii U were no exception. The launch titles for these last two consoles were aimed at the manufacturer's new target audience: families. The Wii was accompanied in 2006 by two popular games, *Wii Sports* and *Wii Play*, while in 2012, *New Super Mario Bros. U* and *Nintendo Land* were released with the Wii U. The same pattern holds for the portable consoles. The franchises chosen as launch titles therefore implicitly reflect the audiences that Nintendo is targeting.

Nintendo's newest portable console, the 2DS, went on sale worldwide in October 2013—except in Japan, where it didn't come out until February of 2016!

Logic would dictate that the 2DS should focus on 2D games… but that was not the case. And if logic doesn't help us in this situation, that's because this console represents a unique situation in which the manufacturer had to *downgrade* to a new console! Having removed 3D functionality from its previous model, Nintendo obviously wasn't going to try to highlight this technological step backwards as a selling point. In fact, the reason for this about-face was that Nintendo was targeting younger audiences again. Recall that the 3DS is not recommended for children under seven years old. From the physical architecture of the 2DS to its outward appearance, everything fits: Nintendo was once again aiming to sell consoles to kids. But what games would they play? "Christmas games," of course: *Pokémon X/Y* and *The Legend of Zelda: A Link Between Worlds*. While these series are very popular among older players, today's children are not as familiar with them. Although they were still hit franchises, it was important that Nintendo continue to draw in new generations of players with games like *Zelda*—hence its policy of continuing to refresh and renew its flagship series.

RENT-A-BOMB

Once again, Nintendo's approach is impressively efficient. *A Link Between Worlds* is a high-quality game, but longtime fans will be a bit shocked by the greater accessibility of this episode. For the first time in the series, it offers an item rental system, making the entire arsenal available to players from the very beginning of the game. As a result, the adventure is more open and less restrictive than its illustrious ancestors. It's entirely up to the player to decide which levels they want to complete in which order. *A Link Between Worlds* occupies a delicate position: boldly winning over a new audience as the launch title for a console with reduced capabilities (the 2DS), while also supporting the deleted feature on its predecessor (the 3DS)! And yet the title accomplishes all of this admirably: the adventure is just as enjoyable in two dimensions as in three. In addition, it is interesting to consider this episode's place in the series as a whole. Before the game came out, observers were calling it a sequel, a remake and an homage to the third *Zelda* game. In fact, the game is all of these things at once. But who can blame Nintendo? To win over the hearts of a new generation, why not reuse a proven formula that had already made millions of kids into fans? Rather than a "link between worlds," perhaps the new game was first and foremost a bridge between two generations.

Nintendo's choice of launch titles has always provided insight into the company's strategy, but this was the first time that this same strategy had guided

the development of its two most popular series: *Zelda* and *Pokémon*. We have talked about the 2DS as a mere variation on the 3DS, and we have even treated it like a joke. But we were wrong. Underneath its childish appearance and its colorful plastic curves, the 2DS was Nintendo's opportunity to introduce young players to two series that were already beloved by vast numbers of old-timers. This approach was probably for the best.

ALMOST FAMOUS

The basic template is the same as for other *Zelda* games, but the addition of just one new gameplay mechanic (Link as a painting) was enough to turn players' all-too-firmly rooted habits on their heads. The world of the third *Zelda* game provides an instant shot of nostalgia, like an old familiar tune. Not to mention the game's many "Easter eggs" that refer back to various older episodes. All of that is pleasant enough; and yet the game leaves us with an unpleasant aftertaste. If only a new world map or a few original items had been added to the mix, this episode might have marked a turning point in the series as important as *Ocarina of Time*, given its success in reinventing the classic dungeon formula. Like its predecessors, *A Link Between Worlds* stands out for the quality of the level design in its puzzle-filled underground labyrinths. The way that players gain access to them, as well as their guardians, are again reminiscent of *A Link to the Past*, but their architecture is completely different. The overall structure of the game, while less strongly linear than in the past, remains within the saga's usual parameters. In the end, *A Link Between Worlds* could have forged its own legend, but instead remains in the shadow of the game that inspired it.

CHAPTER XV

SPIN-OFFS

aving completed our long examination of the canonical entries in the Zelda saga, we will now turn to the other games in which Link and his friends have appeared. From remakes to forgettable spin-offs, from the Super Nintendo to the CD-i, the following is a brief review of the many faces of the elf in the green tunic.

BS: Link in orbit

BS Zelda is the name that Nintendo came up with for this remake of the first *Zelda* game, available for download only—back in 1995! How was this possible at a time when the general-purpose Internet was still taking its first baby steps? In fact, the game made use of an extension to the Super Famicom known as the Satellaview, a system that used satellite television to save data on a BS-X cartridge. Available only in Japan, the service was completely free, although the extension itself cost 14,000 yen, or about 110 US dollars. Shipped with a BS-X cartridge and a memory card, the Satellaview gave owners of the Super Famicom access to a game downloading service, as well as codes and information (in the form of audio and video reports). Almost ten years before the advent of Xbox LIVE or the PlayStation Network, the Japanese manufacturer was already offering a first look at what digital content would one day become. In practice, all Satellaview data was transmitted through a satellite channel owned by the St.GIGA company, then saved on the player's BS-X cartridge. Subscribers could also tune in to a specific TV channel to watch programs designed especially for players.

The first game to make use of this revolutionary service was none other than *BS Zelda*.

An adaptation of the original game with updates to its graphics and sound, *BS Zelda* took advantage of the Super Famicom's increased power. Split into four weekly episodes that were saved on the BS-X cartridge, players were required to play this game in a specific time slot: from 6 p.m. to 7 p.m.! At any other time, *BS Zelda* was simply inaccessible. The map of Hyrule had been slightly changed for this version, and the dungeons were completely redesigned. Another key point was that players were no longer playing as Link, but as the BS system's mascot (with the choice of a male or female avatar). But the most striking aspect of the Satellaview version was its use of the system's internal clock. An on-screen clock always showed the current time, allowing players to participate in a series of events that took place at specific moments. At the appointed times, special new elements would appear in the game. For a limited time, the player would be asked to go on a simple quest (such as going to find a fairy at a specific place), or undertake a mission to increase the maximum number of arrows that the hero could carry. Other events were simpler, like the sudden disappearance of certain monsters. Several different versions of *BS Zelda* were broadcast, each with its own graphical style—one of them even resembled the third episode, *A Link to the Past*—or changes to the world map.

Replaying the first *Legend of Zelda* game is always a joy. While Japanese players were able to enjoy this ingenious event-based system, the new graphical style and the redesigned dungeons, American and European players with no access to Satellaview services were left out in the cold. This unique system continued to operate until June 30, 2000.

GAME & WATCH: LINK ON THE GO

Just a few electronic beeps and chirps are enough to bring the memories flooding back. To anyone who ever owned a Game & Watch, these tiny handheld games from Nintendo are sure to recall many a wonderful moment playing in the schoolyard. And let's not forget that games in this format, invented by Gunpei Yokoi, got Nintendo back on its feet financially after a difficult period. It was in the summer of 1989 that Link's adventures appeared on the Multi Screen line of Game & Watch units. In fact, the *Zelda*-branded Game & Watch was the very last Multi Screen model to ever be released. Nintendo had made every effort to adapt the series' philosophy to this small handheld format. The results were quite remarkable, given the technical limitations; richer than the other Game & Watch offerings, this game was in many ways the high point of the collection. Battles and exploration are translated to the handheld format with great skill. In essence, Link has to find his way through the twists and turns of a dungeon after every battle he fights. Players had to rely on their sense of exploration to find the local map, health potions, and the hammer they needed to defeat the boss (which was a dragon, by the way, and not Ganon) as they explored eight different dungeons, each of which contained a piece of the Triforce that Link had to find. Along the same lines, miniature Game & Watch units (in the form of watches or tiny keychains) were released a few years later, presenting their own versions of the intrepid young Hylian's adventures.

NES CLASSICS: REMEMBERING THE HITS OF THE PAST

In 2004, Nintendo launched its NES Classics line, in which the NES era's greatest hits were ported to its handheld console at the time, the Game Boy Advance. The first two *Zelda* games were part of this collection, along with other timeless classics like *Castlevania* and *Metroid*.

ZELDA VS. ZELDA

In 1989, Nintendo and Sony entered into a partnership aimed at developing a CD-ROM extension to the Super Nintendo as part of the so-called "Play Station" project. Nintendo later decided to break off the agreement and work with Philips, Sony's direct competitor. However, given the lack of consumer interest in the Sega CD accessory that Sega had developed for its Genesis console at about the same time, Nintendo ultimately decided to abandon the idea of a similar accessory for its own home console. Sony continued its own work on a console based on a CD drive; needless to say, this project would eventually evolve into the original PlayStation. Despite the end of its partnership with Nintendo, Philips retained the contractual right to produce four games based on Nintendo licenses for its own new machine, the CD-I (Compact Disc Interactive). And that's how Philips came to produce a *Mario* game (*Hotel Mario*) and three adventures inspired by the *Zelda* franchise (*Zelda: The Wand of Gamelon, Link: The Faces of Evil* and *Zelda's Adventure*). The Wand of Gamelon was the first to be released, in 1993. Developed by Animation Magic, this dreadful episode is utterly forgettable, as are the two chapters that followed it. Nintendo has made sure to point out that these three titles have nothing to do with the saga's main timeline—suggesting that the Japanese developer is somewhat put out by their very existence. In *The Wand of Gamelon*, the player controls Princess Zelda for the very first time. Playable sequences in a side-scrolling perspective are punctuated by short

animated scenes of dubious quality, as the princess rushes to save Link from Ganon's evil clutches.

A second adventure, *Link: The Faces of Evil,* was released at the same time. This time, Link takes center stage, but the story and gameplay are still no better than in *The Wand of Gamelon.*

Two years passed before Philips put out its final *Zelda* game. Once again, the princess is running the show, and once again she has to save Link. This title leaves the side view behind, opting instead for the classic overhead perspective. Even so, the game itself is in no way comparable to Nintendo's in-house productions.

As an interesting side note: Philips chose to emphasize its machine's audiovisual capabilities by using live actors for the main characters in the cutscenes for *Zelda's Adventure.* The result is... disconcerting. Finally, unlike the previous *Zelda* games for the CD-i, *Zelda's Adventure* used edited digital photographs for its environments. Jason Bakutis, a former Hollywood special effects expert who was in charge of the backgrounds for this episode, explains at the Nintendo Player website that the settings in *Zelda's Adventure* were constructed like little stages. First, the creatures were sculpted from clay, then cast in plaster. He then created the final versions from latex and synthetic foam. In the mold, Bakutis had set up a simple framework made of aluminum wire that allowed him to animate the monsters however he needed to for a given situation. The paint, the cloth and fur costumes, and even the teeth—everything was made by hand.

TINGLE

The *Zelda* series' most famous cartographer got his own game for the Nintendo DS, released in 2006 for the Japanese market and a year later in Europe. *Freshly-Picked: Tingle's Rosy Rupeeland* was the brilliant title given to this adventure, starring Hyrule's most miserly, flamboyant and ridiculous imp. Always eager to make a few rupees, Tingle learns one day of a place called Rupeeland. He immediately packs his bags for this magical destination whose name alone sounds like his idea of paradise. But the road is long and full of obstacles. The player controls Tingle throughout his journey, helping him to collect as many rupees as possible. As eccentric as its hero, this adventure game does not measure up to the series that spawned it, but it still stands out for its quirky and good-natured atmosphere. A sequel was released in Japan the following year.

Tingle's Balloon Fight was designed for the DS as well, but was only available to Club Nintendo Platinum members in Japan. In this remake of *Balloon Fight,*

a 1986 game for the NES and Game & Watch, Tingle takes center stage; the graphics have also been updated, and the game has been optimized for use with the handheld console's two screens. The concept is simple: Tingle and his enemies are hanging from balloons in midair. By tapping on the A button, the player has to control Tingle's balloon so that he can maneuver over his opponents and pop their balloons to make them fall. The experience is simple, refreshing and addictive, and can be played by up to four players at once with a single cartridge.

A little game known as *Dekisugi Tingle Pack* was also available on the Japanese DSi Shop; it contained different tools like a timer and a calculator, plus a variety of wacky minigames.

LINK'S CROSSBOW TRAINING: LINK AS SALESMAN

After *Four Swords Adventures*, Link would once again find himself sacrificed on the altar of shameless promotion. To help sell consumers on the Wii Zapper, a new accessory for the Wii, Nintendo chose to associate the saga's illustrious image with the item. The Wii Zapper is a plastic shell in the shape of a pistol grip that serves as a receptacle for the Wiimote and the Nunchuk, supposedly to provide a more immersive experience.

Nintendo had the clever idea to bundle the accessory with a new *Zelda* spinoff called *Link's Crossbow Training*. This little shooting game takes place in the world of *Zelda: Twilight Princess*, with Link in the starring role. It consists of nine challenges, each broken down into three parts. Most of the time, the player simply shoots at targets, some stationary and some moving, but on a few rare occasions Link can move around freely. The gameplay system, based on collecting points by shooting targets, is enjoyable but hardly thrilling, despite the added prestige of the Zelda brand name. This was the second time that the publisher had tarnished the saga's "sacred" aura with this type of purely commercial application. The *Zelda* license is used solely to lure in fans of the series and help to sell the new accessory, with Link providing his "celebrity endorsement" to a game that will occupy players for a few hours at most.

A PROPER DUEL

Thanks to his charismatic personality and extraordinary physical prowess, Link has also appeared in a number of fighting games. For starters, our illustrious hero made a high-profile appearance as one of the fighters in *Super*

Smash Bros., a Nintendo title that brings together famous characters from the company's other games and pits them against one another in truly epic battles.

In the first installment, released in 1999 for the Nintendo 64, Link was the only representative of the series; he stood out for his powerful sword attacks and his impressively diverse arsenal of weapons (bombs, arrows, etc.). The next episode in Nintendo's brawler series, which came out in 2002 with the subtitle *Melee*, then added sweet little Zelda to the list of playable characters alongside Link. Despite her regal appearance, the princess of Hyrule packs a punch, and can transform at will into Sheik (her masculine appearance from *Ocarina of Time*) to unleash a rapid series of attacks. Also joining in the fun are Ganondorf, the indefatigable symbol of Evil, and the child version of Link. In 2008, the series made its way to the Wii with a new episode, *Brawl*. Alongside Link, Zelda and Ganondorf, who appear in a graphical style inspired by that of *Twilight Princess,* "Toon Link" (the version of Link that appeared in *The Wind Waker*) now gets his chance to rumble with Mario, Pikachu and the rest. Finally, in 2014, the Wii U and the 3DS each welcomed a new installment of *Super Smash Bros.* Both were high-quality episodes, but added no new characters from the cast of the *Zelda* series. At this point, the available characters were Link, Zelda, Sheik, Toon Link and Ganondorf. Each of these characters also appeared as Amiibos. In practice, these plastic figurines equipped with an NFC chip were not all that exciting to play with. They are used to save a character for the player to fight against. The console's AI then controls the Amiibo opponent.

Although it is hardly surprising that characters from the *Zelda* series would appear in a game like *Super Smash Bros.*, which was published by Nintendo, it is a bit startling to see Link turn up in a game from another publisher. But sure enough, the young hero was honored with an appearance as the "guest character" in the GameCube version of *Soul Calibur II*, Namco's weapon-based fighting game. That spot was reserved for *Tekken's* Heihachi Mishima in the PlayStation 2 version, and for comic-book hero Spawn in the Xbox version. As for the GameCube version, who better than Link to play the role of the glamorous guest star? Fans who had blasted *The Wind Waker*'s visual style finally had a chance to see what a *Zelda* game in realistic 3D might have looked like. The result is dazzling, the animations are astoundingly smooth and their flawless structure makes for some truly impressive duels. Although he has a shorter reach than characters like Siegfried or Nightmare, Link's natural charisma and his varied range of exciting attacks made him an instant favorite among players.

In another notable appearance that fans had long been waiting for, Link also showed up in *Mario Kart 8*. In a paid DLC package, the hero of the *Zelda* saga made his grand entrance into the *Mario Kart* series, along with a special racetrack.

HYRULE WARRIORS

As is often the case with spinoffs, *Hyrule Warriors* was not developed by Nintendo, but by Omega Force. The studio worked frequently with publisher Koei Tecmo, and was known for its *Dynasty Warriors* series of hack-and-slash games, in which players take on vast hordes of enemies all at once. In this case, it was Omega Force itself that approached Nintendo to propose a project based on its *Shin Sangoku Musou* series (the Japanese name for the *Dynasty Warriors* games). "We went to see them about using our game engine. We thought it would be a good match for the *Zelda* series. We needed the income, and they were happy to add another game to their catalog. So they said yes." Nevertheless, Aonuma and Miyamoto made a number of demands—first and foremost, that all of the usual animations from the *Dynasty Warriors* games be completely revised to fit better with the design of the *Zelda* series. This threw cold water on Omega Force's original plan to reuse the animations from earlier *Musou* games. Nintendo's second demand went the opposite way: while Omega Force had intended to move away from their own series' formula to develop an adventure game more like typical *Zelda* titles, Miyamoto insisted that this spinoff preserve the spirit of the *Dynasty Warriors* series.

Hyrule Warriors was officially announced on December 18, 2013, as part of a Nintendo Direct presentation, and went on sale in 2014 (in August in Japan and September in North America) for the Wii U console. As crazy as the concept might seem, the combined might of the *Zelda* and *Dynasty Warriors* series packed a powerful punch. In this explosive new spinoff, the player controls not only Link, but a large number of other characters (twenty-six in all, including the DLC) as they face off against the forces of evil. As usual, the story is merely a pretext for the action—an amalgam of all the key elements of the *Zelda* saga, from the main characters to the typical story beats involving new items and legendary weapons. And although the gigantic battle scenes would seem to go against everything players would normally expect from a canonical episode, the different qualities of the two series come through clearly without either one dominating the other. The combat system turns out to be every bit as dynamic as in a *Dynasty Warriors* game: the combat is exciting, there's a wide range of playable characters, and the power attacks rain down in a thrilling storm of fireworks. Alongside these primal pleasures, the rich complexity of *Zelda*'s world fills out the missions with objectives drawn from different episodes in the series. Fans will be delighted to discover the many subtle references aimed directly at them.

As an added bonus, the studio also added a welcome touch of RPG structure to the game. Players have to level up their character and, more importantly,

manage the sizable arsenal of available weapons. A smithy allows players to upgrade their weapons, and to add new abilities by merging certain weapons together. In short, there is a huge amount of equipment to work with. Players can arm Link with a sword, a Fire Rod or a boomerang—whatever strikes their fancy! Every new weapon switches up the gameplay with its own completely new set of attacks.

Still, there's no denying that the *Dynasty Warriors* games can be repetitive at times. To add a bit more variety, Omega Force included multiple game modes: Legend mode (the main story mode), with eighteen scripted missions in which the player is assigned a specific character; a Challenge Mode; and an Adventure mode. The latter mode exactly reproduces the map from the very first *Zelda* game on NES—a bracing shot of HD nostalgia that combines brawling and adventuring in a series of missions that can be played solo or with a friend.

At the E3 conference in June 2015, Nintendo announced a port of *Hyrule Warriors* for its handheld console, the 3DS. This time, the initiative came not from Nintendo or Koei Tecmo, but in response to strong demand from Japanese players. This version, called *Hyrule Warriors Legends*, includes the entire Wii U game with all of its DLC, along with new playable characters like Toon Link, Skull Kid, Tetra, the King of Hyrule, and one very special new addition: Linkle, a female version of Link who caused quite a sensation when she was unveiled in November 2015. The game was released in March 2016 worldwide, and included the new StreetPass function supported by the 3DS.

TRI FORCE HEROES

Much like the earlier pair of *Four Swords* games, *Tri Force Heroes* grew out of Nintendo's desire to offer a new multiplayer *Zelda* game. But this installment, developed by the Grezzo game studio, is designed for three players rather than four—a choice that Hiromasa Shikata explains by noting that it's easier to cooperate in a group of three (since four-player groups often split into two pairs, thereby undermining the game's initial ambitions).

Another unique aspect of this episode is its setting. Instead of Zelda as the princess of Hyrule, this game stars Princess Styla and her kingdom of Hytopia. The princess has been subjected to a strange curse: in a world of high fashion, she is forced to wear a hideous outfit, to her immense humiliation. And indeed, fashion is a key element in this episode. The three Links who rush to Styla's aid will have to adapt to the latest local trends to make their way through the game's eight dungeons and defeat the witch responsible for this outrage. As with the YRP team in *Final Fantasy X-2*, each tunic is associated with a specific power: the Goron Garb lets Link swim through lava, the Big Bomb Outfit makes bombs more powerful, and the princess's Legendary Dress makes extra hearts appear. But to create these outfits, players have to collect the right materials by finishing levels and completing special challenges. It's possible to play alone, in which case the two other Links become immobile and invincible puppets that the player can control one at a time with a tap on the touch screen, thereby simulating cooperative play. But *Tri Force Heroes* is best played with three players, whether online or locally; two-player games are not an option.

Besides the 3D aspect, this episode is built around perspective. The biggest gameplay innovation consists of "stacking" the three Links in order to build totem poles of various heights. Players have to acquire a solid grasp of this system's subtle nuances in order to disarm traps and solve the often tricky puzzles presented in this installment. Perfect coordination is the key to success: each player has one secondary weapon that complements those of their teammates. The final touches in this highly symbiotic system are the health and magic meters, which are shared among all three players.

The game is a pleasure to play, and more inventive than some might have expected. The special challenges make the team's work more difficult, but more interesting as well. For example, players may be asked to finish a level without using swords or with a reduced health meter, or to avoid a giant hand that is constantly trying to grab hold of our heroes. While the game is enjoyable with three players, it becomes a chore in single-player mode. Taking on the most complex obstacles, which generally involve reaching high places, turns out to be a hassle, requiring the player to swap awkwardly back and forth among the three characters.

CHAPTER XVI

A Unique Saga

THE ZELDA TIMELINE

Attempting to work out a definitive timeline to include every episode in the *Zelda* saga had always seemed to be an enormous or even impossible task—without direct help from Nintendo, at least. To be sure, there were certain clues that could serve as helpful reference points, but nothing truly convincing.

Places and characters recurred from one episode to the next, but most often with completely different attributes. How could anyone tie all of them together if each episode offered only enough clues to establish a relationship with one or at most two other installments? For example, we know that *Majora's Mask* follows *Ocarina of Time*, and that *Phantom Hourglass* comes after *The Wind Waker*, but what about the relation between *Oracle of Ages* and *The Adventure of Link*?

The creators' own statements are not much more enlightening. Miyamoto had often commented that the *Zelda* games were developed with a primary emphasis on gameplay, rather than any concern for a consistent story. He even went so far as to say that he didn't want to establish an official timeline, for fear of constraining his creative process. That announcement could have brought an end to the debate and silenced any questions... if only Eiji Aonuma hadn't later revealed that there was, in fact, a "general timeline" carefully preserved in a "confidential document" that only Miyamoto, the director of the current game, and Aonuma himself were allowed to see. Nintendo also wanted to avoid "sharing it with anyone else" so that it would remain free to "add new titles before or after any given episode." Before this document's existence was made public, Miyamoto had insisted that *Ocarina of Time* was the saga's very first episode in chronological order. Aonuma had commented along the same lines in his statement about the existence of a parallel world associated with the toon-shading episodes that started with *The Wind Waker*. During the promotion of *Skyward Sword*, for which a release date of late 2011 had just been announced, Aonuma finally admitted (after consulting with Miyamoto) that the new chapter took place chronologically before *Ocarina of Time*. As such, the infamous secret timeline seemed to be in constant development, leaving the creators completely free to include new installments wherever they liked. It seemed impossible that a complete and consistent timeline could ever be established—until Nintendo finally decided to satisfy fans' curiosity and reveal the whole chronology in the encyclopedic *Hyrule Historia*, supervised by Aonuma himself.

In this book, we learn that the saga's timeline is broken down into different eras, corresponding to the major changes that have shaped the kingdom of Hyrule over the years. It all starts from a single shared origin story, with the creation of the world and the Triforce by the three goddesses Din, Farore and Nayru, who then entrusted the goddess Hylia—from whom Hyrule takes its name—with the responsibility of caring for that world. This is where *Skyward Sword* begins, followed by *The Minish Cap*, *Four Swords* and *Ocarina of Time*; the timeline then splits into three separate branches. After that, things get complicated...

Ocarina of Time serves as a turning point in this timeline, with three different possible outcomes that develop into three alternative realities resulting from the final battle against Ganondorf. In the first case, the hero is defeated, leading to the fall of Hyrule and a dark age in which *A Link to the Past*, *Oracle of Ages* and *Seasons*, *Link's Awakening*, *The Legend of Zelda* and *The Adventure of Link* all take place. The second branch is the one in which the hero wins the battle, and then decides to go back to the past (after his seven years' slumber). *Majora's Mask*, *Twilight Princess* and *Four Swords Adventures* then follow. Finally, the third branch arises from the teenage Link's decision to continue his quest after defeating Ganondorf, leading to *The Wind Waker*, *Phantom Hourglass* and *Spirit Tracks*, with the advent of the Hero of Winds.

Obviously, this idea of three distinct timelines seems a bit too neat and tidy. One might be tempted to see it as a kind of "just-so story" aimed at getting a chronology down on paper in response to fans' eager demands—that is, as a response designed specifically to make them happy. In fact, the real key may have been right before our eyes since the very beginning. It's right there in the title, in capital letters: *The Legend of Zelda*. After all, wouldn't it make more sense to think of the different *Zelda* games as a series of variations on the same legend than as episodes in a chronological sequence? As noted earlier, a legend was originally a written tale, sometimes associated with a specific iconography, which is ultimately intended to be read; recall that the Latin word

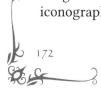

legenda signifies *things to be read.* Moved and impressed by the wondrous nature of the tale, its audience passes the story on to others in turn. Ultimately, the details of the story are of secondary importance, since the essential function of a legend is to convey spiritual or moral values. As the legend is passed down from generation to generation, it is changed, transformed and renewed as it incorporates new elements added by the previous teller. In this way, the different elements of the story are gradually modified by the popular imagination, and the legend eventually becomes a reflection of the collective unconscious. On the face of it, this description seems to fit the *Zelda* series perfectly: each game in the series would in fact represent an embellished, distorted and personalized version of the legend of Hyrule and its savior, Link.

Nevertheless, it is clear that as the saga has evolved, it has also become more cohesive and consistent overall. We can see this in the toon-shading episodes, which are all intimately related to one another, and in *Skyward Sword*, which provides a new prologue to the series. The existence of an official timeline seems to confirm Nintendo's desire to fit every episode into a larger whole from now on. But was that really Miyamoto's original intent? We doubt it, but we will probably never know for sure. One thing is clear: the *Zelda* saga will always remain a legend in the world of video games.

AT THE HEART OF THE ADVENTURE

Despite their lack of any particularly elaborate plot, the *Zelda* games are incredibly captivating, even addictive. The meticulously designed gameplay grabs us right from the start and never lets go. Still, Link's stories never seemed to impress players nearly as much in their own right as other major series with more intricate plot lines. The many iterations of *The Legend of Zelda* are no less fascinating for all that, because unlike most other games, they focus the player's experience on the present moment. Recall that the *Zelda* games, like all Nintendo productions, are based in a model in which the ultimate goal is to entertain the player. The developer's philosophy is to always build everything around the gameplay and players' hands-on experience of the game. That being said, the way in which Link's quests are structured is still quite remarkable. In a *Zelda* game, players themselves move the plot forward simply by taking part in the adventure. One might not think that this was anything special, or anything that distinguishes the series from other games, regardless of genre. And yet, when we look more closely, we see that the *Zelda* games describe and present their world without ever trying to recreate it completely. To make clear what we mean, we will look at three examples from three different genres—an open-world game, an RPG, and an FPS, all of them noted for the quality of their scripts: *Red Dead Redemption*, *Final Fantasy VII* and *BioShock*. In these three games, the player's goal is to find as many clues as they can, hidden in the environment or in lines of dialogue, to help them put together an enormous puzzle: either the history of the world in which the game is set, or the main character's past. The overall framework in which these games take place is much more complex than in any *Zelda* game, but the only effect of the player's actions is to reconstruct the backstory. Even as the player discovers more and more twists and turns in that story, the progression and development that takes place within the game itself is minimal. John Marston, Cloud Strife and Jack all experience their adventure as a search for identity following an accident or traumatic event. In *Zelda*, on the other hand, the player's actions directly advance the plot. The story often begins in the simplest of ways: a young hero with no particular skills finds himself at the center of developments that will reveal his legendary destiny. Each action he accomplishes will bring him closer to his goal: to save Princess Zelda and the kingdom of Hyrule. And while a mythological setting is indeed presented to the player (a creation myth and the history of the world and the people that live there), it ultimately has little impact on Link's actual adventure. There is no need to reconstruct the past, because the game is focused on Link in the present. This narrative schema, in which the player is constantly involved in the story, explains the ongoing attraction of the *Zelda* games. As with the gameplay, immediacy and clarity are the key features of the plot.

Link's lack of a past explains his status as a kind of empty shell, or rather, it results from that status: because Link *has to* be an empty shell, there is no need to evoke his past. Elevated to the status of a legendary hero by the end of the game, the young Hylian initially appears as a child or teenager like any other. It is the events of the game that *form* Link, shape him, and allow him to develop through the player's own actions. Although he is the chosen one who represents the Triforce of Courage, he has no particular physical skills or magical powers. His only distinguishing feature is his extreme daring, which allows him to play this exceptional role: with no divine or superhuman attributes, all he has to rely on is his courage. This leads players to identify all the more deeply with the character, since they experience every plot point that shapes Link's character as it happens, and through their own actions. Seen from this point of view, the *Zelda* series is an exception among contemporary video games, which attests to Nintendo's utterly unique approach. Unlike many other story-driven games, which ask players to painstakingly reconstruct a past history grounded in a rich backstory, and rely on players' empathy to establish a connection with the character they play, *Zelda* games make no pretense of delivering a deep or

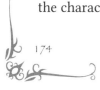

complex message. Instead, the goal is to form a simple relationship between the player and their character, by guiding the player through an experience in which they will come to identify completely with their avatar. This connection is established through gameplay, rather than a multifaceted story based on various more or less obscure events in the past.

A FIXED FORMULA

From its very first episode, the *Zelda* saga established the foundation for what would soon become an unchanging formula. Right from the start, progression through the game is based on two alternating phases: exploring the world, and exploring the dungeons. While both of these sections have plenty of action, players will also need to use their creative and deductive powers to deal with the puzzles they'll have to solve in order to find secret tunnel entrances or gain access to the dungeons beyond them. Although the gameplay changed considerably in the second episode, it also saw the addition of villages in which Link could wander around, talking to residents. The third *Zelda* game would combine these two approaches into a structure that alternated between village visits, exploration of the world, and dungeon exploration.

In this seamlessly efficient system, each dungeon is also tied to a specific theme: Link discovers water, fire, and forest temples, among others. Within each one, he invariably has to acquire a specific object hidden in a chest (boomerang, bow, hookshot, etc.) that will help him not only to solve the current dungeon's puzzles, but also to defeat the local boss. To make his way forward, Link will have to open locked doors with keys that he collects with the help of his compass and map (also hidden within the dungeon). The final key leads to the room where he can finally confront the boss that awaits him at the end of each dungeon.

Experienced *Zelda* players starting a new episode will immediately feel right at home. Unfortunately, this basic formula, established in 1991, has hardly changed a bit since then. Of course, it would be unfair to claim that later episodes contributed nothing new at all. There have certainly been changes to the story and the setting; the appearance of 3D graphics and the addition of new items; changes to the graphical style; and one-time additions like ocean voyages or the ability to change into a wolf. Even so, it is still disappointing to see the same fixed structure repeated exactly every time, so that returning players are never truly surprised. Fans continue to eagerly await the episode that will bring a break in this routine, perhaps by switching up the usual set of items or breaking free of the saga's usual village-dungeon-boss sequence. Or why not go further still and introduce a new hero with a different look—or even the ability to speak? Then again, would the result still really be a *Zelda* game?

As if to emphasize the repetitiveness of this structure, the rate at which new *Zelda* episodes are released has increased considerably in recent years. While almost twelve years passed between the first *Legend of Zelda* and *Ocarina of Time*, for a total of just four games, the twelve years after that saw the release of nine new episodes! The reputation that the series had acquired after *A Link to the Past* and *Ocarina of Time* certainly played a role in this decision to increase the frequency of new releases. For a while, players were getting a new *Zelda* game every year. A remake of *Ocarina of Time* for the new 3DS came out in 2011, followed by an all-new episode, *Skyward Sword*, at the end of that same year. All those new releases surely exacerbated the sense of repetition we mentioned above. The cult status of an episode like *Ocarina of Time* was at least partly due to fans' excitement at having a new *Zelda* game to play after years of waiting, with each postponement of the release date only further stoking players' anticipation.

THE MANY FACES OF LINK

The first and third episodes of *The Legend of Zelda* gave the impression that Link was a child, or at most a young teenager. Indeed, he is often teased about his young age, for example at the start of the third episode, when the soldiers are surprised to see him "still up at this hour." So let's take a look at the character's appearance to get a clearer understanding of the situation—and at the same time, to draw parallels between the evolution of his character design and the saga's overall orientation.

With the advent of 3D graphics, games were able to fill in a lot of new details about their worlds. In the first *Zelda* game, the little sprites that appeared on screen left plenty of room for players to "fill in the blanks" from their imagination. Each player could form their own image of Link, informed by their own personality. Starting with *Ocarina of Time*, the addition of a third dimension meant that Nintendo had to make some bold decisions in the game's art design, and unveil a hero with a more clearly defined look. Recall that the plot of the fifth episode sees Link grow seven years older over the course of the game, in order to finish his quest and save Hyrule from chaos. A few years later, *The Wind Waker* went in the opposite direction, introducing a cel-shaded hero who looked more childlike than ever. This episode marked a major branching point in the saga developed by Miyamoto and Aonuma.

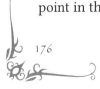

From 2003 on, the world of *Zelda* was split in two: on the one side were the more "mature" episodes for home consoles, and on the other was lighter fare aimed primarily at handheld consoles. *Twilight Princess* had the unenviable task of following up on *Ocarina of Time*, in terms of both game design (overall structure, segmentation of the world and its dungeons) and story. With regard to its content, the result was quite close to *A Link to the Past* for the Super Nintendo. The other branch of the series already includes four episodes: *The Wind Waker*, *The Minish Cap*, *Phantom Hourglass*, and *Spirit Tracks*. This redesign—or this return to basics, depending on who you ask—reveals a world that's closer to what we'd expect to find in a kids' cartoon. The bad guys aren't really scary, the adventure proceeds at a more relaxed pace, and the sense of impending doom is less heavily emphasized. As a result of this new design, or perhaps as a guiding influence on it, the new branch also introduces a game design philosophy that is different from what fans were used to. The main adventure is typically shorter than in earlier games, with an increased emphasis on side quests and general exploration of the world, encouraging the player to wander randomly through the different environments. On handheld consoles, there are fewer dungeons and the difficulty level is slightly lower. Clearly, the purpose of this split was to target different audiences. Obviously, anyone can enjoy a *Zelda* game, whether they're a serious fan or not. But to attract new players unfamiliar with the adventures of the most famous green-clad elf in video games, Nintendo had to make some kind of change.

But the changes didn't stop there. The choice of cel-shading also gave the creators an opportunity to enhance Link's personality. We can now see our young hero smiling, frowning and reacting to his environment. In this way, even though Link is still the same mute and rather unassuming hero we've always known, he seems much more relatable in these cartoon-like *Zelda* games than the strong silent type we find in *Twilight Princess*, for example. Along the same lines, we also see Princess Zelda coming into her own in these adventures—a topic we will return to later on. Paradoxically enough, then, the cel-shading style is much more convincing when it comes to presenting more lifelike and believable characters—as opposed to the frustration that players often feel with the Link of *Twilight Princess*.

Anyone who has finished *The Wind Waker* will surely remember the scene in which Link enters a temple that is frozen in time, where he discovers stained-glass windows depicting a well-known adventure. This was an explicit reference to *Ocarina of Time*, and quietly presented the Link of *The Wind Waker* as the Hero of Time's spiritual heir. There may be a subliminal message at play here as well, as though the cel-shading episodes wanted to step away from the legend and distance themselves from its imposing legacy. To be sure, the

Link of *The Wind Waker* is the hero of a quest as well, but one that cannot be directly compared with those that came before. It's almost as if these games, aimed more at the younger players, were intended as a kind of initiation—a way of preparing them for the mythical adventure enjoyed by older players, for which the younger ones might not yet be ready. "Big brother" Link thus serves as a role model for his "little brother"; the epic scale of the larger adventures contrast with the quieter aspect of the smaller ones. Doesn't it make sense to see this as a message from Miyamoto and Aonuma, who had cleverly managed to split their series into two distinct branches, each aimed at a different group of players, as we have argued? This hypothesis would seem to be confirmed by the fact that the more "mature" *Zelda* episodes are reserved for home consoles, while the lighter quests are developed for handheld consoles. Following this decision, every aspect of the design of the games in question—the world, the background, the overall aesthetic and the game design—had to be modified accordingly.

From this perspective, we see that the technical, artistic and story aspects of a game as ambitious as those in the *Zelda* series are interconnected in a systematic way. Although it is impossible to truly say which of these aspects influenced the others, all of them come together to create an experience that is thoughtful, coherent, and always highly effective.

COMMUNICATING IN SILENCE

Link's characteristic silence required an intermediary between the player and the character, so that he could interact with the inhabitants of the world he was exploring. Navi, the fairy who appeared in *Ocarina of Time* on the Nintendo 64, was the first to play this role.

Since the very first episode of *Zelda*, Link has never said a single word, although we began to hear occasional shouts and interjections starting with *Ocarina of Time*. In fact, Link only appears to be mute, but in fact, we know that he can talk; it's just that his words are never seen or heard by the player. However, the non-player characters that the hero interacts with frequently repeat his words back to him before they reply. Perhaps one reason why the games in this series never allow the player to hear (or, in keeping with the literary genre of legends, to *read*) the young Hylian's words is to underline his status as an "empty shell," inspiring the player's imagination while making it easier to identify with the protagonist. And so it was that a very important character called Navi made her first appearance in *Ocarina of Time*. The reader may recall that Navi was the fairy ordered by the Deku Tree to guide Link in his adventure. As we saw earlier, fairies are traditionally imagined as creatures that guide the destiny of a person of their choosing. Therefore, it is not at all surprising to encounter a fairy in the world of *Zelda*—quite the contrary, in fact. So it is Navi who plays the role of interpreter between Link and the other characters in the game, and between Link and the player as well. Interestingly, the name *Navi* was originally an abbreviation of *Fairy Navigation System*, the phrase used by the designers to refer to her function within the game. Having gotten in the habit of referring to the character by the abbreviation "Navi," they decided to keep it in the final version. When the idea was raised of including a fairy in *Ocarina of Time*, Yoshiaki Koizumi originally wanted to represent her as a pretty girl, whom he probably imagined with curves worthy of a Régis Loisel drawing. Unfortunately for him, the limited capabilities of the Nintendo 64 made that impossible. Instead, he decided to simplify her appearance, finally settling on a winged ball of light. And thus was born the fairy assigned to guide Link and assist him in his quest for the Triforce.

As is often the case at Nintendo, the new character was created in response to a technical problem. The designers behind Z-targeting wanted the system to have a concrete in-game representation. In this case, their solution took the form of a fairy who served as a target lock. Navi would stick like a marker to the enemies that Link aimed at with Z-targeting, allowing the player to see exactly which opponent they were facing at any given moment. Over time, the designers came up with other new ideas: if Navi could aim at enemies, she could also aim at friends or important elements of the environment. A color code was established, with each color corresponding to a specific case: friends, enemies, tips, and so on. At that point, the Navi concept was sufficiently well-established that the episode's script could be changed to integrate her character into the story. Not only does the presence of a fairy make sense in the world of *Zelda* and contribute to its overarching mythology, but the character is also used first and foremost to strengthen the connection between the player and the hero that represents them. As it turns out, Navi is very talkative, which is useful in her role of starting conversations with other characters. The same approach is used again in *Majora's Mask* (although a different fairy takes Navi's place in that game), but then dropped for *The Wind Waker*. Nintendo probably assumed that players were sufficiently familiar with the lock-on system by then, since the same function had since been reused in a number of other games. Nevertheless, the fairy would return once more in *Phantom Hourglass*, both as a story element (Ciela guides Link and turns out to be very important to the plot) and at a gameplay level (the fairy shows players where to point the stylus). Finally, in *Twilight Princess* (but only in the Wii version), a fairy is also used to indicate where the Wiimote is pointing on the screen, but its presence is not in any way relevant to the story.

Nintendo had thus successfully related the addition of a gameplay-specific function to the introduction of a new character in the series. Besides responding to the needs of the new Z-targeting system, Navi the fairy also became Link's ideal assistant by taking charge of conversations, which have never really been Link's strong suit. Even more so than the main character himself, Navi had become the link between the player and the game.

CHAPTER XVII
MUSIC IN ZELDA

I s there anyone out there who's never heard the musical theme to The Legend of Zelda, also known as Overworld? A rousing melody that evokes grand adventure, it has become one of the great video game classics, alongside the music from the first level of *Mario Bros.* These two pieces stand as symbols for the entire Nintendo universe, and are seared into players' memories as the ultimate in video game music. The man behind this impressive feat: Koji Kondo. A longtime friend of Shigeru Miyamoto, he composed the music for a number of video games, then gradually moved away from composition and into a new role as a music and sound director. Still, his name will forever be associated with the *Zelda* series, and his presence is felt in almost every episode. Even as the composers have changed, the saga has developed a rich and unique musical identity that was always designed to keep the player engaged.

Starting with the very first episode, Kondo's powerful melodies made impressive use of the very limited audio capabilities of the NES to bring a sense of epic adventure to the game. There were not many different melodies at the time, but boredom never sets in—as if the magic combination of exciting gameplay and the player's imagination had somehow transcended the limited material and the lack of an orchestra to make the music of *Zelda* sound like a John Williams score (*Star Wars, Superman, Indiana Jones*, etc.) to enchanted players. Kondo's compositions sent shockwaves through the world of video game music—sound quality be damned! As long as the melody is good and strikes the right tone for the game, the player will enjoy it as part of a memorable experience. The clearest proof of this is surely the incredible success of these *Zelda* and *Mario* tunes, which every fan knows by heart and which have appeared in many forms, despite their relative complexity—and the fact that they are actually quite difficult to hum. Of course, if the games hadn't been fun to play, the music wouldn't have been such a hit. That much is clear from the following episode, *The Adventure of Link.*

The second episode's radical change of course was also reflected in a change of composer. Although far less well-known, the music written by Nakito Akatsuka (*Punch Out!*) is also of excellent quality, with inspired themes that fit brilliantly with the tone set by Kondo in the first game. Nevertheless, this soundtrack has faded into obscurity, much like the game itself.

The arrival of the Super Nintendo and the legendary episode *A Link to the Past* marked the first of several revolutions in the saga's musical development. With up to sixteen available voices (as opposed to just five for the NES) and much higher sound quality than its predecessor, the new console gave Koji Kondo an opportunity to considerably enhance his style and his overall approach. Although the melodies are still the most important part of his compositions, reflecting a consistency of talent that commands great respect, the new range of sonic possibilities also allowed Kondo to add subtler shades and nuances to his pieces, which he used to evoke an impressive variety of moods. Virtually every location has its own unique tone, and the synthesized sounds begin to sound more like those of a real orchestra. More important, though, is the sense of magic and mystery that predominates in this musical score. While the soundtrack as a whole is very dynamic, based on powerful melodies dominated by brass instruments (like the thrilling *Hyrule Castle*) or unsettling themes guided by restless strings (*Sanctuary Dungeon*, and the famous overture in which violins evoke falling rain), the score's most consistent element is its sense of wonder. There's an undeniable feeling of grand adventure, like reading an epic that is exciting, enchanting and frightening all at once—and the music, through its narrative dimension, contributes to this sensation. The soundtrack in the first *Legend of Zelda* had this character as well. Koji Kondo gives his melodies plenty of freedom, and lets each theme take its time to develop; he introduces variations and interruptions, and makes use of complex harmonies. While the advancements in graphics quality that the Super Nintendo brought to *A Link to the Past* gave the designers more freedom to tell the story the way they wanted to, that same sense of increased freedom also applied to the composer, who now had a much wider range of options to develop his pieces and their narrative impact. The end result was a highly memorable work that many still consider as the musical high point of the entire *Zelda* series.

A bittersweet, poetic and quirky digression from the main saga, *Link's Awakening* on Game Boy called on the services of Minako Hamano, Kozuo Ishikawa and Kazumi Totaka, three talented composers who, despite the technological step backward imposed by the handheld console, managed to do justice to the spirit of Kondo's score while inventing some unforgettable

melodies of their own—starting with the ones played on the ocarina, an essential element of the plot that would come into its full potential on the Nintendo 64 in the following episode, *Ocarina of Time*. As Kondo's last solo work for the series, that game's score represented yet another revolution, one which went beyond the *Zelda* series itself to make its mark on video game music more generally. Although the cartridge format placed unfortunate restrictions on the sound quality compared to what would have been possible on a CD for the PlayStation, this installment nevertheless gave the composer a chance to try out a completely new approach to writing music, and to the interaction between the music, the game and the player: this was the episode that first used pieces with an adaptive structure. When players first discovered Hyrule Field in this game, they were in for a double shock when the legendary melody of *Overworld* not only fails to play (and indeed, never appears at all in this episode), but is replaced by an adaptive score that changes in response to the player's actions, the passage of time, and the presence of enemies. This adds a highly advanced interactive dimension that considerably enhances the experience and improves the player's immersion, reflecting what must have been a long and arduous process of composition—so much so that this approach, which could have become standard practice in the creation of video game soundtracks, has in fact been used only rarely. The introduction to *Ocarina of Time*, in which music accompanies cinematic sequences like Navi's unforgettable flight, marks yet another major leap forward: in terms of the connection between music and image, Kondo's work here approaches that of a film score composer. Also in this game, players can use the ocarina to play their own melodies, a highly effective immersive tool. Just like the graphics, the sound in this episode is more realistic as well, with sound effects now playing just as important a role as the music. The introduction of 3D graphics turned out to be a key source of creativity for Kondo, who even went so far as to completely change the style of his compositions for the dungeons. These melodies were dynamic and intense in earlier games, but in *Ocarina of Time*, they are much calmer and more expansive, with a greater sense of depth. This new musical approach commands the player's attention right from the Deku Tree dungeon sequence. A few other pieces are almost experimental in nature (like *Forest Temple* and its otherworldly sounds), firmly establishing this soundtrack as one of the best in its genre, and as one that would change the history of video game music. Other developments later in the series were not nearly as bold.

In *Majora's Mask*, Toru Minegishi joined the team for the first time to lend Kondo a hand. This episode sticks to the previous episode's formula in terms of its sound: although the music is still as excellent as ever, providing the perfect accompaniment to the bizarre and disturbing world of the game, it adds nothing new in terms of its form. But ultimately, that's of little importance when the quality is still just as high. The same is true for *The Wind Waker*, for which Kondo began to move away from composition and into a supervisor's role, making room for Minegishi to take over with help from Kenta Nagata and Hajime Wakai. Despite the transition from the cartridge format to optical discs, there are a few small steps forward here but no great leap in the sound quality—a somewhat disappointing result. Nevertheless, the compositions are still finely crafted, calmer and lighter this time, and a number of the melodies here have earned their place among the saga's most memorable themes— notably the Ocean Theme.

We might also mention *Oracle of Ages* and *Seasons*, which were released as a pair, as well as *The Minish Cap*—three minor but thoroughly enjoyable episodes developed by Capcom for the Game Boy Color and Game Boy Advance, with melodies that are certainly less inspired, but still highly listenable.

The two DS episodes, *Phantom Hourglass* and *Spirit Tracks*, benefited from the talent of the official new *Zelda* sound team. Directed by Minegishi with help from Kenta Nagata for the first game and from Asuka Ota and Manaka Tominaga for the second, the team's efforts were again supervised by the great Koji Kondo.

Twilight Princess should have been the perfect opportunity for a new revolution. When a real orchestra was brought in to perform the music for the trailer (composed by Mahito Yokota), it raised hopes for a symphonic soundtrack that would finally do justice to the epic spirit of the majestic compositions written by Kondo and his team. Unfortunately, only three pieces in the score made use of a real orchestra (arranged by Michiro Oshima, the composer for the game *Ico*); although the rest of the score was as well-written as ever, it once again relied on synthesized sounds—and fairly mediocre ones at that, for a soundtrack produced in 2006. Kondo later attempted to justify the absence of an orchestra by arguing that pre-recorded music would not have been flexible or interactive enough. Although this type of music certainly imposes certain constraints, Mahito Yokota later proved with his soundtrack for *Mario Galaxy* that nothing is impossible—while also demonstrating how much real orchestral pieces can contribute to a game.

Miyamoto was convinced, and gave the green light for *Skyward Sword* to use real orchestral arrangements of compositions by Hajime Wakai and Mahita Yokota. As a reflection of the game's aerial setting, the musical atmosphere had *Zelda* fans in seventh heaven, even as it marked a new step forward for music in the series.

Anyone who enjoys orchestral music in video games would do well to pick up a copy of *Hyrule Symphony*, a sublime collection of string arrangements of the

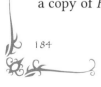

most beautiful pieces from *Ocarina of Time* (along with the original *Overworld* theme and the *Ballad of the Wind Fish* from *Link's Awakening* as an added bonus). Combining nostalgia, melancholy and a stirring call to adventure, this album brings together everything that makes the musical world of *The Legend of Zelda* so charming and unique. In terms of its intrinsic qualities (dozens of memorable melodies, captivating soundscapes, skilled arrangements, etc.) as well as its contribution to the genre and the brilliant ideas laid out by Koji Kondo, *Zelda's* musical tradition is undeniably one of the most important in video game history.

PLAYING GAMES BY PLAYING MUSIC

While the soundtrack has clearly been an essential part of the series' success, one uniquely fascinating aspect of *The Legend of Zelda* has been its willingness to incorporate music into the gameplay itself. Most episodes make use of one instrument or another—and the flute even appears in the very first game! In fact, musical instruments even become central elements of the narrative in some cases, to the point that entire games are named after them, as with *Ocarina of Time* and *The Wind Waker*. And while it's unfortunate that the gameplay system ultimately never gives them any grander status than that of simple gadgets or tools that allow Link to move situations forward, manipulate time, and so on, these instruments still provide a more direct way to connect the player to the music of the game—through the music *in* the game. *Link's Awakening*, with its eight magical instruments on which Link can play the superb *Ballad of the Wind Fish*, was a source of lasting memories for many players, but it was in *Ocarina of Time* that this connection became more concrete. Starting with this episode, players are invited to interact with the instruments, and to perform these melodies themselves. The game doesn't require them to play to any particular rhythm, and the tunes are not especially difficult; nor is there any need to memorize long sequences, since there are generally only a few notes to remember, and they can be viewed in the menu at any time. The idea here seems simple enough: to focus players' attention on the different musical themes they hear as they make their way through the game. Because it is integrated into the gameplay system itself, thereby forcing the player to pay close attention to various melodies, the score becomes a concrete element of players' experience of the game. To reinforce this link, other elements are also tied into the narrative, such as the associations between various secondary characters and their instruments (Sheik and the harp he plays with Link, Malon and her song, etc.) or the way in which different tribes

are represented musically in *Majora's Mask*—the low sounds of the tuba for the subterranean Dekus, pounding tribal drums for the Gorons, and so on. To us, this seems like a great way to derive both gameplay and aesthetic value from musical diversity in a video game score—one of the many fascinating ideas explored by the series.

CHAPTER XVIII

LINK: A CHARACTER AND
HIS EVOLUTION

t first glance, Link's personality seems rather simplistic. But to discover the secrets of The Legend of Zelda, we will have to analyze Link in fine detail in order to reveal a subtext woven subtly into the very fabric of the saga. *Ocarina of Time* is the episode that lends itself most readily to this approach.

IS LINK A HERO?

The manga version of *Majora's Mask*, published in English by Viz Media, includes an intriguing foreword by the two female authors (writing under the shared pseudonym of Akira Himekawa). They tell the story of their first meeting with their partners from Kyoto, in which they asked what exactly made Link a hero. The Nintendo representatives were taken aback, and in hindsight, the manga artists themselves seem to think that it was a foolish question... and yet, they do not provide an answer.

Still, the question is certainly a valid one: what is it that makes Link a hero? Is it because he saves princesses? That's surely one part of the answer, but in the 21st century, it hardly seems very original or impressive. But there's no ignoring the fact that Link has been freeing one person or another for more than thirty years in an unbroken series of successes. Like it or not, the *Legend of Zelda* series still enjoys immense popularity.

This question allowed the two manga artists to separate what makes *Zelda* interesting as a video game from what makes it interesting as a story. Similarly, to understand what makes Link a hero, we will focus here on key moments of the different stories in the series. To do this, we will analyze the character of Link by examining the story in *Ocarina of Time*. Why this specific installment?

Simply because it is a central episode in the history of the *Zelda* series. First of all, from a strictly chronological perspective: *Ocarina of Time* came out almost twenty years ago, and the series celebrated its thirtieth anniversary in 2016. Its central position in the series makes it the ideal link between the saga's origins and its more recent episodes. Secondly, *Ocarina of Time* was the first *Zelda* game to appear in 3D. It therefore represents the point at which the series' classic features first took on their current form. Finally, *Ocarina of Time* laid the foundation for a gameplay system that seems likely to be with us for a long time to come. The importance of this episode is presumably why it was chosen as the first one to explore the third dimension. It also plays a central role in terms of the story, which is the point that will interest us here. Indeed, when *Ocarina of Time* was first released, everything in it was a reminder of earlier episodes; but all the *Zelda* games that have come out since then have in turn been inspired by *Ocarina of Time*. The decision to split the adventure into two distinct parts has its roots in the first episode. The structure of these two quests and the establishment of a dual world, meanwhile, draw freely from *A Link to the Past*. In addition, many existing elements were reused in a different form. For example, we meet characters with origins in several different episodes: the Zoras, who had already appeared in *A Link to the Past*, the owl from *Link's Awakening*, and so on.

Finally, *Ocarina of Time* offers a new interpretation of themes that were already addressed in earlier installments, though not in as much depth. For example, Link's slumber echoes that of Princess Zelda's in *The Adventure of Link*, and his battle against his shadow self in the Water Temple recalls the final boss in that game; his time in the belly of the great fish Jabu-Jabu is similar to his descent into the innards of the Wind Fish in *Link's Awakening*; and so on.

Events like these can also be found in myths and fairy tales. Years spent in sleep, an adventure in a fish's belly or a battle with one's own shadow hearken back to deeply familiar images. Taking the symbolic value of these images as our starting point, we will now explore the symbolism of the story in *Ocarina of Time* to finally answer the question:

What is it that makes Link a hero?

THROUGH THE LOOKING GLASS

In terms of the player's introduction to the adventure, *Ocarina of Time* differs from its predecessors in starting out at a slower pace. Thinking back to the earliest episodes in the series, Link always began his adventure alone, ready to leap right into battle. Not until *A Link to the Past* would players be

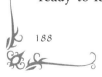

offered an introduction that set up a specific narrative context. And *Link's Awakening* begins with a cinematic sequence that was quite ambitious for a Game Boy title. But in *Ocarina of Time*, this initial section was more extensive than ever before. The adventure begins with two distinct segments. First, we are introduced to Link's day-to-day life. But before long, he leaves this world behind to embrace the adventure that awaits him. We learn a lot about the hero's character from the moment when he has to say goodbye to his loved ones.

A SYMBOLIC SETTING

The moment when Link leaves the Kokiri village is an important turning point in the plot of *Ocarina of Time*, since it marks the hero's entry into a new world. His departure even gets its own cutscene, in which Saria says her goodbyes. To address our chosen subject, let's take a moment to consider the setting in which this event takes place. First of all, we will turn our attention to the bridge.

By joining two opposing shores, a bridge connects two worlds that can differ from one another in any number of ways. As such, it is an especially popular choice among video game developers for introducing players to the world of the game. We find a bridge in Fumito Ueda's *Shadow of the Colossus*, for example, and in *Resident Evil 4*, in which Leon begins his adventure after crossing an old wooden bridge into a place where madness reigns. In both of these examples, the bridge becomes inaccessible right after the player crosses it. In other words, it is impossible for the player's character to turn back and return to his old life. But in fact, going back would be impossible even if the bridge were still usable.

The bridge is just one of many symbols used to express this idea of a point of no return. It represents a boundary that can appear in any number of forms. For Harry Potter, the boundary is simply an old brick wall. Along the same lines, Alice gets to Wonderland by stepping through the looking glass. We might also mention the hero of *Ico*, who is literally absorbed by the walls of the castle at the beginning of his adventure. In *Ocarina of Time*, then, Link's departure represents a process of transformation that is much more profound than it first appears. And since nothing will ever be the same again, there is a sense of finality to this moment.

THE QUESTION OF CHOICE

Like many heroes, Link gets his adventure underway by crossing a barrier that is impossible for other characters to get past. Why? Each story provides its own logical reason. In *Ocarina of Time*, we are told that leaving the forest is deadly for the Kokiri, but we soon learn that Link is actually Hylian. The stated reason is simply the story's justification for a very subtle narrative technique. We can draw an amusing parallel here to a French short story by Alphonse Daudet, *La Chèvre de monsieur Seguin* (*Mr. Seguin's Goat*), about a young goat who leaves her farm to seek freedom in the mountains. At first glance, it may seem strange to compare a fantasy video game to this modern fairy tale; but Link's journey has the same narrative structure as our example. In both stories, the hero's everyday life is presented as a safe haven, while the world outside is described as full of danger. And yet in both cases, the hero decides to leave home. Whereas Link sets out to save the world, the goat is only pursuing her own selfish goals. The sense of greatness in her adventure comes from her heroic battle against the big bad wolf.

But what's so heroic about making a choice? To answer this question, let us make a brief detour by way of the battle between Neo and Agent Smith in *The Matrix Revolutions*, the final film in the Wachowskis' famous trilogy. This episode puts a particular emphasis on the question of choice. However, we will approach the subject of heroism not from the perspective of Neo's choice, but through Smith's inability to understand that choice.

BREAKING THE RULES

As an agent of the Matrix, Smith is a computer program. He is therefore incapable of making a true choice; all he can do is to follow the instructions in his code. This is why he believes so strongly that all events are preordained, since from his point of view, everything is determined by a program. As Smith himself says in *The Matrix Reloaded*, something inside of him forces him to act as he does. He has no choice. That's why Smith rebukes Neo for stealing his prize. The agent's situation shows the extent to which a person can be controlled by external forces when they are unable to make their own choices. And isn't resistance to those forces what defines the hero's role? Solid Snake, the hero of the *Metal Gear Solid* series, is a military clone designed to reproduce the great deeds of his original template. But he refuses to see himself as a simple war machine, and enters an ongoing battle against his genetic heritage, the "program" that controls the functioning of every living organism. This lifelong

struggle is summed up at the very end of *Sons of Liberty*, the second episode in the series. Handcuffed, Snake is left at the mercy of the Metal Gear robot. He breaks his chains and heads into battle, symbolically breaking free of his genetic destiny by deciding to fight against it.

Faced with determinism, choice is essential for anyone who seeks freedom. Harry Potter could never have passed through that brick wall if he hadn't first gotten around the ban on reading his own mail at the beginning of the adventure. From the red pill right up to his final sacrifice to ensure peace, Neo's path in the *Matrix* trilogy is filled with choices.

Does all this mean that Link is a hero because he crosses a bridge that no one else dares to? Obviously not. But this scene is an expression of Link's heroic potential, in which he makes a choice that no one had ever made before. To emphasize this idea, the game gives the player the choice to accept or refuse the Deku Tree's request. Any player with the slightest bit of contrarian attitude has surely tried to refuse at least once—only to immediately discover the futility of this act. In terms of game design, however, imposing an explicit choice gets the player involved in the hero's development. In other words, the bridge scene must be understood as a promise.

Nevertheless, we cannot conclude that Link is a hero simply because he stands up to Ganondorf. As we have just shown, the plot of *Ocarina of Time* requires us to pause and look at its individual events to understand what they might mean. We have yet to define what kind of determinism Ganondorf represents. To do this, we will have to consider all of the events in the game, and make a long detour before providing a response to our initial question.

A PRECIOUS GIFT

At long last, we can venture forth into the vast fields of Hyrule. We will begin our analysis of *Ocarina of Time's* story with the sequence in which Link is trapped in the belly of the giant fish Jabu-Jabu. This segment is the one in which we will find the greatest number of references both to the *Zelda* series itself and to other well-known popular tales. Incidentally, the gameplay system in this sequence has its origins in the previous episode. But more than the connection to other *Zelda* games, it is the connection to myths and fairy tales that interests us here, and that motivates our decision to start from this specific episode.

A MOST FAMILIAR THEME

The theme of being trapped inside a giant fish had already turned up in *Link's Awakening*. In this game, Link had to find a way to escape a dreamlike world created by the mind of the Wind Fish. Although the events that unfold in *Ocarina of Time* are more prosaic, the connection to the earlier game is still distinctly felt. The two sequences are similar, but their respective roles in the story are completely different. Therefore, we will turn to myths and fairy tales to understand what happens to Link in Jabu-Jabu's belly, since this sequence touches on a universal theme that recurs in many different cultures around the world. The image of a hero trapped in the belly of a whale has been the subject of extensive study throughout the 20th century, with psychoanalysts taking over mythologists' role in explaining its underlying symbolism. Over time, the proposed explanations have become highly complex and specialized. But for now, we will simplify this analysis and focus on the similarities between Link's adventure and those of other heroes.

IN THE BELLY OF THE BEAST

When we consider the theme of a hero trapped in the belly of a whale, one tale in particular stands out as a key reference point in our culture: the story of *Pinocchio*, the Carlo Collodi novel that describes the adventures of a wooden marionette that comes to life and dreams of being a real boy. Pinocchio's adventure is a somewhat erratic voyage from one major event to the next. When he finally decides that he's ready to go back to his father Gepetto, Pinocchio learns that he has been devoured by an enormous shark. After various twists and turns, the puppet is himself swallowed by the very same beast, where he finds Gepetto still alive in its belly. Pinocchio and his creator then climb up the shark's esophagus, and wait until it falls asleep at the surface to sneak past its three rows of teeth. Unlike Gepetto, Pinocchio is a very good swimmer, and together, they manage to reach the shore. Pinocchio has changed. He is ready to work in order to earn the money he needs to take care of his ailing father. He has also become a conscientious pupil. A blue-haired fairy appears to the marionette in a dream to congratulate him, and when he wakes up, Pinocchio realizes that he has finally become a real boy.

The adventure of Pinocchio and Gepetto bears certain similarities to the story of the prophet Jonah that is told in the Jewish, Christian and Muslim traditions. Although he was chosen by God to deliver his holy message to the city of Nineveh, Jonah tries to escape by sea. God summons up a storm along

the fugitive's path, leading the sailors to throw the prophet overboard. Lost in the middle of the ocean, Jonah is swallowed by a "great fish" sent by God, which regurgitates him onto the sinful city's shores three days later. Finally accepting his divine mission, the prophet heads to Nineveh under clear skies. The tales of Jonah and Pinocchio in the belly of an enormous fish have another curious point in common: in both cases, the fish in question came to be seen as a *whale* in traditional retellings. We might ask what reasons led Walt Disney to represent Collodi's giant shark as a whale. Was it a way to make the animal a bit less scary for kids? A nod to Herman Melville's classic novel *Moby Dick*, or perhaps an implicit reference to the religious tradition that recast Jonah's fish as a whale?

In any case, these two stories are representative examples of a widespread theme found in virtually all the world's cultures. They focus in a simple and striking way on the change that the hero undergoes when he escapes from the animal's belly. In light of this, we are led to wonder whether Link is also transformed when he emerges from inside Jabu-Jabu.

TRANSFORMING ENERGY

The stomach, which often stands in symbolically for the digestive system as a whole, is the place where "dead" matter is transformed into nutritious elements that provide the living body with the energy it needs. The same logic of symbolic transformation that takes place in the whale's belly also applies to the stomachs of other monsters: wolves, dragons, and so on. It is therefore interesting to note that in *Ocarina of Time*, the two dungeons before Jabu-Jabu's also take place in locations that can be related to stomachs. At both the Deku Tree and Dodongo's Cavern—at the moment when Link confronts the boss, in the latter case—Link enters the location through a "mouth." Beyond the symbolism of the mouth and the stomach, transformation is also a key feature of the (Deku) tree and (Dodongo's) cavern environments. This idea is more sophisticated than that of a hero who gets swallowed up, but it occurs in myths and stories every bit as famous as the tales of Pinocchio and Jonah that we referred to above.

Caves are associated with the earth, and reveal the forces hidden within it. The magma flows that are responsible for earthquakes and volcanic eruptions also help seeds to grow into plants. We can easily see how this transformation might be metaphorically linked to that of a hero trapped inside of a cave.

Trees, meanwhile, are an extension of the transformations taking place underground, and represent a concentration of forces that are drawn in through

a vast network of roots before joining solidly together in the trunk, then spreading out once more into branches that reach up toward the sky.

In sum, all the evidence points to the conclusion that the first part of Link's adventure symbolizes his transformation as an individual. And indeed, each of the first three dungeons he encounters (tree, cave and animal's belly) evokes the idea of change in its own way. The first part of this adventure will therefore change Link significantly.

At the end of each dungeon, the boy is rewarded for his skill with the acquisition of a precious stone. Together, three of these stones form the key he needs to open the doors of the Sacred Realm, the sanctuary where the Triforce rests—and the first objective Link has to reach.

THE INITIATE'S EXPERIENCE

Link is a member of the Kokiri tribe. As it happens, this tribe consists entirely of children who never grow up. However, the game's narrative timeline shows that the hero does in fact get older: Link jumps ahead seven years into the future shortly after he acquires the sapphire. We then see that the first quest in *Ocarina of Time* was actually an initiation ritual, once again illustrating the idea of change and the necessity of Link's trip to the whale's stomach.

An initiation ritual is a test that introduces a novice into a secret domain. In his book *The Quest: History and Meaning in Religion*, the Romanian ethnologist Mircea Eliade defines "initiation" as follows: "The term *initiation* generally denotes a body of rites and oral teachings whose purpose is to produce a decisive alteration in the religious and social status of the person to be initiated. In philosophical terms, initiation is equivalent to a basic change in existential status." The first of these initiations is called a "puberty initiation," because it celebrates the individual's promotion to adult status—a description that would seem to apply to Link's quest.

THE INITIATION

Many cultures mark the passage from childhood to adulthood as an important step in life, by organizing carefully orchestrated celebrations designed to suitably commemorate the event. Jewish culture marks this change by celebrating the bar mitzvah or bat mitzvah. In the Catholic tradition, a child's first communion plays a somewhat similar role. These contemporary ceremonies have many equivalents throughout the world, all of them rites of passage. The anthropology literature is filled with accounts of such events in primitive societies. Based on observations from around the world, pioneering scholars like James George Frazer were able to derive a schema for the dramatic progression of rites in this category.

The celebration depicts the neophyte's death, which actually signifies the "symbolic death" of the child he has been up until now. In certain cases, the elders may try to frighten the initiate as much as possible, or even physically torture him, to bring his experience as close as possible to the natural fear of death. After a period of isolation, which symbolizes the metaphorical death of the child and is a time to acquire new knowledge, comes his rebirth as an adult.

The puberty initiation rite is also a time for more advanced learning about the group's ancestral culture, its origins and the work of the gods that created it. These teachings are imparted during the isolation phase by a specific instructor, typically a mentor or godfather.

We have taken the time to describe this schema as part of our analysis of the story in *Ocarina of Time* because each of these steps is faithfully reproduced in Link's own journey. By a simple process of analogy, we can easily recognize the dungeons as periods of isolation. At the end of each of these sequences, Link gains new information on different aspects of the founding myths of the nation of Hyrule. The education that triggers the neophyte's moral transformation is thus represented very clearly in these scenes.

As for the symbolism of the hero's death, it appears not only in the isolation phases, but even in the figure of Link's instructor for the first quest (the section in which our hero is still a child). During the first part of his journey, Link is confronted with changes within himself. Through a series of tests, he glimpses his own evolution from the child that he was into the adult he will become. To ensure the success of this initiation rite, he is guided by a most unusual mentor: an owl.

THE OWL'S TRUE FACE

The instructor accompanies the neophyte on his journey to the world beyond. In *Zelda*, this role falls mainly to the mysterious giant owl. An anonymous figure who appears throughout the course of Link's adventure, he teaches his charge about the unique features of each region he explores, the powers of the local fairies, or Hyrule's royal family. Although his teachings do not focus on the legends of the past, he follows and guides the hero in his adventure even as other characters keep a certain distance. As a symbol of the forest, the owl is linked to the hero. But even beyond their common origins amongst the trees, his role as an instructor is justified by another of his many symbolic values: the owl is traditionally associated with death. This connection to death is found in the cultures of ancient Greece and Egypt, China, and in Native American traditions. And because it lives its life at night, the owl also symbolizes melancholy, cold and isolation. This relation to death and the night was already highlighted in the story of *Link's Awakening*, in which the owl revealed to our hero that he was trapped in a dream world. By accompanying our young Kokiri throughout his adventure in *Ocarina of Time*, the owl guides the soul of the deceased to its new home for the periods of isolation (the dungeons). It plays the *psychopomp* role (from the Greek word meaning *guide of souls*) that is reserved for the instructor. As a teacher, however, the instructor is not only associated with death. Therefore, the owl in *Ocarina of Time* has another reassuring feature that softens the coldness of its symbolic associations. When the grim-faced horned owl turns its head around, it reveals a different, gentler face: that of a barn owl. As a nocturnal animal, the barn owl is also associated with the cold and isolation of the night. But its ability to see in the dark makes it a powerful symbol of clairvoyance. The barn owl also represents Athena, the Greek goddess of wisdom. In this way, the game stays true to the logic of many rites of passage by allowing the face of wisdom to shine through behind the face of death, when the owl reveals its gentler side by turning its head.

This interpretation, in which Link is being guided along a path to the great beyond, should not be particularly surprising. We got a hint of this connection from the warning given to Link by a fellow Kokiri at the very beginning of the adventure, who tries to stop him from leaving the village by citing a local saying which reminds us that "he who leaves, dies!"

THE GORONS' ROLE

What is the Goron tribe's role in this journey? Hidden away high up on Death Mountain, which is a calm but still active volcano, the Gorons are associated with fire. Somewhat undisciplined and rough in appearance, they are the exact opposite of the Zoras—aquatic humanoids with a more distinguished look who live in a region that is the source of all the kingdom's water, which they are sworn to protect.

Women and water are symbolically linked in many different cultures around the world. For example, they find a powerful association in the Taoist principle of yin. Along the same lines, we can also speculate about the symbolic value of the Goron sequence and its place in the story. As we have just observed, the Gorons are associated with fire. And just as yin represents both women and water, men and fire are governed by the yang symbol and the power of the

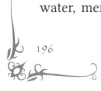

sun. So when Darunia declares that Link has become a member of the Goron community, he thereby implies that our hero is no longer a child, but an adult who is ready to capture the "Zora jewel." In short, Link is well on his way to becoming a man.

THE SECRET OF THE SACRED REALM

Our hero's symbolic journey in *Ocarina of Time* can be summarized as follows: after leaving his childhood behind by turning his back on the land of the Kokiri, Link overcomes a challenge to become a man in the land of the Gorons, and then discovers the secrets of life as an adult with the Zora princess. From this point of view, the quest in the Sacred Realm—a place so mysterious that it has no real representation in the game—can be interpreted as a quest for a woman.

After gathering the three Spiritual Stones and unlocking the gateway to the Sacred Realm, Link completes his initiation and becomes a man. And indeed, that is exactly what happens when he takes hold of the legendary sword that resides at the center of the Sacred Realm. The powers imparted by this sword correspond perfectly to the phallic symbolism often associated with that object. When Link draws the blade, he is transported seven years into the future, and grows that much older as well. When he later returns it to its pedestal, he goes back to the past and finds himself in a child's body again. In light of our interpretation, this aspect of the sword's function clearly confers certain powers of virility on Link's legendary blade.

THE HERO'S DEATH

Although Link has successfully overcome the challenges of the first quest, the way in which events unfold seems more indicative of defeat. The castle is under attack, and the princess is forced to flee in haste. As for Link, he finds himself watching helplessly as Ganondorf enters the Sacred Realm, having taken advantage of Link's carelessness to follow him to the gateway. To understand this situation, and to determine the role occupied by Ganondorf in relation to Link's status as a hero, we will continue our analysis by extending our interpretation of this adventure as an initiation rite. We will therefore begin with the game's two final dungeons, the Shadow Temple and the Spirit Temple, which mark the end of the hero's second quest—the one he began after reaching adulthood.

THE SOURCE OF LINK'S TRANSFORMATION

In our analysis of the game's first quest, we evoked various types of initiation rites. Although they differ from one another in terms of the type of initiation involved, they all have one idea in common: the death of the neophyte. Jung's analytic psychology explains the unconscious role of this symbolic death.

The Swiss psychoanalyst Carl Gustav Jung disagreed with Sigmund Freud about the importance of sexuality in the activity of the unconscious mind. Jung believed that other instincts also had a role to play. In his opinion, the survival instinct was just as important as sexuality. This instinct involves a fear of death. For Jung, it is this fear that underlies tales of travelers trapped in deep caves or in the belly of a whale. But these voyages into the depths also offer a chance at growth and development that can lead to a new life. Myths include many references to this process of rebirth, but they often relate to the experience of a newborn baby. For example, in Eiji Yoshikawa's epic novel *Musashi*, Shinmen Takezō spends three years closed up (isolated) in the highest chamber of the castle of Himeji. Much like a newborn, he gets a new name when he emerges: Musashi Miyamoto. In George R. R. Martin's series of fantasy novels, *A Song of Ice and Fire*, Daenerys reveals her divine nature by casting herself into an inferno from which she emerges unscathed, but as bald as a newborn baby (in the original story, though not in the *Game of Thrones* television series). To take another example from the world of video games, we find Raiden wandering the halls of Arsenal Gear in *Metal Gear Solid 2*, also as naked as a newborn. Note that each room of that vessel is named after a part of the human digestive tract; Hideo Kojima, the creator of the series, wanted to evoke Pinocchio's adventure. And with that, the circle is complete; we can return to *Ocarina of Time*.

THE FINAL CROSSING: THE SHADOW TEMPLE

If we had to identify just one dungeon in *Ocarina of Time* that most symbolizes death, it would have to be the Shadow Temple. Located under the cemetery in Kakariko Village, it is decorated with sculptures of scythe-wielding skeletons, and its corridors are simply a long line of guillotines. The cries of cursed souls complete the dark portrait, while hinting at the temple's vast extent. Finally, to get to the temple's final boss, Link has to take a boat which sinks as soon as he arrives at his destination, leaving him no way to go back from whence he came.

While the deathly symbolism of the earlier elements is easy to understand, the boat requires a bit more discussion. Associated with the idea of a transition or crossing (in this case, crossing over into the afterlife), boats are often seen

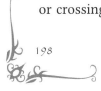

as a vehicle for guiding the souls of the deceased. In Nordic mythology, this boat is called *naglfar*; in Greek mythology, it is guided by old Charon down the rapids of the river Styx; and in the Egypt of the pharaohs, it was said to carry its passenger through the dangers of the twelve regions of the underworld. In short, the boat serves as a temporary link between two regions, as opposed to the bridge, which symbolizes a more permanent connection. The boat that Link uses in the Shadow Temple represents the ultimate crossing.

A DIVINE BOUNDARY

In myths, only gods are able to live on beyond death. In Scandinavian mythology, Odin faced a number of tests in his quest to acquire enough power to become the father of all the *Æsir* (the main gods in the Nordic pantheon). These included being hung from the great ash Yggdrasil for nine days and nine nights before being reborn as a god. In the same way, Siddhartha Gautama had to pass through a long cycle of reincarnations before becoming the Buddha. Let us also recall the story of Jesus Christ, who returned to life after being crucified on Mount Golgotha. Of course, none of these examples provides an explanation for why death should be associated with an ascension to divinity, but together they are enough to demonstrate the frequency of this idea across cultures.

To understand the symbolic value of a hero's victory over death, we must first understand that gods possess a state of consciousness far superior to that of mortal men. In fact, godhood is the highest possible state of consciousness. Death, on the other hand, corresponds to the lowest level—a state of nothingness. Therefore, a hero who can return from the land of the dead is able to transcend his own consciousness in order to pass beyond the darkness. And by circumventing the fundamental laws of the universe imposed by the gods themselves, he presents himself as their equal. Death is the great teacher of existence, revealing the vast secrets of the world to the soul that is able to escape from its clutches, since such a soul does not limit his perception of the world to its material aspect. Instead, he sees reality from a spiritual perspective. This is the situation illustrated by Link's passage through the Shadow Temple.

THE EYE OF TRUTH

In the kingdom of Hyrule, this much-coveted truth is intimately tied to our hero. But before we consider its content, we will first turn our attention to the element that represents Link's entrance into the circle of initiates who are

privy to that secret: the Lens of Truth. Found at the bottom of the well in Kakariko Village, this unique item allows Link to tell what is real and true from what is false in the Shadow Temple—that is, to see paths that would be invisible without the Lens, but which are nevertheless essential to the advancement of his quest. In the kingdom of Hyrule, as elsewhere, the underworld is an impassible labyrinth for mere mortals.

Alongside the hero's own two eyes, the Lens of Truth acts much like the third eye possessed by certain gods. The eye, as the organ of visual perception, is universally considered as a symbol of intellectual perception as well. This third eye therefore represents a higher stage of evolution—and conversely, a person with only one eye is assumed to suffer from a certain degree of mental weakness. This is certainly the case for the cyclops Polyphemus in the *Odyssey*, who is easily fooled by Ulysses. Similarly, the devil is also frequently represented as a one-eyed monster.

Beyond its function as a "divine eye," the Lens of Truth in *Ocarina of Time* is an object whose very origins are related to the notion of death. In particular, the well in which it is hidden is located near a cemetery. Plunging down into the deepest bowels of the earth, the well is a window onto the world of the dead, through which it lets in the light of the heavens above. For this reason, the well in Kakariko Village is a necessary step on our hero's path to the Shadow Temple. In other words, having passed through this dungeon, Link achieves a higher state of consciousness—the only way for him to confront Ganondorf and save Hyrule.

THE HOUSE OF THE GODS: THE SPIRIT TEMPLE

After the Shadow Temple, our hero rushes off to the Desert Colossus, located in the western part of the kingdom beyond Gerudo Valley. His journey to the heart of darkness is followed by a voyage filled with light. Independently of the hero's actions, there are many elements here to indicate that the founders of Hyrule saw this place as being close to the home of the gods. In fact, all of these elements can be subsumed under just one: the desert.

The Bible is certainly the work in which the symbolism of the desert is most fully developed. Described from many different perspectives, the desert is both a hostile environment that is home to demons, and a holy place in which true believers can be closer to God.

This simple observation tends to support the argument by which the second part of Link's adventure is seen as a quest for divinity. But we have not yet defined the true power of the desert. The desert draws its symbolic power

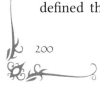

from the sense of solitude it inspires. Spreading out into the distance with no apparent end, it is a fundamentally undifferentiated and sterile environment in which reality hides behind mirages. Its undifferentiated nature recalls the lack of distinctions in the earliest moments of creation, when all the universe was at one with God. Crossing through the desert therefore symbolizes the hope of returning to that initial state of unity. From our current perspective in the context of a quest for divinity and truth, the Gerudos' desert appears as a mysterious region that conceals true reality. To reach the Spirit Temple, Link must cross the Haunted Wasteland in which an eternal sandstorm rages. The danger of this voyage lies in the reduced visibility that can lead the careless traveler astray. This is precisely what will happen to our hero unless he finds the Lens of Truth, thus gaining access to a higher stage of consciousness after his passage through the Shadow Temple, as discussed earlier.

This search for truth which leads beyond death and into the light is no less than a mystical initiation. From this perspective, the second part of the game can be seen as an extension of the first quest. For the sake of completeness, however, we must take a moment to consider the content of this great truth if we hope to truly understand the game.

THE SECRET OF HYRULE CASTLE

We have interpreted Link's progression through the last two dungeons (the Shadow and Spirit Temples) as a mystical initiation, opening the doors to a divine state that will reveal the secrets of Hyrule. To unveil the truth that Link discovers there, we must turn our attention to an unobtrusive but essential element of the game's setting: Hyrule Castle. The castle is truly a character in its own right, one that Ganondorf covets just as strongly as Princess Zelda herself. Our analysis of its symbolic value will serve as a foundation from which we can analyze the first three dungeons of the second quest.

INNER STRENGTH...

The castle is an essential part of any good fairy tale, because one of its symbolic roles is as a reflection of the hero's own inner state. The story of *Sleeping Beauty* provides a particularly clear example of this. The heroine of this story is a princess who has been cursed by an old fairy, who condemned her to die as a young woman by pricking her finger on a spindle. Another fairy intervenes to lighten the curse: in the end, the princess will slumber for a hundred years, and will only be awakened by a kiss from a prince. Not long after her fifteenth birthday, the princess injures herself and falls unconscious. To save the princess from awakening in a world in which everyone she once knew has died, the good fairy puts all the castle's residents to sleep—except for the king and queen, who have to leave. Finally, to prevent anyone from entering the castle during the coming century, the fairy blocks all access to it with a thick network of brambles. The overgrown plants wither away and disappear after a hundred years, thereby clearing a path for the prince to enter. He arrives at the princess's bedside and gives her the long-awaited kiss. As promised, Sleeping Beauty wakes up, and the whole castle comes back to life along with her. In sum, when the heroine is cursed, the palace is too. And when the curse is lifted, it is lifted from both of them.

Going further, the symbolism of the castle as command center also extends to the symbolic function of the world around it. In this sense, everything that happens in the world of Hyrule can be interpreted as a reflection of Link's state of mind.

...AND A SYMBOLIC SETTING...

To come back to the game: although Link has never set foot in Hyrule Castle, *Ocarina of Time* makes use of this symbolic function to relate the hero's state to that of the palace. Given our interpretation of the first quest as an initiation, this relationship explains why it is Ganondorf, rather than Link, who acquires the power of the Sacred Realm. Ganondorf's appearance in the adventure parallels Link's process of initiation. Throughout the first quest, Ganondorf remains more or less absent from the scene. His appearance in the story follows an interesting progression: before encountering him in person, Link had already sensed Ganondorf's presence in a dream, and then furtively spotted him through one of the castle's windows. In short, Ganondorf's presence in the game starts as a dream, but soon becomes reality. Each of Ganondorf's appearances occurs in conjunction with an important event in Link's learning process.

The dream serves as our introduction to the game, and precedes the death of the Deku Tree. Link sees him through the garden window after his meeting with Zelda. Finally, their first face-to-face confrontation occurs just moments before he enters the Sacred Realm. The castle plays an essential role in the villain's gradual introduction into the story: even as he moves towards center stage, Ganondorf is also moving from the inside of the castle to the outside, with his confrontation with Link taking place at the threshold of the drawbridge.

...FOR THE BIRTH OF EVIL

In *Ocarina of Time*, the castle is clearly influenced by Ganondorf's presence. As he emerges, dark clouds accumulate over the building, and his ascension to power completely transforms the palace. If the castle is a reflection of Link, the image of Ganondorf coming out of the castle symbolizes the emergence of a new side of our hero. As long as this aspect still slumbered within Link, Ganondorf remained inside (where we see him subjected to the king's authority), and could only appear in the private realm of dreams. But now that it has become too strong, this aspect reveals itself and breaks free. This, then, is Ganondorf's true role with regard to our hero. Ganondorf personifies Link's dark side. Within the overall context of the series, he represents a side of Link's personality which has been quietly growing in the realm of shadows, and which must be brought under control before it affects the realm of light. This symbolism explains the structure of the worlds on display in *Ocarina of Time*, *Twilight Princess* and *A Link to the Past*. In fact, we can even go further with this idea by observing that, in the latter two examples, Link has to use a mirror in order to reach the shadow realm where Ganondorf reigns, because it reflects the darkness that secretly lives within Link's own heart.

A HERO SEEKS PURITY OF HEART

Mirrors appear frequently as symbols in video games. For example, the heroes of *Final Fantasy III* reach the final boss's lair by passing through a mirror. *Silent Hill 2*, the survival horror game from Konami, begins with a long shot of the hero, James, lost in thought as he stares into a mirror before passing over to the "other side." But the mirror is no more than a cinematic tool. What's important about it is the idea that the enemy is most often the expression of a weakness or vice that lurks in the hero's own heart. It may be vanity, fear or even an overly strong attachment to his image of his parents. And when the enemy tries to convince the hero to join him, it is the influence of this vice that is being expressed. In *Star Wars*, when Darth Vader tries to persuade Luke Skywalker to cross over to the dark side of the Force, it is in fact because Luke feels that desire rising within himself. Yet at the same time, Luke also personifies the good that lies deep within Darth Vader's heart. These two tendencies eventually collide, and when Luke Skywalker's father ultimately betrays the Emperor he once served, Darth Vader dies and becomes Anakin once more.

THE FOREST TEMPLE

In *Ocarina of Time*, the nature of Link's dark side is directly related to the initiation he goes through in the first quest. But to suppress this darkness, he must first be aware that it exists. This is the theme that develops in the Forest Temple, the first dungeon in the second quest (that is, after Link has become an adult), in which Link confronts a ghostly avatar of Ganondorf. This battle indicates that he has begun to identify the problem within himself, even if the enemy's ghostly nature also suggests that his awareness of it is still somewhat vague. Besides the form of the boss, this "revelation" is also expressed in the particular item Link finds in this dungeon: a bow. By its nature and function, this weapon requires the archer to recognize his target and focus on it in order to strike home. In the Japanese tradition, the Zen discipline of archery requires a form of concentration that aims to purify the mind. The arrow at the center of the target reflects the archer's internal state at the moment when he releases the tensed bowstring. This is the moment when he learns whether or not he has reached his objective: total mental clarity. Therefore, Link must focus on and identify with his alter ego by aiming his bow at the enemy he hopes to strike. This notion of an objective or target is also expressed through the colors of the other ghosts that haunt the temple. Each of them has a color that aligns with the theme of one of the other temples: green for the Forest Temple, red for the Fire Temple, blue for the Water Temple, and purple for the Shadow Temple. Once Link has defeated these four ghosts, he will be ready to face the fifth. This final spirit represents the Temple of Light where Link will find the truth, as we mentioned earlier.

The introspective nature of the temple is also reflected in its location deep within a forest, a common symbol of the unconscious realm. This symbolism is confirmed by the mazelike path that Link must follow in order to reach the temple. But it is even more clearly illustrated by the lost Kokiri that he finds there. In fact, there are only two ways out of the Kokiri village: the one that Link takes at the start of the adventure (the bridge), and another that leads even deeper into the forest. Symbolically speaking, the Kokiri that head out in this second direction are displaying a kind of autistic behavior by pulling back from the outside world, which symbolizes withdrawing into oneself. For this reason, it is difficult to approach them.

In short, the Forest Temple is a microcosm of the entire adventure. But we have not yet defined the nature of the darkness that Ganondorf represents. Once we have done so, we will be able to draw a connection between the first and second quests, and understand the role of the fire and water dungeons. But above all, it will allow us to understand the character of Zelda.

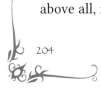

ESCAPE OR ABDUCTION?

While maintaining our interpretation of Ganondorf's character as presented above, we must also acknowledge that Zelda follows the same path: she, too, emerges from the castle. In her case, however, she is running away. At this point in the game, Zelda's experience has all the usual features of an abduction. The image of a young girl being kidnapped appears frequently in myths to represent a woman's passage from childhood to adulthood. The myth of Persephone expresses this idea very clearly: while she is still living with her mother Demeter, Persephone is abducted by Hades, god of the underworld, who wants her for his wife. Demeter then asks Zeus to bring her daughter back. But because Persephone has tasted food during her time in the underworld, she is condemned to stay there forever. As the goddess of agriculture, Demeter threatens to express her anger by making the world barren. Zeus then proposes a compromise: Persephone will stay for six months with her husband, then return to her mother for the other six months of the year. This shared custody arrangement was the ancient Greeks' explanation for the changing seasons. In any case, the abduction led to Demeter's young daughter becoming Hades' wife. Other Greek myths define this as the moment when a young girl becomes an adult.

Zelda's escape resembles a kidnapping in that the symbolism of abduction is tied to a sense of being forcibly torn away from one's home. And indeed, in order to save her from Ganondorf's clutches, Impa is forced to take the princess away from the place where she grew up. Just like the victims of abduction in ancient myths, the princess is taken away against her will from the world where she had lived throughout her entire childhood. From this perspective, Zelda's story is an echo of Link's journey of initiation. But she is also hiding another secret—the secret that drives both Link and Ganondorf. To understand it, we will have to return to the analysis that we presented earlier.

OF GODS AND MEN

We have described Link's second quest as a quest for divinity. And at the end of that quest, Link finds Zelda. This would seem to suggest that the princess has a divine nature. In terms of the plot, this is hardly surprising, since the princess possesses the Triforce of Wisdom. At our level of analysis, we can thus conclude that Zelda represents a new element: the spirit. This point of view provides a partial answer to the question of what makes Ganondorf a mortal enemy of the princess. In fact, because he personifies a vice, he can only be harmful to the virtue represented by the spirit.

RETURN OF THE KING

The spirit is a source of justice and moral knowledge. The psychologist and mythologist Paul Diel defines it as a set of guiding values that serve to orient our behavior towards that which is right and good, and towards justice and truth. Gods are powerful symbols of the spirit.

Other elements of interpretation can be drawn upon to support the hypothesis that Zelda represents the spirit, especially those elements that relate to the king. Often considered to be of divine ancestry, kings are also a symbol of the spirit. This is why Ganondorf is kneeling when we see him through the window of Hyrule Castle, indicating a situation that is still under control by the forces of good. Like any man, however, a king can be corrupted by bad habits or fall victim to jealousy, greed, and the whole range of negative human emotions. In such cases, he is often accompanied by a bad counselor to whom he listens uncritically, and who can sometimes take power for himself.

A weak king represents spiritual weakness. The kingdom is then exposed to malicious forces. And since the state of the land reflects the hero's psychological state, these invading forces symbolize the vices from which he would normally protect himself, but which he ultimately gives in to. *The Lord of the Rings*— both the series of novels by J. R. R. Tolkien and Peter Jackson's trilogy of film adaptations—is the perfect example of this principle. It's easy to recognize the pattern: the One Ring has cast its spell over kings and weakened the world of men. But Frodo agrees to carry the great evil of his time on his shoulders, thereby allowing King Aragorn to return. As a princess, Zelda represents the king's symbolic pedigree, in both its positive and negative aspects. In *Twilight Princess*, we encounter the theme of corruption in Zelda's possession by an evil spirit, and in her physical assault on Link at the end of the game.

But the end of this corruption is shown in a cinematic sequence in which we see her falling unconscious onto the throne. This return to the throne indicates that evil is no longer in control. At the same time, the fact that the princess is unconscious reflects a power vacuum, which means that the fight against evil must continue. Let us also recall that the return of the king is highlighted in the closing credits of *A Link to the Past*. Taken together, these examples are enough to convince us that Zelda represents the spirit, which Link seeks to protect from the corruption and vice represented by Ganondorf. This, then, is the secret that the princess was hiding.

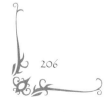

THE ETERNAL FEMININE

So why does the series focus on a princess rather than a king? First, note the classic nature of this narrative template: a knight saving a princess is a very common structure in fairy tales. In most such stories, however, the hero marries the princess and becomes king himself. But Link has never married the princess.

We must also mention women's uplifting role in fairy tales and other myths. The story of Theseus in the Minotaur's labyrinth will help us to understand this idea. To kill the monster of Minos, Theseus made his way deep into a labyrinth "from which no one ever escapes." Ariadne comes to his aid by giving him a ball of golden thread to help him find his way back out. The usual interpretation of this story is that, in order to kill the monster within himself, Theseus had to explore the furthest depths of his soul. This was a perilous inner journey, and Theseus was in danger of losing his way and never coming back. But Ariadne guided him back to the light. With *Faust*, Goethe paid homage to this uplifting role of women through his notion of the "eternal feminine." Near the end of *Ocarina of Time*, Zelda guides Link by opening his path to the exit from the final castle. In this scene, we see her guiding a hero at risk of being lost forever, just as in the tale of Ariadne. After explaining this danger of being lost forever, we will be ready to consider Zelda's dark side.

CAPTIVATING, THEN CONTROLLING

Although Zelda is not among the game's characters, her's dark side appears for the first time in *Link's Awakening*. In this episode, Link meets Marin. Over the course of the game, a mutual crush develops between the two characters. But the story takes place in a world of illusion that Link is trying to escape. And as he progresses towards that goal, Marin becomes more and more insistent, finally scolding Link for his attraction to "that Zelda." This rebuke clearly shows that the outside world, the world of truth, is associated with Zelda. It also shows that Marin's function is opposed to Zelda's uplifting role, since Marin tries to keep Link trapped in illusion. Marin personifies the risk discussed earlier of getting lost in the labyrinth forever. That risk arises from a fascination with a given place that ultimately becomes all-consuming and controlling. We encounter the same situation in *Kingdom Hearts: Chain of Memories*, in which Naminé appears as the controlling version of Kairi. In this game, Sora makes his way through the Castle of Oblivion, whose white walls symbolize the risk of amnesia that threatens all those who come there. In *Ocarina of Time*, this controlling aspect first appears with Link's imprisonment by the Gerudos. But Link is able to deal with the situation, and turns this experience into a part of his initiation.

Elsewhere in the series, the controlling character also appears in the form of Midna in *Twilight Princess*. Like Marin, this princess belongs to another world. However, her controlling nature manifests itself in a very different way—mainly in the heart-rending goodbyes she makes us suffer through at the end of the episode. Even as it lets us go, the game does its best to make us want to stay, inspiring feelings quite similar to the ones that players felt when it was time to say goodbye to Marin. By forcing us to move forward, the game teaches us to face this feeling. So there is an interesting educational aspect at work here, and an approach to game design that goes beyond the gameplay framework itself.

BODIES AND SOULS

In the course of our analysis, we have had occasion to explain the symbolic value of the first quest (initiation as a rite of passage into adulthood) and that of the Shadow, Spirit and Forest Temples, as well as the roles of the Zelda and Ganondorf characters (with the former representing the spirit and the latter representing Link's dark side). At this level of understanding, however, Ganondorf's role still appears somewhat vague. He embodies a vice, but which one? Our analysis of the Fire Temple will allow us to answer this question. In turn, that analysis will lead us to an understanding of the symbolic values of the Water Temple and the role of the Sheik character.

THE CURSE OF ETERNAL HUNGER

We began by interpreting Link's adventure as an initiation test designed to guide him from childhood to adulthood. We gave an initial interpretation of the Gorons' role based on their association with fire. But we didn't go into much detail at the time. By analyzing the events that take place in the Fire Temple, we can now develop our account a bit further.

In the Fire Temple, the second dungeon in Link's second quest, the Gorons have been imprisoned, condemned to be eaten by the temple's boss, Volvagia. We focus on this detail because of how it relates back to the Gorons' situation in the first quest. When Link first encountered the tribe led by Darunia, he found them starving, and helped them to gain access to their food by re-opening the entrance to their cavern. And when Link meets them again seven years later,

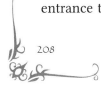

the Gorons have gone from predators to prey, locked up in the Fire Temple. To explain this reversal of their situation, we will set aside myths and fairy tales and cite the words of Captain Barbossa in the first *Pirates of the Caribbean* movie. He explains that after he and his men had seized the treasure of Isla de Muerta, they had indulged in every pleasure available to them. But the more they ate, the hungrier they became. And the hungrier they became, the more they ate, until they were continually consumed by an insatiable hunger. This is a recurring theme in many myths as well: he who gives free rein to his appetites runs the risk of constant hunger—exactly what the Gorons experience in the Fire Temple as victims of an endless appetite.

CONTROLLING THE VOLCANO

The fact that we see the theme of hunger following the Goron tribe from one quest to another shows that it is not arbitrary. Like any symbol, hunger has both a positive and a negative side. *Ocarina of Time* is all about psychological urges. The Gorons only eat rock, which is an element of the earth. The earth has a material aspect incompatible with the spirit, which is associated with the sky. And it is here that we discover the true nature of the vice represented by Ganondorf as the embodiment of Link's dark side.

SLUMBER

This situation relates directly to the sequence in which Link takes hold of the legendary sword. This is the exact moment when he is plunged into a seven-year slumber. By falling asleep, Link leaves the kingdom under the control of its instinct, represented by Ganondorf. In *The Lion King*, Disney's full-length animated feature, we see the same course of events: when King Mufasa dies, his son Simba flees, allowing his uncle Scar the usurper to take over. During his exile, Simba finds refuge in an oasis, where he nonchalantly stuffs his face all day while his people suffer through a drought.

PSYCHIC ENERGY

As soon as he opens his eyes, Link begins a process of regaining control of himself—a path that becomes clearest in the Forest Temple. We saw earlier that the weapon he discovered there aligned perfectly with the symbolism of the

dungeon as a whole. In the Fire Temple, the Megaton Hammer also aligns with Link's needs. The hammer is a symbol of the need to make a choice. In this case, Link must choose to no longer be ruled by impulse. A judge's use of a gavel is partially inspired by this symbolic meaning. In English, when a message or argument is repeated with great force, we say that it has been "hammered home." But in order to make this choice stick, Link must find the strength of will that he seems to have lost, if we rely on our interpretation of his seven-year slumber. Now, the problem with hunger is that it diverts psychic energy and redirects it towards the satisfaction of that hunger. A person in this situation no longer has any motivation to do anything else.

THE FLOW OF ENERGY

This psychic force appears in many myths and belief systems as a kind of universal energy that connects all things. In the Western tradition, it is referred to as the *anima* or *pneuma*; in India, as *prana*; in China, as *qi*; and in Japan, as *ki*. The concept is also known as *mana* in Polynesian culture. We find this universal energy in many contemporary myths as well, including the Force in *Star Wars*, the Lifestream in *Final Fantasy VII*, and Eywa in *Avatar*. In *Ocarina of Time*, psychic energy appears in the form of Hyrule's largest river. And indeed, the kingdom's water supply suffers from problems that reveal its symbolic function. As long as it is flowing freely, water appears clean and under control. But in the case of stagnant water, as in a swamp, it is a synonym of melancholy and a lack of mental life. In *Ocarina of Time*, the river's source is frozen. This reflects the psychic sterility that comes when one's energy is monopolized by instinct. Nothing can be created by a person in this condition, because all of their energy is focused on consumption. In the game, the frozen water source leads to a drop in Lake Hylia's water level, which then represents the level of Link's psychic energy. The Water Temple's role is thus to re-establish a balanced flow of psychic energy, and to rebuild the necessary strength to rid the kingdom of the vice that Ganondorf represents. In his introspective journey, Link is joined by an unwavering companion: Sheik.

THE MENTOR'S SECRET

By pushing him to find Zelda, Sheik (who is in fact none other than the princess in disguise) provides the advice that will guide Link towards the light. Like all the other characters in the game, Sheik also represents a part of

Link. From this perspective, the advice he offers actually comes from the hero himself. And by representing the internal voice that strives to influence the spirit, Sheik plays the part of the soul—Link's soul. While the spirit symbolizes a state of psychic balance, the soul represents the drive that seeks to reach that state. The soul is the intuition behind all that is just and good. Considering his role, it is reasonable to conclude that Sheik is the owl's heir. Throughout the second quest, Sheik embodies a soul who has been wounded by the pressing urges of instinct. His body is even partially covered with bandages. At the same time, the soul's inspiring function appears explicitly in his artistic abilities: playing the harp and writing poetry. Sheik thus represents the soul, the drive that guides us towards the spirit. These two aspects of the personality are very closely related—hence the character's double identity. In this way, *Ocarina of Time* represents the soul and the spirit as the same person. Nevertheless, for the majority of players, Sheik is really a separate character in his own right, just like Ganondorf, who represents instinct.

A REVEALING DESTINY

As a continuation of the first part, Link's quest for divinity gives us an opportunity to consider the character's heroic nature. In our analysis, the scene at the bridge foreshadowed the great feats to come. But the quest for divinity allows us to see that these promises were already present in the earliest stages. Indeed, this aspiration to a state of divinity reveals that it is not only Link's journey, but the story of our young hero's childhood as well, that is comparable to the path walked by the gods.

THE ORPHAN

Link has a unique feature that he shares with many mythological gods and heroes: he is an orphan. Because orphans live without any attachment to the past, they are often presented as being free of the constraints of tradition. They therefore represent the freedom to become anything we choose. This is why a hero is often someone who breaks free of the rules that govern most mere mortals. Heroes are also frequently born under unusual or miraculous circumstances. This idea is an extension of the symbolism of the orphan.

EXPOSED TO DANGER

There is something else unusual about Link. In this case, it is something that took place when he was only a baby. The biographies of great heroes often reveal that they were subject to extraordinary dangers in their earliest childhood. Greek mythology abounds with well-known examples, including that of Zeus, threatened by his father, Cronus, who had already devoured all of Zeus's brothers. Much like the image of the hero as orphan, the idea of a young hero exposed to great danger continues to inspire contemporary novelists and screenwriters. The danger in question is often one that causes the death of the hero's parents; if his mother had not sacrificed herself, Harry Potter would surely have succumbed to Voldemort's attack on him as a baby. Link follows the tradition in this respect. In *Ocarina of Time*, we learn that he was taken in by the Deku Tree as his dying mother was trying to escape from a war.

THE LAST OF US

Alongside his status as an orphan and his exposure to danger, we find another detail that confirms Link's unique character: he is the last of his community. Although most of the Kokiri show no animosity toward our young Hylian, the chief Mido's contemptuous behavior towards him nevertheless reflects Link's precarious position within the community. Even though Saria is a close friend of Link's, she too considers him to be different from the rest. The fact that our hero had no fairy to accompany him for such a long time eventually came to isolate him from the rest of the village. This is often the fate of a hero in the making. We find this idea expressed even more subtly in *Metal Gear Solid*, in which the character with the least complex genetic heritage is the one who is victorious in the end.

The clearest example from traditional stories is probably Hop-o'-My-Thumb, derived from the French tale of *Petit Poucet*. The youngest in a family of seven children, Hop-o'-My-Thumb stands out for his unusually small size. But it is he who figures out his parents' plans to abandon their children, and develops a strategy to save himself and his brothers. He is also the one who defeats the ogre and becomes a close friend of the royal family.

A SPECIAL CONNECTION

One final point completes our understanding of Link's unique childhood: his special connection to the natural world. Threatened by Cronus, Zeus was fed

and protected by the goat Amalthea. And the baby Jesus was born in a stable where, according to tradition, the ox and the ass came together to worship him, although they are usually described as rivals. As for Link, he is adopted by the tree that protects the forest, is later guided by a giant owl, and even tames the wild mare Epona. This benevolent relationship with nature is also developed in *The Minish Cap*, where Link discovers the secrets of local plants and animals with the help of his talking cap, Ezlo. This is also one of the hero's unique features in *Twilight Princess*: when he transforms into a wolf, he gains an especially enlightened connection with nature.

LINK IS THE HERO OF OUR OWN STORY

We can now review Link's journey from beginning to end. In his first quest, Link feels adult urges rising within him (he dreams of Ganondorf) and prepares to leave childhood behind (he leaves the Kokiri village). He later catches a glimpse of those deep-seated urges, which seem to be under control (he sees Ganondorf through the window of Hyrule Castle, kneeling before the king). But he is then overwhelmed by those same urges (Ganon emerges from the castle and knocks him down). He ultimately loses control of his desires (he falls into a deep sleep and leaves Ganondorf in control of the world).

In the second quest, Link becomes aware of the evil consuming him: he meets Sheik, understands the path he has to take and the objective he has to reach in the Forest Temple. He then re-establishes the flow of psychic energy within himself (in the Water Temple, he thaws out the fountain and fills Lake Hylia with pure water) and enters a period of deep introspection (he discovers the eye of truth and makes his way through the Shadow Temple). Finally, he reaches a state of higher consciousness by passing through the desert mirages and acquiring the mirror shield to light up the darkness. He is then ready to face his alter ego without fear. Seen in this way, Link's journey is simply an allegory for the changes we all go through in life. And it's because this story belongs to all of us that Ganondorf threatens to return and torment Link's descendants. After all, every child has to pass through the ups and downs of adolescence on their way to adulthood. What makes Link a hero is that he acts both as a prophet, in showing us the path that leads to the spirit (Zelda), and as a pious man, by refusing the demands of instinct (Ganondorf). *Ocarina of Time* narrates an epic tale that resonates with each and every one of us—and as the bearer of an extraordinary destiny, Link symbolizes the hero that lives deep within us all.

CHAPTER XIX
ZELDA AND GANON

PRINCESS ZELDA

Princess Zelda. Her name appears in the title of the saga, which is often simply referred to as the *Zelda* series. And yet she is surely the least well-known of the saga's major characters. A truly symbolic figure, the princess represents the series rather than personifying it. First and foremost, Zelda corresponds to one of the three triangles that make up the Triforce. Unlike power and courage, the wisdom that Zelda personifies is the only genuinely spiritual value associated with the three golden triangles. Needless to say, she was never destined to be a warrior. Calm and reasonable, she is usually the source of the knowledge that guides Link in his adventures. But despite her many admirable virtues, she initially appears as little more than an untouchable icon—a mere symbol. And yet when we look a little closer, we see that Zelda represents much more than this. Her role is to help Link act like a hero, and to reveal him to the world as the chosen defender of the Triforce. Before her abduction, Zelda was the heir to the throne of Hyrule, and appeared as an Olympian figure pondering the world from atop a high pedestal; only after she was taken prisoner by Ganon would she become the focus of a quest. Prior to that event, Link did not desire Zelda, any more than he dreamed of saving the world. But when the princess was captured by Ganon, it awakened the hero within him. In this sense, Ganon also plays the role of a catalyst; without him, Link would never have become the hero we know so well today.

While the early stages of the saga present Zelda as an archetypal princess—especially in the second episode where she plays the role of the sleeping princess, in a direct reference to traditional stories and legends from our childhood like *Snow White* and *Sleeping Beauty*—her character becomes more fully defined with each passing episode, and ultimately grows into an independent character in her own right. Zelda's transformation is divided into four distinct stages, over the course of which she develops from a sweet, shy little girl into a bold, experienced and responsible heir.

After spending the first three episodes being kidnapped and rescued, Zelda dives head-first into the action in *Ocarina of Time*. Marked by change at every level, this installment for the Nintendo 64 is also the one in which the princess experiences a metamorphosis of her own. To begin with, it is Zelda that hides behind Sheik's warrior disguise. This discovery adds new layers of complexity and depth to her character, and a corresponding richness of symbolic interpretation. In her guise as Sheik, Zelda becomes a very exciting protagonist for the player. A charismatic and highly skilled character with an apparent gift for combat, Sheik draws our attention so effectively that Link is left in the shadows. Unlike the hero of the series, Sheik can even speak for himself! His speeches are far more interesting than Link's silent gesticulations—especially since he seems to know a lot about the ongoing quest. After lagging a bit behind the rest of the cast, the princess finally begins to play an active part in the story; she introduces herself by interacting with the player, and becomes that much more charming as a result.

With the introductions out of the way, Zelda breaks free of her old image in *The Wind Waker*. On the GameCube, she no longer appears as an immaculate princess, but as a tough little pirate at the head of her own crew! The goal is to demystify Zelda by catching players off guard and showing them that the character is not who they think she is. A genuine "woman of action," introduced by the name of Tetra at the start of the adventure, the Zelda we meet in *The Wind Waker* is freed from the rules of decorum that went along with her former status as a princess. Hardly unexpected, since she was unaware of her destiny at the time. Totally emancipated, she reveals a mischievous and even mocking side, along with amusing and downright comedic character traits that make her even more fun for players to spend time with.

As with *Ocarina of Time*, the themes addressed in *Twilight Princess* would leave their mark on the saga as a whole. Defined by its emphasis on maturity, this chapter returns Zelda to her role and appearance as a princess—and a rather clichéd one at that, to be sure—even as it imbues her with a wisdom that befits her divine heritage. She appears as an adult here: radiant, but also deeply troubled by the responsibilities that rest upon her shoulders. It is a darker vision of Zelda, in her role as the true heir to the crown. Leading an army on the verge of defeat, the princess decides to save her people by laying down arms and surrendering to Zant. For the first time, she finds herself in a truly hopeless situation. Her failure as a ruler is matched by one in her relationship with Link: for the first time, it's not Zelda who haunts our young hero's romantic dreams. Next to Midna, one of the most endearing characters in the entire series, Zelda

pales in comparison—even as she grows into a more serious and responsible figure in this episode, fully accepting her role as a princess for the very first time with total dedication and devotion.

The final stage in Zelda's evolution arrived with *Spirit Tracks*, the second episode to appear on the Nintendo DS. This time, Zelda is right beside Link for every step of his journey. Freed of her physical shell, she flits about in a ghostly form, playing the advisor's role previously occupied by fairies like Navi and Ciela. By his own admission, Aonuma wanted to bring the princess even closer to the player with this approach. She reveals a highly talkative and mischievous side in this episode, continuing the transformation that had begun in earlier installments: at the start of the game, we see her engaging fully with her role as a leader and taking steps to save her kingdom. Other than the two games for CD-I (and *Tetra's Quest*, only available in Japan), *Spirit Tracks* marks Zelda's first appearance as a playable character—a strong sign from Nintendo, even if the designers had to come up with a specific function for her on the gameplay side before deciding to put her character in the spotlight, in accordance with the publisher's longstanding creative philosophy.

At the end of the day, Zelda is the only character that really evolves over the course of the series. Unlike Link, who never changes a bit, and Ganon, entrenched in his antagonist's role, the princess makes use of her divine wisdom to develop and grow as a person. And just like Link and Ganon, she is an inseparable part of the series—which, like the Triforce, needs all three of its elements to exist.

GANON

Like Zelda, then, Ganon is an essential part of Hyrule's world. He joins a long line of famous Nintendo villains alongside Bowser, Wario and Mother Brain. Since his appearance in the very first *Zelda* game, Ganon has become the saga's most iconic antagonist, and the source of all evil in Hyrule. Born of the Gerudo people, a tribe of women living in the desert, he was destined to become their chief, according to the legend which foretold that a man would be born once every hundred years to become the tribe's leader. Hungry for power, Ganon would not rest until he seized the Triforce and all its power for himself. To achieve his dark intentions, Ganon abducts Zelda on a number of occasions, thereby drawing Link's ire. Associated with the third part of the Triforce, he represents power, in contrast with Zelda's wisdom and Link's courage. And yet, like Zelda, Ganon does not appear in every episode of the series. At times, he remains hidden behind a more obvious threat, only to reveal himself much later

(*A Link to the Past, Twilight Princess, Oracle of Ages* and *Seasons*). In *Twilight Princess*, he achieves a semi-divine status and manages to corrupt Zant, an inhabitant of the Twilight Realm who sees him as a god. These two characters then become intimately linked, such that neither can die without bringing the other with him. At the very end of the adventure, Zant sacrifices himself to eliminate the one who had manipulated him, once and for all.

Ganon's appearance changes over the course of the series. At first, he takes the form of a huge anthropomorphic pig. His silhouette also appears on every "Game Over" screen in *The Adventure of Link*. Starting with *Ocarina of Time*, he takes on a humanoid appearance, and goes by the name of Ganondorf. In the final battle, however, he transforms into a more frightening boar-like form, similar to that of earlier episodes. These differences can be explained by the fact that *Ocarina of Time* takes place before the three preceding episodes in the saga's overall timeline. On this view, Ganondorf would indeed be the leader of the thieves, born of the Gerudo tribe, and able to transform into a powerful pig-like beast known simply as Ganon. Based on the information provided in *The Wind Waker*, it seems that the Ganon character is the same individual from one episode to the next, whereas the other two representatives of the Triforce, Zelda and Link, go through various incarnations (e.g. Link in *The Wind Waker* is not the same person as in *Ocarina of Time*). The character's continued presence throughout the ages reinforces his status as the saga's main threat, eternally opposed to the hero whenever they meet. And indeed, his role and his motivations never really change throughout the series. The only sign of change is in *The Wind Waker*, when he seems touched by a sense of nostalgia and regrets the loss of the Hyrule of old.

ZELDA

THE HISTORY OF A LEGENDARY SAGA

A NEVER-ENDING LEGEND...

aving reached the end of the book, it should now be clear: the Zelda saga is one of a handful of series that have fundamentally shaped the history of video games. Each episode left its mark on its era, influencing not only the platform for which it was published, but above all, the players who tried their hands at the game.

Thanks to the impressively consistent quality of its adventures, the series has remained incredibly popular right up to the present day, and continues to enjoy a universally positive reputation among players. There's a *Zelda* game for every kind of player, from the youngest to the most experienced; together, these games have contributed to a vision of video games in which gameplay and pure fun take center stage.

It is often said that the success of a series can be measured by the influence it has on its competitors. But the fact is that few other games have attempted to imitate *Zelda's* style of gameplay. That unique style is intimately bound up with Nintendo's core philosophy, and leaves little room for variation. Still, we can readily cite a number of worthy heirs, including *Ōkami* and *Darksiders* as well as *Alundra*, *Crusader of Centy*, *Secret of Mana* and *Golden Axe Warrior*. We might also mention *Legacy of Kain*, the mythical saga developed by Crystal Dynamics with the participation of Amy Hennig. This much-respected creator worked on the *Soul Reaver* episode, which explicitly drew on the legacy of *Zelda*; she later moved on to Naughty Dog, Inc., where she worked on the *Uncharted* series. All of these productions have one point in common: they offer the player a chance to explore a world like no other.

With almost twenty episodes under its belt, *The Legend of Zelda* has remained one of Nintendo's most riveting series. Taken together, the games that make up the saga have already sold more than sixty million copies worldwide—which is presumably why the Japanese publisher insisted on a proper celebration of the prestigious saga's thirtieth anniversary. More than most of its other productions, the *Zelda* games have always served as a showcase for Nintendo's prowess as a developer, even as they have contributed to its commercial success. Now an unavoidable part of the landscape, the series remains one of the most iconic in video game history— and the legend is far from over.

SPECIAL THANKS

Nicolas Courcier and Mehdi El Kanafi would like to thank:

—Damien, for his unwavering support;
—Thomas, for his help, for his reliability, and for everything;
—Fred, for always being there to lend a helping hand;
—Georges Grouard, for blazing the trail that we walk upon today;
—Carolyn.

⊛ ALSO AVAILABLE FROM THIRD ÉDITIONS:

- *The Legend of Final Fantasy VII*
- *Metal Gear Solid. Hideo Kojima's Magnum Opus*
- *Dark Souls. Beyond the Grave*
- *BioShock. From Rapture to Columbia*